ISBN 978-1-332-21645-1
PIBN 10299561

1 MONTH OF
FREE
READING

at

www.ForgottenBooks.com

By purchasing this book you are eligible for one month membership to ForgottenBooks.com, giving you unlimited access to our entire collection of over 700,000 titles via our web site and mobile apps.

To claim your free month visit:

www.forgottenbooks.com/free299561

Similar Books Are Available from
www.forgottenbooks.com

THE NEIGHBORHOOD PLAYHOUSE

Leaves from a Theatre Scrapbook

BY

ALICE LEWISOHN CROWLEY

THEATRE ARTS BOOKS : *New York*

In somewhat different form the "Epilogue" of this book was published on the 30th Anniversary of the Neighborhood Playhouse School of the Theatre, © 1958 by Alice Lewisohn Crowley.

The quotation from Stark Young's review of *The Little Clay Cart* is reprinted from *Immortal Shadows* by Stark Young. Copyright 1948 by Charles Scribner's Sons and reprinted with their permission.

The quotations Joseph Wood Krutch makes from his own reviews were copyrighted in 1924 and 1926 by *The Nation* and are reprinted with its permission.

Library of Congress Catalog Card No. 59-13239

Designed by Stefan Salter

Published by Theatre Arts Books, 333 Sixth Avenue, New York 14, N. Y.

Printed in the United States of America
by the Vail-Ballou Press, Inc.

CONTENTS

TABLE OF ILLUSTRATIONS

by Joseph Wood Krutch

The renaissance of the American theatre dawned in the years just before World War I and came into full flower during the twenties. This renaissance involved a sharp break with the rather shabby tradition of its past and there has been no such break since. Whatever in our theatre is admirable today has grown out of the achievements of the teens and the twenties. Until then there had been no major American playwright and very few who so much as aspired to anything which could be called serious writing. Neither was there any art of the theatre which was more than an imitation of the rather elementary pseudo-realistic methods of the nineteenth century English and French stages.

The American ambition to produce plays which might challenge comparison with the best contemporary literature in other forms and a determination to explore the possibilities of stage craft as an independent art were born so short a time ago that not a few of those who first inspired them are still living and active. The designs and costumes of Aline Bernstein exercised a profound influence on subsequent leaders in these fields. Moreover there would be no Arthur Miller or Tennessee Williams today if there had not been an O'Neill then and no such directors as, to take a single example, Kazan, if there had not been in the "little theatres" of the teens and twenties half a dozen adventurous spirits who sensed possibilities which the plodding "practical men" of Broadway neither suspected nor wanted to suspect.

It is also a simple historical fact that the first significant experiments which led to the renaissance were made by the enthusiasts who launched three "little" (or as we should now say "Off-Broadway") theatres. By no means all of either the "new playwrights" or the adventurous directors and producers made their first appearance in these "little theatres." In fact, it is telling evidence of the acuteness and vision of these theatres that the possibilities they suggested and the response which audiences made to them very soon inspired imitation on Broadway itself. But it is no less evident that it was they who led the way.

Until now there has never been any history of one (and by no means the least important) of the three pioneering little theatres. Adequate accounts of the origin and development of both the Provincetown Theatre and the Washington Square Players have been written, but no such history of the Neighborhood Playhouse existed. Now one of the two sisters who founded and guided—who indeed simply *were*—the Neighborhood, has told the story both of its external history and of the ideas and ideals which it embodied. It is a fascinating account and it illuminates a mystery as fully as a genuine mystery can ever be illuminated.

A good deal of a mystery it was, even in the days when it was playing so significant a role in the theatrical life of the city, and a mystery it has remained. I am not sure which was the first of its productions I saw but I rather think it was the bill (fully described in Mrs. Crowley's pages) which presented the slight but unconventional and strikingly effective one-acters of Lord Dunsany. When, a few years later (in 1924), I became drama critic of the New York *Nation* I naturally covered each of its productions and continued to do so until public performances ceased. And though there were no evenings in the theatre to which I looked forward with more pleasure there were also none on which one was less sure what to expect or when one felt, somehow, further removed from the profes- sional "show business" to which even the Provincetown and the Washington Square Players were more closely related.

To begin with there was, of course, the fact that nothing "Off-Broadway" could have been further "off," either physi- cally in miles or in atmosphere. The journey to Grand Street in the heart of the great isolated, self-contained, exotic and teeming East Side took one into a world most of us seldom visited on any other occasion and one which was, in many respects, as "foreign" as though it had been located on a dif- ferent continent. Grand Street was an adventure in itself. I, at least, knew very little about the theatre to which I was headed beyond the fact that it was somehow connected with the Henry Street Settlement house and that it had been founded by the two Misses Lewisohn who had inherited from their father both wealth and a philanthropic impulse.

Given these circumstances it would have been strange if what one found in this theatre had not been decidedly dif- ferent from what one found on Broadway or at some lesser distance "Off." But what was most surprising was the fact that, different as it was, it was also relevant to a whole theatri- cal movement beginning to flourish up town. How did it happen that a settlement house on the East Side had some- thing very significant to contribute to what seemed a very different world? And what was this unique something which it did contribute?

The first of these questions (and to a considerable degree the second also) is answered so fully by Mrs. Crowley herself that one need add very little. A settlement house on the East Side had something to contribute because Mrs. Crowley and her sister had seen what this something might be. As young women they found themselves almost equally drawn toward social service and the arts. Contact with Miss Lillian Wald, the guiding spirit of the famous Henry Street Settlement house, made it almost inevitable that they should want to join her enterprise. Their interest in the arts made it no less inevitable that they should soon find themselves asking how the welfare which Henry Street was promoting might include as a major element contact with the arts and artistic expression. The Misses Lewisohn wanted to bring various arts to the East Side but (and this is perhaps the real secret) they also saw the possibility of eliciting art from it. They saw that it need be no mere matter of anything condescendingly handed down. Those who came to the settlement were not to be merely instructed and presented with "culture." They were to be helped to become the creative artists they potentially were.

Hence it was, as the pages of this book make clear, that the work was begun at an elementary but creative level. The first projects of what was only later to become the Neighborhood Playhouse were informal "festivals" of pageant, song, and dance centering around the traditions of Grand Street itself. Only very slowly and after many experiments in various directions did the performance and interpretation of existing dramatic texts become a major part of the enterprise, while productions intended as much for an uptown as for the Grand Street community evolved more slowly still. One is tempted to say that what happened here was a recapitulation of the evolutionary history of the theatre itself which had first come into being in much the same manner. And one is led to believe that the uniqueness of the contribution made by the group was a result of the unique process which developed it.

Few other little theatre groups have ever experimented so

widely. The actual texts chosen for performance were of every conceivable kind—ancient and modern, realistic and fanciful, poetic and tendentious. They included Shaw, James Joyce, Lenormand and Browning, but also Yeats, Dunsany and Percy Mackaye; also the ancient Hindu *Little Clay Cart* and the Chassidic *The Dybbuk*. Even more remarkable was the variety of influences to which the Misses Lewisohn deliberately exposed their pupils and fellow workers—beginning with that of the dramàtic coach and reader Sarah Cowell Le Moyne, and including Boleslavsky, Dalcroze and Yvette Guilbert as well as what they themselves brought back from tours of observation in Egypt and India. Obviously the intention was to explore as completely as possible everything which might help recapture those elements of ritual, poetry and mysticism which had tended to disappear from the realistic and commercial modern stage. And it was the extent to which they succeeded in doing just that which made possible their unique contribution.

When in 1915 the first public performances were given in the newly completed Playhouse almost a decade of experiment lay behind them. By the time the Neighborhood had become a well recognized part of the New York theatre and commonly associated in the public mind with the two other important little theatres the special character of their performances was also recognized though perhaps not clearly defined. Perhaps only those of us who can now look back are in a position to understand just what the differences between the three were but they may be stated somewhat as follows. The Provincetown and the Washington Square Theatres were primarily devoted to dramatic literature—especially modern literature. Of the two, the first was the more concerned with the native playwright and also with radical social and moral ideas; the second was less earnest, more "sophisticated," and especially drawn to plays which seemed to illustrate what was being called "the continental" as opposed to "the puritan" attitude. Both contributed to the intellectual revolution which was one of the most striking phenomena of the teens and twenties. Both the intention and the achievement of the Neighborhood were more different from either than they were from one another. It was less concerned with intellectualized convictions, with morals, or sociology, or manners, more with song and dance and ritual as direct expressions of the beauty and joy of life; or, as one might sum it up, less interested in drama as literature than in what the theatre and theatrical presentation can accomplish as an independent art.

That this is true cannot be realized simply by glancing through the record of productions offered between 1915 and 1927. They included works by a great variety of essentially literary playwrights and many of them were extremely interesting in one way or another. But as one who saw most of them can testify, the most memorable were those in which the unique character of the group's intentions and talents were most striking. And among such I think it was *The Little Clay Cart* (1924) and *The Dybbuk* (1926) which most strikingly demonstrated artistic achievement of a kind which one could have found in no other New York theatre.

The first of these happens to have opened early in the first season that I functioned as a professional reviewer. This was a remarkable theatrical year for it included also the premières of *What Price Glory* by Maxwell Anderson and Lawrence Stallings, Sidney Howard's *They Knew What They Wanted* and O'Neill's *Desire Under the Elms*—all plays original enough and powerful enough to be remembered thirty years later as proof that the American playwright had emerged as a figure to be reckoned with.

Different as the three were they were also obviously of the

same time and in a similar theatrical tradition. All three were not only realistic in manner but also plays which owed their impact to the deliberate challenge they offered to the genteel tradition which they affronted. All three were "timely" and almost journalistic in their obvious relevance to the contemporary scene. *The Little Clay Cart,* on the other hand, came from far away and long ago—from a different time and a different world. It was stylized rather than realistic and so sophisticated that it seemed naïve. It was relevant not to this age, but to all ages and its message was both as gentle and as timeless as the message of the others had been violent and timely. They stated truths of the moment. It revealed without stating a truth which is eternal.

Had I been asked in advance I would probably have said that my own convictions concerning what the theatre should be were best illustrated by the three modern works. But once I had been exposed to the magic of *The Little Clay Cart* I fell completely under its spell. It had taken the Neighborhood group almost two decades to learn how it might open to our time the timelessness of this Hindu classic and I cannot resist quoting a little of what it then moved me to say in *The Nation* for December 24, 1924:

"From a revival of an ancient Hindu classic, *The Little Clay Cart,* one might expect chiefly the exotic and the quaint. Actually, however, the impression produced goes infinitely deeper than either of these words would indicate, and they suggest reflections not only upon the whole theatrical art but upon civilization itself. Here, if anywhere, the spectator will be able to see a genuine example of that Pure Theatre of which theorists talk, and here, too, he will be led to meditate upon that real Wisdom of the East which lies not in esoteric doctrine but in a tenderness far deeper and truer than that of the traditional Christian who has been thoroughly corrupted by the hard righteousness of the Hebrew. He will see acting which has abandoned all pretense of literal imitation but which is yet strikingly beautiful and impressive; staging which belongs frankly to the make-believe of the child at play but which is nevertheless artistically satisfying; and, in addition, a play which is artificial yet profoundly moving because it is not realistic but real."

Scarcely more than a year later I wrote as follows in *The Nation* for January 6, 1926:

"Last year the company at the Neighborhood Playhouse recreated upon its stage one of the most serene of masterpieces; this year it has chosen to show the other side of the picture and to produce a play whose beauty is of a dark and fearsome kind, for Ansky's *The Dybbuk* manages by means of the skillful use of atmosphere and ritual to externalize the passion and tortured mysticism of the Medieval Jew much as the airy charm of *The Little Clay Cart* externalized the untroubled serenity and the daylight wisdom of a people completely at home in a kindly world. Written by a man who had escaped intellectually from the religion of his fathers but who discovered late in life how profoundly that religion still engaged his emotions, the play uses an ancient legend as the means whereby the spiritual life of a people may be invoked; and it clothes this legend with an outward garment of ritual, tremendously effective upon the stage for the very reason that it was unconsciously intended for a dramatic purpose—for the purpose that is to say of being an outward and visible symbol of a spiritual attitude. By means of their wailing chants, their solemn ceremonies and those songs of wild exultation into which their suppressed passions now and again broke out, the Chassidic Jews revealed to one another the tumult of their souls. Removed to the stage, the same means hypnotize the spectator into a poetic faith in the legend itself and make real for him the mood which it generates. . . .

"Some who saw the original production of *The Dybbuk* in the tiny Habima Theatre in Russia tell me that the performance at the Neighborhood Playhouse is inferior, and perhaps it is, but I, having no standard of comparison, find it very lovely indeed and another proof of my contention that nowhere else in America are plays requiring a non-realistic atmosphere and style done half so well as here."

Mrs. Crowley's book recounts in detail both the outer and the inner history of the enterprise which she and her sister created and guided. She describes its earliest beginnings and also the developments which led to the announcement at the close of the 1926–27 season that it would offer no more productions to the public.

Its heyday had coincided pretty closely with that of the two other most important little theatres; and it is in the nature of such enterprises that they perform a certain function and that, having performed it, they come to the end of their careers. The Provincetown Theatre, having "discovered" O'Neill and launched the careers of at least ten or a dozen other writers, actors and men prominent in other fields, had accomplished its task. The professional theatre had absorbed both its lesson and a considerable number of those who had contributed to its success. It ceased to exist because its personnel had scattered to the four winds. The fate of the Washington Square Players was different. Instead of dissolving when it realized that it, also, had accomplished what it had set out to do it simply transformed itself into the professional, "On-Broadway" organization still known as the Theatre Guild. On the other hand, the guiding geniuses of the Neighborhood Playhouse embarked upon new pilgrimages concerning which something is said in the Epilogue to this volume.

This also was inevitable both because Mrs. Crowley and

Miss Lewisohn were so obviously seekers who would never be content with what they had already found and because a permanment professional theatrical organization had never been a principal object of their ambition. Every step which led from original community experiments at Henry Street to the fully developed theatrical organization was taken with a certain reluctance. When public performance came to be a major part of the program that meant a step away from the original intention because it involved the establishment of a professional acting company some members of which had, to be sure, been trained at the Playhouse while others were re-cruited from the professional theatre. The existence of a pro-fessional company meant that adequate paying audiences had to be attracted and to that extent the Playhouse of necessity became commercial as well as professional.

The disappearance of the Playhouse from the theatrical scene was a shock and a loss to those of us who had come to depend upon it for some of the most rewarding evenings of every season. But we realized even then that we had no right to complain. It had for a number of years done more than merely provide those evenings. It had made a permanent con-tribution to theatrical art in the United States.

by the Author

These memories of the Neighborhood Playhouse
are in no way thought of as an historical record;
dates, definitions, personalities, or even reference to the legion
that contributed time and personal service to a cultural enterprise have been sadly neglected. I have attempted rather to
recapture values which stimulated relationship to a creative
image.

The Neighborhood Playhouse grew from the need to integrate media of production at a time when photographic representation dominated the commercial stage, when lyric forms
expressed through the dance, or through song, were relegated
to the music hall, opera bouffe, or opera ballet. Actually our
experience grew from a source wholly foreign to the theatre
of that day. It developed spontaneously by way of festivals
given by members of the children's clubs at the Henry Street
Settlement in Manhattan's lower East Side, at the turn of the
century. These initial offerings, notwithstanding their imperfections and crudity, were the germ which animated a
decade of intensive experiment in various aspects of theatre.
Quite apart from their naïve form these festivals stimulated
an indefinable mood for the audiences as well as for the children taking part. This may have been due to the response to
a timeless image. For the festivals were motivated by myth
and ritual associated for the most part with the traditions of

the people of the neighborhood. Later on plays in which the senior members of the clubs participated were given at Clinton Hall not far from the Settlement.

The partnership between my sister Irene Lewisohn and myself which began with the children's festival productions continued uninterruptedly over the years at the Neighborhood Playhouse. In fact Irene was responsible for the productions by the children and their training as well as for the training for the festivals by older, more advanced groups. The lyric programs as parent of the Neighborhood Playhouse productions provided not only the germ but the basic form of later productions, such as *The Little Clay Cart,* a Sanskrit drama, and *The Dybbuk,* based upon a Chassidic legend. In both, the mood outweighed the structure of the drama; in both, a lyric quality was their intrinsic feature.

Although the link with the Henry Street Settlement continued through personal relationship as well as through the fact that the amateur groups taking part in the productions were associated directly or indirectly with the clubs and classes of the Settlement, the Playhouse had from the beginning its own identity and freedom to develop in a wholly individual way. It was to the credit of Miss Lillian Wald and the directors of the Henry Street Settlement that the Neighborhood Playhouse had the benefit of being included under its charter as a nonprofit activity freed from taxation. It was for this reason also that we were able to hold performances on Sunday.

On February 12, 1915, these various enterprises moved to a home of their own on the corner of Grand and Pitt Streets on the lower East Side of Manhattan.

Looking back over the years thudding with experiment and constantly shifting adjustments, I would be at a loss to indicate the force of the compelling image that dominated the group, except as a potential value-seeking creative form. Our task was apparently an attempt to extract an essence out of the dramatic material of the productions rather than to convey the art of good showmanship. It seemed as if the whole process involved in staging, wrestling with our own inexperience as well as with undisciplined students, working with faulty material, as well as with tools which in themselves have no value—for every object in the theatre serves only to create an illusion of reality—in fact all the obvious as well as the deeper problems of production were carried on as an instinctive urge that could not be defined. What is more exacting than building, shaping, and reshaping a scene, to destroy and reexperience it in the course of rehearsals? Or to labor with paraphernalia which has no intrinsic substance? In fact the whole concentration upon doing and undoing is designed to experience that intangible subtle element realizable only as symbol. Though this magical factor eludes all definition it may at times be sensed in the theatre through the mood, atmosphere, or imagery of a creative situation. Or again perceived as something which conforms with our senses yet enables us to transcend the immediate or photographic reality.

It is not surprising then that theatre with all its trickery and sham, its often obvious and tawdry manipulations, can lead us to the heights and depths of human experience if we succeed in penetrating the outer layer for the essence or image.

In retrospect it seems natural that our adventure did not move along a broad straight thoroughfare but that it followed its own spiral course much as a mountain trail which winds back and forth, yet offers the climber a new perspective at each turn. Though the mountain peak with us remained invisibly present, the way moved laboriously through trial and error around the image which the Neighborhood Playhouse carried for its eager, searching family.

These pages have grown in much the same way. They were

begun shortly after the closing of the theatre with the hope that through them some of the unresolved problems might become clarified and a new way found for further experiment. But I was too involved in the conflict of releasing from the old ties and the gripping dynamis to find the right perspective. Some years later I tried again only to find that I was too detached to relive it as a personal experience. These incompleted manuscripts were rescued by an old friend, Clara Bogart Burrage, who, through devoted interest in the material, assembled scattered pages, edited, transcribed them and harbored them in her attic for years. I am also grateful to my nephew, Walter P. Lewisohn, for his cooperation in the early versions. The thirtieth anniversary of the Neighborhood Playhouse School of the Theatre called me again to the task of resuscitating the orphaned child. For by this time the students of the school were clamoring for the story of their ancestors.

Irene's vision and enterprising spirit carried on undauntedly after the closing of the Neighborhood Playhouse. We are indebted to her and Rita Morgenthau, our associate from the Henry Street days, for establishing the School, where training was based upon the experience of the Neighborhood Playhouse. This enterprise had already assumed a significant place, including a place in the educational world, at the time of Irene's death in 1944. Another product of Irene's vision was the Costume Institute which after its successful experimental years under the direction of Irene, Aline Bernstein and Polaire Weissman was incorporated in the Metropolitan Museum of Art in 1945. These and other creative enterprises initiated by Irene are referred to in the Epilogue.

Memories such as these have numberless alluring aspects. To convey them adequately would require the combined efforts of the original "family." In fact were the story told by another of the old colleagues, it would undoubtedly present a wholly contrasting picture, for any individual enterprise conforms in large measure to the outlook of the observer. In finally releasing the manuscript I am only too conscious of its limitations and prejudice. I am equally aware that it suffers from the tricks of a faulty memory. It has been my fate to have been long removed geographically from the world of the American theatre, and this accounts for the dearth of contemporary analogy or comment. May I therefore repeat that these reflections are thought of primarily as an attempt to revive something of the ardor vitalizing a pioneer experience. Yet curiously much that we lived and pressed so hard into life seems now to take form and the pattern once dimmed to grow clearer.

Though there has been no direct attempt to evaluate these "memories" from a psychological angle, still any experience of theatre is enhanced by the new psychological standpoint opening up areas of understanding below the level of rational consciousness. For the opportunity of even a fragmentary insight, I wish to make deep acknowledgment to C. G. Jung.

I also wish to express my appreciation for the encouraging interest of Theatre Arts Books, and particularly for the indefatigable cooperation of Robert MacGregor and Hermine Isaacs Popper, and my gratitude to Alice Owen for her great help in bringing this book to the attention of the publisher.

To each and every one who shared in the Playhouse adventure during a decade pressed with the intensity of the experience, these memories are dedicated. As craftsman, designer, author, composer, producer, player and audience, each played a role in the quest for a unified creative experience. It is my humble attempt and privilege to share with you a glimpse,

prejudiced though it is, of the old Grand Street days of growing into theatre. May I hope that these "scrapbook leaves"
may serve as a kind of sounding board to old collaborators
and students.

To you, Irene, what can I say. Your presence, creative impulse, energetic spirit lives in every memory. Your vision,
transcending the old epoch, lives on through the gallant group
of teachers, students, players of other generations, enabling
them to play their phantasy of theatre.

June 8, 1959
A. L. C.
Zurich

CHAPTER ONE

THE BEGINNINGS

The original image of the Neighborhood Play-house entered the secret door of our nursery when my sister Irene and I were three and six years of age. It came as a sudden vision vividly contrasting with the drab life of city children, so startling that it was guarded as a secret never to be divulged. But later it emerged out of hidden depths of memory as an expansive hillside on whose treeless crest a temple stands severe in form, of sparkling stone which appears white in the brilliant sunshine. Children are seen coming toward the temple from all directions, some leaping, some dancing down more distant slopes. Approaching it they form in procession, carrying garlands which they place upon an altar in the portico of the temple as they sing.

To children whose only access to nature was the spacious areas of Central Park banned by cryptic signs—"Keep Off the Grass"—the vision had the magical effect of enabling them to escape from the restricted order of the nursery and its Draconian law of being stockinged, petticoated, washed, combed, and pinafored in twenty minutes for breakfast. This spontaneous play of imagery carried, unknown to us, the roots of drama in uniting the spirit of instinctive play with that of a divine presence indicated in the temple, which conformed, as we later learned, exactly with the design of a Doric temple.

Though the vision was long forgotten before the festivals at the Henry Street Settlement became a yearly event, it nevertheless played an unconscious role, as a dream in childhood often does upon the later personality. For us this childhood experience became the germ of the Neighborhood Playhouse. The idyllic landscape surrounding the temple could hardly be considered prophetic of the setting of the future Playhouse building at the corner of Grand and Pitt Streets. But the dignity of the simple brick structure with its welcoming green doors was soon to have a fateful meaning to old and young who realized their deepest experience through the conflicts, trials, disappointments, suspense, joys of working for the productions of the Neighborhood Playhouse.

My first contact with the Henry Street Settlement and Lillian D. Wald was inspired by my father, who had often spoken about her genius as an organizer in the field of social work, which was surpassed only by the charm of her personality. To my mind she conjured a being who, with a wave of her hand, could convert arid wastes into happy playgrounds, cramped homes into surroundings of dignity and beauty. Then came an invitation to accompany my father to dine with Miss Wald at 265 Henry Street.

The awe of meeting a woman of miracles was for the moment forgotten in the experience of my first taxi ride to the lower East Side. There taxicabs were not only unusual but apparently machinations of the devil, for as we drove through the crowded streets, children shouted scornfully, "Get a horse! Get a horse!" A pebble thrown through the taxi window and landing in my lap was a sharp comment on the intrusion of rank uptowners. The taxi moved at a snail's pace in order not to interfere with lines of pushcarts and peddlers and an occasional hurdy-gurdy with children crowding around it. We passed through streets littered with garbage, the children's playground.

No. 265 was reached at last, modestly tucked in a row of red brick Georgian houses, a relic of early New York's fashionable quarter, now tenements. Though architecturally the building had nothing to distinguish it from the surrounding houses, a brightly polished knocker added a hospitable touch. We picked a circuitous passage up the steps crowded with children playing "jackstones," and almost before the resounding echoes of the knocker had died away we found ourselves inside a haven of dignity and cordiality. Only a door separated this reposeful colonial setting from the noise of the children and the haunting eyes of the immigrants outside.

We were ushered up a flight of stairs to Miss Wald's room, and once in her presence every other consideration vanished. The welcoming smile, gay voice, cordial gesture, the handsome face, ovaled by dark hair in striking contrast to the blue cotton Visiting Nurse uniform—this was the lady of miracles. She was vigorous, and, most overwhelming of all, she was joyous.

The Leading Lady, as Miss Wald was called by her associates, led us downstairs to the dining room where the starched and happy company, the Settlement's Visiting Nurses and their co-workers, were waiting for the gong to announce dinner. Lively spirits sparred across the table, and presiding at its head, Lillian Wald played not one part, but innumerably changing characters. In her role as hostess, her hands seemed to work automatically as she mixed the crisp green leaves in the salad bowl, while she clarified some problem about unions, interlarding her conversation with whimsical stories.

Dinner over, we left the building guided by the Settlement kindergarten and dancing mistress. Crossing the square, we found ourselves in the public school, where a large group of waiting youth impetuously greeted our attractive young guide, Henrietta Schwartz. A piano started and young couples began to dance with awkward jerky movements, but with amazing alertness to master time and step, and with eagerness to absorb.

When we returned to 265, members of the Boys' Club, Miss Wald's "Heroes," were sitting patiently listening to a short bearded man, Robert Ely, discussing civic behavior. These youths seemed far older than their years—quiet, serious, weighted with responsibility, but always intent upon their "chance."

Meanwhile, the Leading Lady was felt here, there, everywhere, she herself the first to hear a knock at the front door and to respond to an incoherent, stumbling appeal for a nurse; or to receive a delegation of pushcart vendors who had come for guidance concerning some new ordinance affecting their trade. A young woman needed data on local conditions, while a university student of sociology patiently waited his turn to confer about a labor dispute. They were all received graciously, put at their ease, counseled with, and when leaving, took with them a sense of friendliness, a glimpse, no doubt, into a wider world.

At last it was time to say good-bye. Miss Wald, unharried, unperplexed, was as much at ease as when she first greeted us, with the same smile, the same buoyant energy and exuberant sympathy. The question I had so long asked myself was dimly shaping its reply. A settlement was   . ? Could this be it? A garden of human sympathy? Miss Wald? Was she not the chief gardener, sowing, grafting, pruning, joyously happy in her garden? She seemed to receive whatever came, to give all she could, to ask nothing more than to sow, to plant, to tend.

This introduction to a new world left a deep impression, although I did not become associated with the Settlement for another year. My father's death the next year, after that of my mother two years before, brought changes, inner and outer ones, and the need for a new orientation to life. Again my partner in the questioning search was Irene. Like children in a mythical tale we were sent into the stormy world with a heavy bundle to seek our fortunes. Free in a sense, because that bundle contained among other things nuggets of gold, yet they added considerably to its weight. For freedom cannot be purchased ready made. It too is a growth like a plant. We were gripped by the burden of responsibility, an incredible weight for youth. For whether the bundle is too full or too empty, the result is the same. This, it seems to me, is true of any inheritance, spiritual or material, positive if realized, yet the task of a life-time.

At that epoch the inner voice of the avant-garde was exteriorized. Individuals began to be conscious of the swarms of foreigners, immigrants from central and eastern Europe flocking to our shores, who, oppressed in their own lands, naïvely anticipated a literal interpretation of the Declaration of Independence in the new world. Baffled and confused by what greeted them, many lost all sense of identity in yielding their image of life and liberty to the demands of sweated industry. The unregulated conditions of labor had generated infectious disease of the spirit and body that spread like fire.

In response to this chaotic situation, valiant spirits joined forces in the overcrowded ramshackle tenement districts of the cities, forming small cooperatively conducted centers, a kind of brotherhood-sisterhood, reminiscent of the Middle Ages, in an attempt to bridge the chasm between the serf and overlord. These were the social workers. Their settlements served as laboratories or experimental stations where students of sociology and other searchers could find a relation to immediate problems such as public health, child labor, the unending conflict between employer and employed, and so forth. But above all, these settlements responded to the overwhelming need for personal service to the dwellers in the neighborhood, offering medical care, citizenship and language guidance clubs, classes, craft opportunities in terms of a human cultural experience.

To these same settlements flocked many young people from overprivileged homes, irrespective of race, social status, or traditional values, there to touch elbows with a foreign world, divorced from their background yet of it. As volunteers they sought to serve in some simple capacity which would have been taboo at home. For here was a breath of reality, a verve, an impulse unperceived through the stolid wall of brownstone, high-stooped dwellings in upper Manhattan.

The Henry Street Settlement was one such oasis in the surrounding din and chaos, Miss Wald its presiding genius. She, Jane Addams, Florence Kelley, will live on as rare statesmen of a new order, for they functioned through a sense of relationship—could one say as Great Mothers?—instead of through the rigidity of a patriarchal system. Theirs was a never-ceasing patient effort to interpret the inner core of America to their neighbors through their understanding and gracious hospitality to the human being lodged within the exploited worker, himself housed in a derelict home. Serving as a voice for the disenfranchised population, they paved the way to the good-neighbor policy which became an effective instrument for international relations several decades later. Franklin Roosevelt, Herbert Lehman, Adolph Berle, Raymond Fosdick, Paul Warburg, George Alger, and other younger and older men, my father in a measure among them, came under the spell of these women who plied the art of resolving conflicts not only in relation to the industrial world but in the lives of countless human beings.

It was not unnatural then that my steps (and soon Irene's) should turn toward the Henry Street Settlement. But the choice was not without conflict. For at one end of the spectrum of my values was a passion for acting and the desire for study, at the other end, a social conscience, more correctly the memory of those hopeless eyes of pushcart vendors that greeted me on my first visit to Henry Street. Coupled with these was the need to relate to an unknown world, to find a root. Irene and I pondered this perplexing situation, and although the conflict between the personal and collective demands remained unclarified, some unknown force compelled the surrender of the inner way. Could this decision have been induced by the need to relate to children submerged in the world of materia as we? For our personal values did not conform with the traditional world of family or of producing a family. Could it have been, though unperceived at the time, that the nursery vision was insinuating in us a new attitude at cross purposes with the world of immediate reality and its definition?

G. B. Shaw and the Fabians had cast a spell over youth at that time, at least over my youth. Various brands of new literature had to be consumed, to find some answer to baffling problems which naturally remained unanswered. For where were the promised values in social welfare leading—heralded by bath tubs, plumbing improvements, and so forth—unless there was a leeway for the spirit? Children were hoarded in the public school with its drab commonplace curriculum, or on the streets which harbored mounds of garbage instead of a glimpse of the green world of nature. Clubs and classes, parties, dances, excursions, valuable as they were, did not touch those fundamental chords out of which culture unfolds. Such were the reflections of the observer in me, searching for an image that was not registered among the values of a collective social enterprise geared as settlements necessarily were to immediate conditions. The search, however, was to find a channel through the experiments of the Neighborhood Playhouse.

CHAPTER TWO

CLUB TRAINING AT
HENRY STREET

Our comings and goings between the Victorian brownstone house in Fifty-Seventh Street and the helter-skelter life in Henry Street were full of adventuresome contrasts. No matter what was concealed behind the expressionless façades uptown, their outer propriety remained unchanged; but the lower East Side was a never-ending kaleidoscope of movement and color. Curbs were hemmed with pushcarts and their jungle of garish display, their crossbars garlanded with the yellowest of yellow shoes, bright feathers, stockings and ribbons, combs, suspenders, underdrawers, corsets. These variegated offerings were a constant source of interest to the moving throngs crowding the cobbled streets, jostling, shouting, playing, and arguing.

Suddenly we were part of it, touching elbows, trying to avoid collision with the hurdy-gurdy dancers, hearing laughter, feeling the bustle, the thrill of confused activity, caught up in the stress and the eager on-push of youth. Then as suddenly we would leave the mêlée behind for the loveliness and calm of the Settlement. There even the clubrooms were planned with a consideration for an aesthetic sense to which both the children and their elders instinctively responded. The brasses and coppers on the mantels, or the Russian bowl on the table, provided the link between the colonial decorum and the foreign homelands of the neighbors.

This relationship between the old and the new countries was always preserved. At Christmas time, the Christmas-tree candles and the Chanukah lights burned in the same room, uniting the spirit of the Christian and the Jewish midwinter feast of light. Once the Henry Street Settlement offered its unfailing hospitality to the bride of a young Armenian who had just arrived. The Gregorian church wedding was carried out with punctilious respect for every detail of the ceremony, including the sanctified wine and the almond cakes. Then there was the celebration when a busful of Chinese mothers, many with bound feet, and their bobbed-hair children, were welcomed with traditions of their background in the spirit of the New Year.

At Henry Street, classes and clubs, dancing and other social activities followed one another in successive rounds, yet each time with the spontaneity and charm of a first occurrence. The club leader played a significant role in the children's lives. She was not only teacher but confidante, and in that way became a link between the family and the outer world. She soon learned something of the family background of each child, was informed about the ninth baby that was coming and how six-year-old Jenny would now have to do the housework. She knew when Sammy wanted his working papers and that Poppa had to go to court about a lapse in his peddler's license; and of course something had to be done about each.

As young club leaders we were left to our own devices. In this new field, each felt free to follow his way, none of the older members offering advice. But if we found ourselves with a problem beyond our depth we could turn to our director of the children's club and class work, Rita Wallach (Morgenthau), an inspiring friend of every child. To her, there was no ugliness or dullness in the make-up of a child, either individually or collectively; yet there was no suggestion of false sentimentality in her relations with them.

She could discipline without disciplining, for whatever she administered in the way of punishment had also the grace of humor.

Visits to the children's homes gradually broke through the wall of reticence between the foreign-born mother and the new world. When language obstructed, there were some tangible articles to be exhibited and admired, perhaps a bit of old brass or a blouse, hidden away because they belonged to the old country, not here where all were Americans. At the mothers' meetings when we all laughed at the oldest and staidest who had to dance with a broomstick in lieu of a partner, she would suddenly become nimble-footed, and forthwith emerged steps and gestures of the folk dances of her youth in the old country. So we began to see, behind the ungainly appearance of the women, the unkempt helpless aspect of the men, a yearning for values of the spirit and gratefulness for any gesture of understanding. This was certainly true in any dealings with the children, always eager to learn, alert, bubbling with ingenuity in performing all the pranks of the devil.

Perhaps the most venturesome effort of our club days was the street pageant given in 1913 to celebrate the twentieth anniversary of the Henry Street Settlement. Relating the social history of the street, it marked our only experience in pageantry. It was completely "homemade" in design, organization, and direction.

The first episode presented the purchase of Manhattan, followed by episodes showing a glimpse of succeeding generations and types of the varying peoples who had inherited the neighborhood. Though simple in design, it was planned for a cast of five hundred, among them mothers and infants en masse début, and a horse, the postie of Dutch colonial days. We had tried to conceal the horse incident from the policeman on duty, but the moment of confession finally came. The officer, visualizing a stampede, turned to Irene with a solemn wink: "Little one, I guess you'll have to can that horse idea." Nevertheless the postie appeared, gaily caparisoned, and won much acclaim for its wholly creditable conduct the night of the performance.

A glimpse at contemporary history was suggested in the last scene by more recent comers to the neighborhood from Russia, Poland, Italy, Ireland, wearing their characteristic dress. Old and youngest in arms united in a gay round of their native folk dances.

Costumes were made by the older women of the neighborhood in a small flat, loaned for this purpose by Harriet Knight, one of the residents. Here, night after night, through winter and spring, the pageant's wardrobe was assembled under the direction of Aline Bernstein and her sister Ethel Frankau. They did not know at the time that this experience would lead them into further adventures in costuming, though hardly to emulate the original standard of economy, as no costume for the pageant might cost more than fifty cents!

The street pageant contributed a field for other initiations. Henry Street was paved for the occasion as an offering of the city. The Edison Company contributed the lighting, the Police and Fire Departments gave every possible assistance, and the school in the neighborhood opened its doors so that the schoolrooms could be used for the dressing of old Manhattan. In busy, crowded New York it had been possible to enlist the wholehearted cooperation of city, school, and library authorities.

The night of the pageant ten thousand people, old and young, crowded the streets to overflowing and looked on from roofs, windows, and stoops of the neighboring tenements. As one of the neighbors expressed it, the whole street was "flooded with love." Besides the many self-invited, there was a grandstand for Miss Wald and friends of the Settlement, including the Mayor and other officials. At the end of the returning procession, when the Visiting Nurses in their starched blue uniforms joined and marched by the grandstand, a rousing cheer for Lillian Wald echoed and re-echoed from street and housetops. The firemen in their dress uniforms stood at attention, guarding firehorses in shining harness. And the old church in Henry Street, the last remaining one in New York with a slaves' gallery, added its tribute with pealing bells.

The various episodes developed and trained in the Settlement's gymnasium could only be assembled at the time of the performance, since the street was not available until then. Notwithstanding the many weeks of rehearsing, the ultimate result remained problematical in spacing, timing, and continuity up to the first performance, which was also the première of the band. But even more problematical, what of the pandemonium after the final procession, when the five hundred inhabitants of early Manhattan, variously assorted, returned to the schoolhouse?

This unpredictable, terrifying possibility resolved in an astonishing episode. Old and young entered the building in complete silence, nor was a sound to be heard as each went to the room assigned. Removing the costume proved to be the epilogue of the pageant. Had each member of the cast been stirred by a unifying experience? Something analogous perhaps to the coming together of different tribes under one honored chief? Whatever the influence, the effect came through as a wholly unconscious and stirring tribute.

CHAPTER THREE

FESTIVALS

Although the children of the neighborhood had inherited an old culture from their ancestors, in the city practically no contact remained with its source— nature. To our young friends spring meant a circus party, with ice cream and cake, or perhaps a frowzy maypole in the distant park. For on Henry Street spring seemed to bloom in an orgy of refuse. Then the streets became a veritable cornucopia of garbage, and within the doorposts of the orthodox Jewish home, a violent equinoctial combat with dust and dirt foretold the coming of the Passover. A similar spring cleaning ritual took place in the homes of our Irish and Italian neighbors, though perhaps with less intensity.

Somehow these realistic dramatizations of renewed energy and abandon seemed to overlook the wonder and joy of awakening life in nature, a feeling for the mystery which has echoed in the heart of mankind from time immemorial. With original man, the transformation of day and night and the cycle of the seasons were not casual events, nor was nature an unqualified provider. It was peopled with divine or healing powers, but also with demonic creatures always present to destroy. Day and night to original man was an experience without certainty in one sense, yet of endless duration, so that the divine and demonic inhabitants, though not visually present, were nevertheless more potent than if they had been mere friends or enemies from another tribe. We can realize, then, how the day and night shielding fabulous beings became superrealities, arousing wonder and fear, demanding propitiation, obedience, service.

We can also realize something of the overwhelming and enduring influence of such experience if we stop to consider that it was not until the so-called age of enlightment—the eighteenth century—that reason invaded nature, driving out the last remnants of its elfin inhabitants, an act of violence as devastating in its implications as any succeeding horrors of destruction. For in destroying the belief in the spirits of nature, man became possessed by them, impersonating caricatures of gods and heroes in assuming himself to be all-powerful as well as omniscient. It was inevitable that through its conquest, nature was emptied of its healing superstitions; yet these images of the soul projected upon the screen of nature are our real ancestors, and as such, carriers of great cultural values. Think of the banality of a world wholly robbed of creative imagination and substituting the voice of the loudspeaker roaring "thou shalt" and "thou shalt not" for the free-to-wander spirit inherent in us all.

Though I may seem to have wandered far afield, it was some such feeling of loss by foredoomed city dwellers that evoked our early festivals at Henry Street, with the doubtful hope that some fragment of creative imagery might thrive in the barren soil of the overcrowded neighborhood.

In the club-meeting periods we had attempted to explain to the children something of the significance of the age-old rituals of spring, and gradually we wove dance and song around their symbols. From the moment the free games gave way to rhythmical movement relating in a purely imaginative way to the myths, the pandemonium that usually climaxed the game and work period subsided into a calm and reverent mood. The myths we told in the story hour, combined with rhythmic movement and song, had the effect of a magic potion, charming the eager and soothing the wild. Thus the seeds of the festivals were sown.

The first festival occurred several years before the street pageant. It was based upon three impressions of spring as perceived through the background of a Japanese, a Greek, and a Hindu child. Myths, legends, fairy tales upon this theme were told in the clubroom throughout the year as preparation, and at the appropriate time an invited audience —chiefly parents of the Settlement children—came to the Henry Street gymnasium to watch the performance on an improvised stage. The production was not a monument to theatre, but somehow behind its crudity, something lived.

The following spring a more ambitious attempt was woven round the theme of the Passover, the first of a series of Biblical festivals. It revolved around the Song of Miriam with its epic note of triumph over the redemption of the children of Israel from the yoke of the Egyptian: "And Miriam took a timbral in her hand and all the maidens went out after her with singing and with dancing." Rites, chants, and psalms observed during Passover in the orthodox synagogues were incorporated into the body of the festival, not as dogmatic creed, but as a thread upon which to link the spring myth of Israel. It was not a pageant nor any attempt at representation. Hemlock boughs provided the setting, the costumes were uniform in cut but dyed by one of the club leaders in a color scale characteristically Eastern. The music was a hybrid collection of themes selected to invoke a mood.

The Chanukah, or midwinter, festival, incorporated some synagogal ritual and chants, but also images that were not traditional, yet suited to the universality of its theme. For in this celebration of the winter solstice, the mystery of light, we recognized a common symbol the world over, the Yule log, the lighted Christmas tree, the Chinese lantern, the Chanukah lamp.

As many of the children came from orthodox Jewish homes, where the law of the father dominated, we had to cope with the traditional taboo on creative play. Neither at home nor at school, where the child was forced into a mechanized system, was there a chance for fantasy, unless playing "mama" to a baby sister or brother could be described as a form of fantasy. Moreover, there were startling prejudices against the most natural instincts. For example, for a little boy to touch the hand of a little girl, or to stand beside her, was taboo. "Oh, she's a girl." To what extent she carried the taint of Eve we could never discover, since the explanation was not suitable for "teacher." With the green world of nature equally prohibited by the close walls of the East-Side streets, it was both a struggle and a challenge to evoke a mood which would allow those taking part, and those observing, to participate in images rooted in universal symbols, and in that way to touch levels of experience beyond their own.

But perhaps just because the way to the life of the spirit was blocked with endless obstacles, it held unbounded fascination. No one could say "what a festival was," but even while practicing, a strange feeling made you still. You could begin to see things that weren't there before, and when the music played and you carried flowers to the altar, you held your breath. Yet when the festival was over, the flowers were gone and the altar was only a table again. This first step toward symbolic imagery explains why gradually and unsuspectedly the instinct of creative play competed with and then triumphed over the pandemonium and battle cries of the same children during their free play periods.

The children's festivals had no claim to artistic pattern. Their value, far and above the actual presentation, lay in the fact that they touched some common ancestral chord which produced a surprising response. However one defines the effect of a timeless, ageless image suddenly awakened, that spark remained the kernel of what in later years was accepted as the spirit of the Neighborhood Playhouse.

In fact, these early homemade festivals would have no reason to be mentioned had they not held the core of the later festivals or lyric productions at the Playhouse. As the years went on the festival—no longer limited to the children —acquired a growing significance, reaching its climax in the production of Walt Whitman's *Salut au Monde* in 1922. The training of the Festival Dancers became Irene's special province. She designed and directed the choreography, and the casts were drawn from her classes in dance, and Laura Elliot's classes in song and choral speech, which in turn revolved around the festivals.

Mrs. Elliot, a singer of distinction, and teacher to notable opera stars, had abandoned her career to apply her gifts to furthering music among working groups. We first met through the Women's Trade Union League, for which we had been asked to arrange a music and dance program. Our shared exploring spirit led into various experiments in voice, in combination with movement and sound. Developed first for the festivals, these experiments were to be invaluable later on to many of the Playhouse productions. Indeed, one of the rare and priceless contacts of all the years began when Mrs. Elliot took charge of the choral work at Henry Street.

In the lyric programs, the theme alone dominated. Mobilized through movement, the production was perceived as an orchestra, the dances serving as part of the orchestration. Irene's designs were meticulously worked out, nothing left to chance or sudden flair. Inspired by the vision of the exact relationship between movement and music, she could stimulate her group to tune into her values, and in consequence the dancers were ready to mutilate size or ego for a chance to work. The concentrated intensity of a festival rehearsal was electric.

Irene's pioneering contribution to the theatre through these lyric productions can only be appraised in retrospect. Today the dance has achieved an art form in and of itself, but at the Playhouse more than four decades ago, the relation of free movement to music was a pioneer adventure, for dance in this country still had no distinctive form other than that of ballet as an appendage to opera or opéra-comique. (The unique exceptions were Isadora Duncan and somewhat later Ruth St. Denis, each of whom brought a new dimension to the dance by giving scope to her own personality, instead of disguising it through the artful formalities of classical ballet.) Under Irene's direction the Festival Dancers acquired a special flair for a form that was in the making.

Although the festivals continued to have a separate identity throughout the Playhouse years, they did not live a life apart. The nucleus of the Playhouse acting group had its first experience in the early festivals, and, over the years, the continuity was never broken in relating dramatic training not only to the dance but to choral speech and pantomime. The conflict arising from the opposite needs of lyric forms and drama created a dynamic verve which became more and more intensified over the years. We could not conceive of theatre divorced from lyrical roots any more than we could help working in forms still in the making. Such later and maturer productions as *The Little Clay Cart* and *The Dyb-buk,* though more rounded as drama, could not have carried the folk spirit combined with a mystical image had it not been for the long experience of the festivals, and the continuity of work in the classes with their directed training for the lyric programs. If for no other reason, the first festivals, with all their imperfection and naïveté, have the value of an ancestral root.

CHAPTER FOUR

SARAH COWELL
LE MOYNE

The beginnings of the Neighborhood Playhouse
are unimaginable without the association of
Sarah Cowell Le Moyne, an association which had grown
out of her performance in Browning's *A Blot in the 'Scutcheon* some years before. Her personality which had impressed itself upon the whole production brought a vision
of what theatre might be. Drama, poetry, gesture, movement,
costume, speech were fused into an unbelievable unity.

An hour before I saw her performance, Mrs. Le Moyne
had been nothing but a name to me, but from that moment
I seemed to have one quest, to meet her for the chance of
working with her. However, it was a matter of months before the end of the quest was in sight and her sought-for
address was in my hands, the Everett House, Union Square.
The following morning, long before the hands of the hall
clock at the staid old Everett House pointed to nine, I installed myself in the lobby until it was agreeable for my
unsuspecting hostess to receive me. Finally I was ushered
into a large Victorian sitting room by her faithful "Parkyn."
I waited apprehensively. How would I be able to tell her
what the performance of *A Blot* had meant to me?

The door opened and she came in, sweeping graciously
toward me. Every word, every thought, seemed suddenly to
disappear. All I could remember afterwards was that Mrs.

23

Le Moyne and Gwendolyn of *A Blot* appeared to have nothing in common but their sex. Her hair was drawn back severely now and was quite gray; her face was lined and worn; and, strangest of all, what had become of her height! But the moment she began to talk, all the vivid impressions of *A Blot* returned, her distinction of speech, her nobility of carriage, her poise. I can still see those blue eyes with their kind, yet half amused, interest in this curious young thing so removed from her world.

With a welcoming smile, she seemed to search me through and through. Before many minutes, I had managed to tell her of my consuming desire to study with her.

"You wish to study seriously? What qualifications do you think you have? Do you know your Bible? I adore it, with all its wickedness!—What language! What character! Yes, we've lost it all. And that, my child, is the trouble with youth today—it lacks style and elegance. Naturally, that is reflected on the stage.—But you say you want to study? Take this line or two and read them to me."

I gladly plunged into "Youth and Art," blissfully unconscious of exuding a sentimental vapor so dear to the heart of the young beginner. Mrs. Le Moyne soon interrupted:

"To read Browning is a long and difficult road. Take Grace Ellison, for example. She worked on Mildred with me for an entire year. I starved her, beat her, in the process," she said, looking me straight in the eye.

Still I was undaunted, even that process seemed to me a small price to pay for the privilege of playing Mildred. Mrs. Le Moyne continued her epic of discouragement. She did not like to teach; she really despised pupils, for no one any longer had a passion for work; no one had any idea of language.

"Take the well-dressed women one meets today, beautifully gowned, princesses to look at; they open their mouths—slatterns! Would they dare reveal their bodies as they do their minds?"

When she finally rose, I was convinced that it was useless to pursue the quest. She escorted me down the long corridor to the elevator. Suddenly, I felt her arm drawing me to her and holding me quite close. "If you really want to work with me, let me know. It may prove a great expense and a waste of time for us both. But, think it over and write to me," and she was gone.

The Everett House became a magical source of life, but also a scene of many hazards, for one never quite knew when to expect the heel of the master's slipper, aimed with comparative exactness, in lieu of criticism, or a peremptory dismissal for the criminal neglect of a consonant. To Mrs. Le Moyne, each word was charged with magic, and failure to achieve the right nuance was tantamount to invoking brimstone and pitch. Although she knew it was never possible to plumb every overtone of thought and the majesty each word contained, to master the word as an instrument was to her a lifelong task. A poem of Browning's was like a precious stone, to which there clung the rare stuff of the mind to work over until each inflection of thought, every shade of color, in the imagery of the word had been polished until it glistened, sparkled.

How often she would say, "There are ten years' more work on that, dear child," perhaps alluding to "My Last Duchess." And yet, with the subtlety of Browning himself, she had already characterized the cold, calculating aestheticism of the Duke who starved his last Duchess while she pecked like a bird at a crumb of life. Who but Browning could compress a novel into a few verses? And who but Mrs. Le

Moyne could convey it to us as if it were our own experience?

We had begun work on *Pippa Passes,* and gradually I was learning to recognize the difference between the technique Mrs. Le Moyne used as a reader and that she used as an actress; for she had developed both gifts. As reader, she seemed to be painting landscapes and types with clear, pure color. As actress, she would chisel a character till it seemed to endure for all time, like her characterization of the Monseigneur in *Pippa Passes.* I can still hear and see him, craftily catechizing his servant; still recall the amazing transition from politician to prelate, from prelate to a man caught and facing God for a moment, some eternal truth brought back to him through the divine-like innocence of a child.

While I was stumbling through the role of Phene, with Mrs. Le Moyne supplying all the remaining parts, she interrupted one day, saying: "I've spoken with Henry Miller. He's interested in the idea of a production of *Pippa.* Would you like to play Phene?"—Really play? From that moment, all energy, thought, purpose was directed toward that possibility. Preparation now became vastly more concentrated, the suspense almost unendurable, until plans for the production were launched.

Then in the fall of 1906 came rehearsals. The stage was like a barn, shorn even of its stalls; the old Majestic Theatre, big and empty and cold. One sat, hour upon hour, on a cane-backed chair, waiting—for what? Nothing happened; everyone was nervous, ill at ease. Mrs. Le Moyne now sat back like the rest of us, waiting. Then, the call to rehearsal. Hats are still worn, no one abandons them, not even the men. Henry Miller, in shirt sleeves and hat, chewing a cold cigar, prances up and down the aisles.

"Begin"—he indicates a reading. How strange—where is the beauty of the verse? The director stumbles over the words; in themselves, they don't interest him. What he does want is force, vigor, something primitive, alive. He thunders, storms, curses, and the actors go right on, oblivious of the grueling. Later, at a stage rehearsal, though feeling that I am gaining ground, I find something ominous in Henry Miller's icy tolerance.

At last, the first dress rehearsal! Jules and Phene, newly married, glide from the church steps and enter Jules's studio. Phene listens to the outpourings of the sculptor's soul, dreading to speak the piece she has been taught to recite by those vicious students who, jealous of Jules, have pawned off their Greek model as the beautiful bride known only by way of letters.

The drama lies in the inner conflict taking place in the bride and groom. Phene, in reciting the poem uncomprehendingly, nevertheless senses that it forebodes her doom; if she does not recite it, she has been warned, great harm will befall Jules. And Jules, listening intently, feels the full impact of the trick. In a burst of rage, he destroys one piece of sculpture after another, when suddenly, the voice of Pippa in the distance, singing a ballad of Kate the Cornaro, a former queen of Cyprus, beloved of her little page, recalls him to the human values in the diabolical situation. He sees before him a bewildered girl "in utter need of me, in contrast to the Queen who never could be wronged, be poor. Need him to help her."

JULES

Shall to produce form out of unshaped stuff
Be Art—and further to evoke a soul
From form be nothing? This new soul is mine!
Oh, to hear
God's voice plain as I heard it first, before
They broke in with their laughter!

Scatter all this, my Phene—this mad dream!

What the whole world except our love—my own,
Own Phene? . . . Stand aside—
I do but break these paltry models up
To begin Art afresh.

In a flight of imagery, he pictures their future on some unsuspected isle in the far-off seas.

The scene is over. Have we both failed? Suddenly there is a burst of applause from the actors watching. Henry Miller rushes upon the stage shouting, "This scene will go big! It'll be a hit! Be sure you make your voice carry, Miss Leigh." [1]

Yet for me, it sounds hollow. The real characters have not come through. Could one ever learn to step from the dream figure, the will-o'-the-wisp, to the living personality, its flesh and blood? This was the great question-mark staring at me. I found that Mrs. Le Moyne, in spite of her vital nature and her art, was also at the mercy of some secret doubt. Sometimes I would find her in tears in her dressing room after the performance because she had not given life to the Monseigneur.

Poor *Pippa Passes* went the way of many special productions on Broadway. It had a short career, about three weeks, distinguished particularly by Mrs. Le Moyne's superb characterization of the Monseigneur, which no shabby theatricality of production could mar. Like the art of many of her contemporaries, it had to be accepted as a solo, with a Victorian chorus and setting.

I wonder if our existence has not lost something of that wholehearted reverence for a master which brings with it an orientation to life? For Mrs. Le Moyne, life had a fuller

---

[1] My stage name.

meaning whenever it touched an experience of the poet's. How tender the hillsides of Italy were to her, for Browning, in treading them, had increased their beauty. This did not mean that she was a shadow of Browning, trailing a sacrosanct image. She was utterly herself, but that selfhood held as its treasure a mirror radiating the colors of the poet's soul.

Perhaps it was this ability to absorb and release spontaneously that gave Mrs. Le Moyne the quality of artist and teacher. As an artist, she had a wholehearted contempt for the artificial or mannered in theatre. She could not act for the sake of acting; any more than she could teach for the sake of teaching; so she demanded of her pupils whatever she asked of herself. It was that directness, that intolerance of all but the dictates of the image, which made her loved by her closest friends and, in her last years, by the little group of students at the Playhouse to whom she revealed something of the volcanic fires out of which the reality of the artist is shaped.

ↄ

The senior clubs of the Henry Street Settlement had been urging me for some time to form a dramatic group, but the thought of working with people who had obviously neither time nor the appreciation of acting as a long and absorbing study did not appeal, so I resisted all overtures. Then one day a manuscript of *The Shepherd* by Olive Tilford Dargan came to hand. Here was a play whose conflict, the revolutionary movement in Russia, had been brought close to our doors by vivid personalities escaping from tyranny and seeking refuge in New York to carry on some of their activities. The parents of many of the Settlement club members had also been victims of Russian oppression and pogroms. *The Shepherd,* which voiced the conflict between revolutionary methods and Tolstoian non-resistance, accentuated the drama in the background of many of this group. To produce and play in it had therefore a special meaning.

The cast was composed of members of the senior clubs, along with some artists not associated with the neighborhood. Irene was to play the young revolutionist, and I a princess with revolutionary sympathies who takes an active part in the movement. Rehearsals for *The Shepherd* were launched early in 1912 under the direction of Mrs. Le Moyne, who had consented to help with the production. From the moment she took command Mrs. Le Moyne ruled with the spare-the-rod school of direction. The players soon found that the instinct for theatre had to be tested through a new type of discipline, not customary for young or recent Americans. None dared question her authority. We all submitted to her czar-like direction with a meekness the most nonresistant character in the play might have courted. At first it seemed to her a hopeless task to fashion English from the mixture of the Settlement's East-Side idioms, but even her passion for pure English succumbed to the fervent, realistic character of the Russian peasant that she could extract from the group.

As the technical side of production was not familiar to Mrs. Le Moyne, she suggested asking Agnes Morgan, formerly a member of Professor George Pierce Baker's 47 Workshop at Harvard, to develop that end. Mrs. Le Moyne had met Agnes through Helen Arthur, a young woman lawyer to whom I had previously introduced her when she needed legal advice, and with whom she had become friends in spite of her antipathy to "all feminists who invade the profession of men." So accompanying Mrs. Le Moyne to the next rehearsal to meet the cast of *The Shepherd* came the lithe, shirt-waisted, and stiff-collared Helen Arthur, dapper, bright-eyed, keen; and her friend, the quiet, serious, watchful Agnes Morgan. It was then and there agreed that they would assist with the production. This was the beginning of an association which continued with unfailing enthusiasm for the Playhouse throughout the years. Agnes Morgan was to join us full time a few years later, and in 1918 Helen Arthur left her job with the Shuberts on Broadway to become our business manager. Meanwhile the association was voluntary and extra-curricular, but never had five people cast in such different molds joined forces with more congeniality.

The performances of *The Shepherd* were held in Clinton Hall, which had been established in the neighborhood a

short time before as a center for trades union meetings and
political discussions, as well as for religious and social gatherings. The auditorium had only a platform, with no equipment for performances, and we had to create the illusion
of Russia's vast and frozen land on a small temporary stage.
A more serious difficulty was the question of where to dress.
At performances we found ourselves trudging up and down
slippery, snow-covered fire escapes to and from a makeshift
dressing room. If we shivered and stumbled on to the stage,
at least we had the advantage of not for a moment escaping
the atmosphere of the play.

At rehearsals, Mrs. Le Moyne towered like a Gulliver in
our midst, lashing, scourging, protesting, but always flaming
with a desire to mold, to create. We were caught in the grip
of the moving situation the play presented, too intent to
question its construction till toward the end of rehearsals,
when I began to have the disquieting feeling that the play
was somehow slipping. Then the discovery at the final rehearsal that there was no play at all! What had become of it?
Even the vivid challenge sounded wooden, the characters
like pasteboard replicas of revolutionaries. Had we hood-
winked ourselves through all these weeks of rehearsing? At
the first performance, no doubt remained: the drama of
The Shepherd existed only in the imagination. It was a
play of ideas, but the ideas never really emanated from the
characters, which served merely as voices for the author's
thesis. The lesson of all those weeks of dealing with starving
peasants was that a play lives only through its power of
characterization. We had also learned that an audience does
not necessarily agree with this conclusion, judging by the
excitement that the play aroused.

From scathing criticism at rehearsal, Mrs. Le Moyne was
our stanchest champion at performance. If she found some-

one near her in the audience who seemed insufficiently impressed, she would exclaim at the closing curtain (as if to herself): "The finest amateurs in the world." Next day, we would be throttled for the weak performance and would crawl away to tend our wounds.

The actual value of *The Shepherd* lay in the fact that the strenuous rehearsals produced an esprit de corps that seemed destined to continue. This varied group of club members, students, artists had learned that a production of a play was anything but a social function. What, after all, constitutes a production? What does it attempt to express or unfold? What are its values for the audience, actors, director? In the years that followed, each successive production was an attempt to discover, each an exploration toward an unknown goal—to extract its hidden value, relate its different elements, attempt to realize and therefore convey a sense of wholeness.

Meanwhile, the reward for the strain and labor, the long hours of grueling or patient submission to discipline was in the ultimate sense of spontaneous release that came through at performance. And something more, the inspiration of Mrs. Le Moyne's masterly influence.

We needed a name, so we called ourselves "The Neighborhood Players," our only claim to organization.

The Silver Box was chosen for the next production, no doubt because in it Galsworthy, who had not yet become popular on Broadway, offered the very instrument we had so lacked in *The Shepherd,* an opportunity for characterization, and what was exceptional in a play of that day, an organic development of a part. The rich, spoiled son and heir, the conventional mamma, the charwoman who accepts the burdens of life, the harlot, the down-and-out man who harangues the world at large; these constituted the dramatis personae, which though set in a British frame was indigenous to any land.

Through hard and persistent work, Max Kaplan, who played Jack, had evolved gradually from one of the nameless peasants of *The Shepherd* to the cuddled lapdog person of the rich young son. Probably no one in the audience on the opening night would have suspected that Max's initiation into wearing evening clothes had occurred the night before under the supervision of Melville Ellis, distinguished as the Beau Brummel of the theatre world. The quality of Max's performance was so moving that after the final curtain of the opening performance Doris Keane, glamorous star of the American and British theatre, rushed onto the rickety stage and throwing her arms about his neck, exclaimed, "You must play Oswald [in *Ghosts*]!" Max capsized with embarrassment. Later, he recovered his poise and courage sufficiently to ask, "Who is Oswald?"

Gertrude Stein once said that the success of English diplomacy was largely due to the fact that the Britishers were the only people who had excelled in combining speaking with eating. The rehearsals of the dinner table scene in *The Silver Box* showed the process in the making. They were conducted largely in our home where, for weeks, dinners and tea parties were made the occasion for acquiring familiarity with Anglo-Saxon customs at the board. The role of Jack required fortitude in facing situations entirely new to Max. For me, life was equally exacting as Mrs. Jones, the "char," whose homework demanded a daily stew of bacon and potatoes. To acquire that careless flip of the potato peel and concentrate my emotion in my back, while my husband harangued the home, his wife, and society at large, required earnest, persistent practice. Bushels of potatoes were sacrificed to my study of the role.

CHAPTER SIX

PLANNING A HOME

Those early years, we had been schooled in the ways of the wandering players, perpetual poachers. Our rehearsal preserve was the dining room of the Henry Street Settlement after dinner hours; our theatre was where we found it, the gymnasium, the improvised stage at Clinton Hall, the neighborhood streets. So the thought of a home of our own had grown to more than a wistful dream. Although the idea of a new building was to carry further the work of the festivals and plays, its possible scope and value extended beyond our own productions. In fact, we thought of it first as a center for the creative expression of artist, craftsman, and student, not limited strictly to the neighborhood. Even as image, it anticipated the opportunity for the old and the young, the initiated and the potentially gifted in the arts, to contribute their part to an individual adventure in theatre.

The building was planned for utmost simplicity. Decorative values were indicated merely through architectural proportions, the use of materials, and the play of light and shade produced by a special system of indirect lighting. Not only were hangings and upholstery eliminated but the same frugality was observed in relation to the stage lighting equipment, and so forth, so that ingenuity and imagination might be the directing forces in all departments. The building was also planned for the running of motion picture shows, projected as an experimental venture.

Months were required to study the complex needs of the building: adequate rehearsal and classroom space, dressing rooms, workshop for making costumes and properties, scene dock, greenroom, lunchroom, and office. Children's classes had also to be considered, besides the more obvious problems of stage and auditorium. The preparation and execution of the plans absorbed two years, largely because many city departments had to be consulted about peculiar problems the Playhouse presented. These included the unprecedented plan to operate for both motion pictures and plays. Also, we sought permission to operate Sundays, for the Neighborhood Players and the Festival Dancers were to alternate in presenting weekend programs, while the motion pictures were planned for nightly midweek performances.

The city officials, however courteous, maintained a justified doubt. Was it a theatre or not a theatre? In each situation, the influence and rapport of Lillian Wald with the city departments paved the way to the cooperation of the department chiefs in the building of this wholly untraditional enterprise.

In the spring of 1914, after each brick, hinge, and nail had been chosen, Irene and I went abroad to make contacts with the foreign theatre and to see the new technique in stage lighting in Germany. We were amazed at the extravagance with which whole lighting systems were introduced today and discarded tomorrow. The elaborate mechanism of revolving stages and huge plaster cycloramas of the German theatre did not always add the promised glamour to the performances. *A Midsummer Night's Dream* at the Reinhardt theatre suffered a total eclipse under the maneuvers of the revolving stage. Moreover, the effect of the German interpretation of

Shakespeare, with the substitution of burlesque for comedy and farce for fantasy, was not a happy innovation. On the other hand, there was rare beauty in the intimate theatre of Germany. The subtlety of direction and the quality of playing in Reinhardt's production of Wedekind's *Frühlings Erwachen* remains one of the great experiences of theatre.

The Dalcroze School was an important experiment in dance at that time, so we went to Hellerau to observe its work. There was an atmosphere of the Greek gymnasia about the school. The students, men and women, moved about freely in their dance costumes, which were one-piece bathing suits in effect, over which they wore, when not in class, a brightly colored mantle cut doctor-of-law fashion.

The auditorium, an immense room devoid of decoration, was lighted by an indirect system, again screened to afford the play of light and shade. The stage consisted of a mass of steps designed for proportion and line. Accuracy and precision, the relation of movement to musical notation, were the foundation of the system. As Dalcroze himself said, it was a system and not an art form. Later we studied and adapted the method in combination with other techniques for our own group training.

One day, while we watched the classes, Pavlowa was also present as visitor. I still recall her quick perception and her pleasure in the work. Years later, when we met again at the Neighborhood Playhouse where she had come to attend a performance of *An Arab Fantasia,* she was still as alert and responsive as a bird perched for flight.

The Dalcroze visit was early in the fateful summer of 1914, and much that we saw and felt in the air of Germany was to be explained in August. We were haunted by the sense of crass, obvious sensualism, a proficient efficiency rather than skill, indeed a dynamo of objective power. In Germany, theatre, music, audience, workers, the simple and the great, seemed pressed into a military mold.

In England, the stormy battle between Parliament and the suffragettes was raging. Hunger strikes! The figure of Sylvia Pankhurst waiting on the Prime Minister's doorstep entreating an opportunity to present a petition of East-End working women. A scuffle with the police, then Sylvia Pankhurst shoved back into prison, threatening a hunger strike which might end in death. Meanwhile, suave and decorous Parliament lords and ladies, cabinet ministers, politicians, sipping tea on the terrace, with an air of "all's well with the world." Delegations, marches, and bands, festivities and trooping of the colors for his Majesty's birthday, turbulent meetings of non-enfranchised women laborers. All this curious mélange and color interspersed with the serenity of Oxford, and visits to quiet hillsides and bleak moors. And then suddenly, that night of horror, August 2, 1914. Mobs waiting outside Parliament for the deciding vote. Finally it comes; awed silence, as if a realization of the consequences has dawned for a moment. And then, the long, long night of marching steps, rumbling gun carriages, muffled drums, and farewells!

Returning to America was like stepping upon another planet. The guns, the ominous treading, the partings, were still as gripping to us as when we had been in their midst five thousand miles away, but only the slightest reverberation seemed as yet to have reached the United States. After a moment of wavering between the collective problems and our own, we plunged with furious zeal into the work of completing the new building. Each nail hammered, each brick laid, now became a challenge to liberate values of the spirit, in opposition to negative and destructive forces elsewhere in command, forces directed to crush the impulse of life. But even such a challenge did not anticipate the dynamo of creative energy that a decade of working, struggling, loving, suffering for an image might release.

In February 1915 the completed Playhouse building finally emerged. Its red brick Georgian design, its apple green shutters and front door were modestly in keeping with the character of the neighborhood's early nineteenth-century architecture. There it stood, on the corner of Grand and Pitt streets, and beside it the familiar landmark of the drugstore with its perennial exhibit of trusses in the window. The white signboard, swinging from the building like those of the old inns, carried the insignia in simple lettering:

THE NEIGHBORHOOD PLAYHOUSE

From the time we knew that we were to have the dignity of a home, we had been haunted by the problem of the kind of production that should initiate it. Neither research nor travel revealed the desired drama. Apparently the opening would have to be a homegrown product fashioned in the tradition of the festivals.

Finally a theme drawn from the Book of Judges was elected. Jephthah, a Gileadite chief, hired by the Israelites to protect them from invasion, vowed that if the Lord would grant him success, whatever object he should first perceive on his return would be a sacrifice to the Lord: "and behold, his daughter came out to meet him with timbrels and with dances." This was the nucleus of the drama around which chorus, mime, and dance were woven.

Heretofore the musical themes for the Biblical festivals

had been taken from old Hebraic chants, and classical themes
were used for the dance motives, a necessary compromise
because the composer of that day was unfamiliar with the
dance as an independent form. Lilia Mackay Cantell, a young
American pianist and composer, grasped the experimental
work necessary for our requirements. She had written a
score for *The Shadow Garden,* a children's production, and
was now eager to produce one for *Jephthah's Daughter.*

Soon *Jephthah's Daughter* was assembling in every available corner of the Settlement and in every crevice of the new
building that could be wrested from the builders' hands. It
was like the occupation of territory by a friendly enemy;
every few days we attacked a new frontier of scaffolding.
The vicissitudes of a homemade production had to be faced,
not least the opening date, February 12, 1915.

To this day, the production of *Jephthah's Daughter* remains a kind of nightmare. I can no longer recall its actual
beginnings or its end, only that there were weeks of agony,
with a kind of tenacity and faith that nothing could destroy
or deflect. At last, the dreaded moment of opening the doors.
The audience assembled terribly on time. Irene and I, both
playing in this dance drama, were in the dressing room
"making up" when the manager reported in dismay that
the seats were still being fastened in and that the setting was
unfinished. There was only one answer—the audience must
wait until Helen Arthur, not yet manager, was corralled to
beguile the waiting group with her inexhaustible fund of
anecdotes. This saved the face of the Playhouse and introduced the audience to the homelife of theatre.

Jephthah's Daughter bore much criticism. Our orthodox
Jewish neighbors were scandalized at the free interpretation
of the Bible text. Caricatures of us appeared in the Yiddish
press showing "Miss Neighborhood Playhouse" slamming

the door in the face of the Yiddish playwright. The radically
inclined were disappointed that the Old Testament was used
as source, rather than Andreyev or Gorky, and the conven-
tionally minded were shocked at the bare feet of the dancers.
Still another chorus raised its voice in behalf of strictly
American culture, protesting that only poor material and no
good could come from this East-Side venture. Notwithstanding the criticism and the production's many imperfections,
Jephthah's Daughter concluded its scheduled run. Whatever it lacked in finish was compensated by its fervor and
originality.

The season of 1914 just before World War I had brought
Diaghileff and his Russian Ballet to London. The introduction of that imperial Russian art to the West brought a new
dimension to the stage in its daring scale of decorative values,
and a barbaric, effete sophistication to the dance. When we
saw Diaghileff's *Petrouchka* in London, nothwithstanding
that it had reached the zenith of classical ballet technique,
we visualized the Stravinsky score in terms of a purely folk
experience, suited to the dimensions of the Playhouse.

To announce *Petrouchka* in the repertory of our second
season, just preceding the Diaghileff première in New York,
would have been a ridiculous gesture had we not been aware
that the super-exotic and the purely folk productions were
linked merely by way of Stravinsky's score.

To our Grand Street neighbors this new kind of ballet,
independent of opera, was a mystery. One bearded father of
Israel, seeing *Petrouchka* announced on the billboard,
walked diffidently into the box-office for a ticket. Putting
down his fifty-cent piece, he cautiously asked,

"What is it that plays tonight?"

"Petrouchka, a ballet," answered the ticket seller.

"And what is dat?"

"Oh, you know, it's dancing."

"Oh, tanzing! I don' tanz." Picking up his fifty-cent piece he walked slowly away.

The spirit of *Petrouchka* was infectious. The high key of color and gaiety of the costumes designed by Esther Peck was strikingly accented at the climax when dancing crowds whirled and swirled in counter rhythm to the gently falling snow. Though the brilliance of Stravinsky's orchestral score had to be compressed for two pianos, played by Charles Griffes and Lily May Hyland, the mood and vitality came surprisingly through.

The dances, authentic and wholly in character with the setting, were arranged by Louis Chalif. Our long and friendly association with Chalif had begun in the early days at the Henry Street Settlement, when we had inadvertently discovered him dancing on an East-Side roof garden. Soon after, he had become our enthusiastic instructor in national and Russian folk dances. An emigré from Russian oppression, Chalif soon held a distinguished position in New York because of his pedagogical talent in simplifying complicated classical ballet technique for teachers of dancing. His summer courses were attended by students from all parts of the country. Now his enthusiastic and generous assistance was invaluable to the Playhouse *Petrouchka.*

The part of Petrouchka, the traditional puppet figure, suddenly brought to fame through Stravinsky's score and Diaghileff's presentation, was played by Irene with a peculiar appeal and charm; for she conveyed the tragic aloneness of the puppet in the midst of the excitement and discordant gaiety of the crowds, jostling, bargaining, dancing at the fair. Some members of the Diaghileff company who attended a

Neighborhood Playhouse, at 466 Grand Street, Harry C. Ingalls, architect

opened February 12, 1915.

2. UPPER: Sarah Cowell Le Moyne as the "Monseigneur" in *Pippa Passes*.

OWER: *The Silver Box* by John Galsworthy, produced in 1913 at Clinton H

Center, Mrs. Jones, the charwoman, Alice Lewisohn;

at right, Jack Barthwick, played by Max Kaplan.

performance were perplexed by the sex of the dancer playing Petrouchka, listed in the program as Ivan Litvinoff. Only when Irene's arm inadvertently slipped out of the sleeve of her costume during the dance did one of these experienced Russians detect that the puppet was being played by a woman.

While New York was being stormed by the glamorous Diaghileff *Petrouchka,* the Grand Street production continued its modest run of the scheduled six weekend performances, winning a crescendo of interest. The delight *Petrouchka* evoked called for another series of performances the next season. Had the conditions for revivals permitted, it could long have remained in the Playhouse repertory.

CHAPTER SEVEN

MOTION PICTURES

No sooner had *Jephthah's Daughter* been launched at the Playhouse in February 1915 than preparations, already in progress, were focused upon the opening of the motion pictures. The nickelodeon, offering sensational wares in a shoddy setting, was in those days the only popular low-priced entertainment in the neighborhood. A dignified, well-arranged motion picture show in a suitable setting would, we felt, fill a need.

Another need was for music that harmonized with the motion picture image. In the "movie" of that epoch, pictures were seen but not heard; or the piano accompaniment, if provided, had little or no relation to the picture. To synchronize them was a new idea. Lily May Hyland, who was engaged to develop this innovation in coordinating sound and visual image, was at home in a vast repertory of music and lent herself indefatigably to what proved to be a long series of endurance tests for her.

The first picture program, given on February 22, 1915, left an indelible impression of a kind! The doors opened early, and we gathered near them waiting for the audience. Mr. Tobin, the doorman, beamed each time a wayfarer straggled in, and he would point majestically to the ticket office where a brightly lighted sign announced the program, and the price of admission—five cents. Children were the most adventuring. They came with their five pennies tightly clasped in hand, the very young having to reach up on tiptoe to take the ticket, though the box office had been planned with the children in mind.

The music began. The picture revealed a dog at play, not conducive, we feared, to enticing the passer-by! During the climax of the next picture, showing a mother cat nestling her kittens, a burly laborer near us heaved out of his seat and jerking his neighbor, who was by this time snoring, said, "Oh, hell! Let's get out of here before she gets the next litter."

It took time and effort to live down the impression of this historic occasion, but by degrees we were making personal contacts with the magnates of the motion picture exchange, often ex-racing bookmakers, with the inevitable cold cigar in the corner of the mouth. At first these officials were on their guard, but when they realized there was nothing to be lost and that the Playhouse was a bona-fide "house," they became interested and amused at the idea of providing a whole program for five cents. Gradually, they warmed up to the situation, and as in those early days we were free to select every picture we showed, the exchanges began to vie with each other in presenting their best.

In order to keep the house filled with our limited audience, a daily change of bill was necessary. A dramatic or lyric interlude was introduced in addition to supply color, fantasy, or comedy, as the case might be. During the next three years, the picture programs, presented four nights of the week and on Saturday matinées, thrived in the hands of Grace Mills who had come to us as manager shortly after the opening. So a sympathetic clientèle had already been established when Helen Arthur became manager of the Playhouse in 1918. Her wide theatre contacts, her humor, creative wit, and popularity brought a further extension to the motion picture experiment.

A remarkable spirit of accord and good will developed between the exchange which provided the pictures, the personnel of the specialty numbers or interludes, the operating staff, and the audience. The neighborhood testified numerically to its satisfaction, if one could judge by the masses who pushed their way in. How often Mr. Tobin's quiet appeal: "Kindly, ladies! Kindly!" would swell into a stentorian, proud finality: "Positively no more room!" We sometimes wished his standard of "room" had not been measured by a subway crush. The Playhouse, which had fostered a new litter of kittens, developed into the most popular movie center in the neighborhood.

Helen Arthur was often able to lure stars down from Broadway to take part in the interludes, not only for an opportunity to try out but also for an amusing adventure. Besides these volunteer performers and other distinguished people who presented "specialties" for a nominal fee, the featured interludes gave opportunity to young professionals with an idea, as well as to gifted amateurs. It was through these motion picture programs that Albert Carroll made his début at the Playhouse and developed his lyrical gifts as dancer and impersonator. Blanche Talmud, Lily Lubell, and several others who later became the vertebrae of the lyric and dramatic bills, gained experience through the movie nights in creating and developing a technique for their gifts, as well as having the advantage of frequent contact with the audience. They were the well-loved stars of the Grand Street stage, when Douglas Fairbanks and Mary Pickford were starring on the screen.

Friday was the popular night for family gatherings. Jewish fathers with their forelocks, mothers with a shawl over the sheitel, sometimes led by young Miriam in her American clothes, were ushered to their seats by the high school girl ushers in their brown uniforms. But of all the performances, the Saturday matinées for the children were the most alluring. The youthful audience would assemble at the doors hours before they were opened, cold or storm shiveringly ignored, for the promised thrill of *Jack and the Bean Stalk,* or the antics of Charlie Chaplin, and whatever the interlude of the day provided.

It became an unwritten law that the smallest children were always given precedence. Those whose feet didn't reach the floor inherited "bald-headed row." Often during the intense scene of a movie or an interlude number, a row of tiny heads would appear leaning on elbows resting on the stage, as close up as it was possible to go. Some of these youngsters established a banking system at the box office, bringing a penny at a time for deposit until their capital had accumulated to five cents. Frequent were the visits of these anxious young depositors to Miss Kaplan, the treasurer, to check their balances.

Within the doors, the house was transformed. The children possessed it. It was their show, their Playhouse, their Miss Arthur, their Mr. Tobin, their ushers. And if, by chance, their Miss Talmud or their Mr. Carroll performed in the interlude, the warmth would explode into frenzied delight.

Although the children were untrammeled, and delightfully free, the very repose and beauty of the building commanded their respect, and the quiet, unobtrusive but nonetheless vigilant presence of Helen and her ushers established a point of view of the relationship of an audience to theatre. Children and grownups alike felt instinctively that as audience they were receiving every consideration and soon, very soon, they responded by unconsciously bringing their share of consideration in the way of more courtesy, less aggressiveness. Nothing in life since then has seemed as infectious as the spontaneous joy, the fresh laughter, or the concentrated hush of that audience of children. No other audience was so exacting of its performers, or once won, gave them such unbounded response.

There was a warmth and intimacy with our movie audiences, a personal "feel" that carried continual flavor. Mr. Tobin at the door, Miss Kaplan in the ticket office, gradually came to know by name large sections of the audience. Often, one or the other would say: "Mr. so-and-so was here again tonight, fourth time this week." Local events were frequently celebrated, and there was a constant interchange, a rapport with the neighborhood.

If that response and understanding, that genial flow between audience and theatre, was the keynote of community theatre, then in that sense our motion picture experiment achieved its end. It created a place, it responded to a demand, it won respect and was approved. And if success can be registered by numbers alone, then as an experiment it went far beyond fantastic evaluation. Yet our adventure into the movie world had touched more than our audience, for as far as we knew, the Neighborhood Playhouse had been the first to institute dramatic or lyric interludes in a motion-picture program.

Offering the best pictures we could acquire, under admirable conditions and for only five cents, had exacted a wide-awake improvement campaign on the part of our competitors, who began to realize that cleanliness, orderly conditions, and even less blood-and-thunder display were definite assets. One by one the dark, smelly, ramshackle nickelodeons, with all their attractions concentrated in glaring posters, or in the vocal capacity, heft, and grotesquerie of the "grabber" whose job it was to "pull" in an audience off the street, blossomed out with fresh paint, brighter electric lights, and more hygienic allurements.

After five years of an increasing response to the programs, a change took place in the movie world. Almost overnight, the market had become glutted with a cheap, standardized type of picture. Stakes too had gone up in the movie race. The exchanges not only quadrupled their rates for pictures but found that they could control the stakes more easily by instituting a "service." So all pictures, good, bad, indifferent, those that proved popular and those that did not, were furnished to exhibitors in packets marked "service," and we found ourselves with no freedom of selection. While there might have been a certain value in achieving a stampede to see a best-seller at the Playhouse, there was no point in exhibiting standardized successes to an audience we had come to respect. Faced with this grabbag situation, it was evident that the time had come to retire.

Nevertheless it was hard to abandon the nightly audiences, and we knew that closing the pictures would be an even greater loss to the children. Though we recognized a certain ruthlessness in denying what had been deliberately stimulated as a standard for wholesome entertainment, we found no further door open to pioneering. Motion pictures combined with other features and adequate music could now be found in many parts of the city.

The day finally came for the last movie audience to pass through the doors. The walls seemed to groan and the seats to creak under the pressure of the crowded house. All the audiences throughout the years seemed literally to have fought to be present at that last performance, September

1920. There were tears in many eyes, and many a strong grip of hands at parting. The motion pictures not only had answered a neighborhood need but through the interludes, musical programs, dances, one-act plays, they had made it possible to develop response and find a place for lyric forms.

CHAPTER EIGHT

THE CHILDREN'S
PERFORMANCES

Although the festivals had grown beyond the exclusive province of the children of the neighborhood, the children's classes remained a vital and uninterrupted element, even when the strain of production was at the highest pitch. A flock of children gathered with the greatest eagerness on Saturday mornings for their studies in dancing, diction—dubbed by them "fiction"—and song. In their bare feet and simple smocks of assorted colors, they gave the rooms the atmosphere of a garden. There was an irresistible charm in their spontaneous rhythmic exercises, guided with exactness yet unobtrusively by Blanche Talmud, and in the meticulously musical approach to song, under Frances Brundage's direction.

Puppet plays, designed and manipulated by the children on their own improvised stage, with a curtain that really pulled, were an extra Saturday afternoon enterprise. These plays, not only managed by the children but sometimes written by them, were presented occasionally for their parents on Sunday afternoons. This creative puppetry was Esther Peck's contribution, growing out of her personal association with the children. Her designs for the settings and costumes of the children's Christmas productions never lacked a rare feeling for color combined with the naïveté of the child. Esther, one of the earliest of our colleagues, was a designer by profession; the Playhouse was her avocation. She remained a stanch and devoted associate until the doors of the Playhouse closed.

The members of these classes were selected from the clubs of the Settlement on the basis of their eagerness for study, an imaginative sense, and a degree of physical coordination. In their classes, under the guidance of "Miss Irene" and Miss Talmud, rhythm leaped joyously into dance, posture, choral song, and ultimately into dramatic pantomime and festival. These classes were never formal but always intensely alive. Indeed, they were part of production, just as production was part of the classwork.

The annual Christmas performance given by these Junior Festival Players was an offshoot of the original midwinter and spring festivals. Each year at this time, the multitudinous activities of the Playhouse and Settlement would be automatically relaxed so that the grownups could participate in the spell the children cast. Without heralding and fanfare, these holiday performances seemed to emerge as though from some sequestered attic, fully blown. Though spontaneity was the keynote, something more than the effervescence of childhood—perhaps one could say the spontaneity of artistry— came through at performance. For their sense of responsibility toward production and their insatiable demand for rehearsals could never have been emulated by their seniors. Irene was the mothering spirit of this department and she fought for the rights and opportunities of her brood with a zest that no technical or business problem could deflect.

Among the collection of children's productions, the original performance of Debussy's *La Boîte à Joujoux* in 1916–17 holds its delight in memory, not as make-believe, but as vivid reality. The intense suspense of the battle, the soldier doll whose wound was both tenderly and intelligently stanched by the French doll, the gesture in giving and receiving the rose; then, the fellow dolls' participation in the wedding, the departure of the bride and groom leading the lamb and goose—all of it opened a door into a fairy world that was the very stuff and substance of experience as perceived, sensed, realized by the cast. What matter that they ranged in age between eight and twelve? They brought to us a muted pathos in those gay, yet breathless, moments of suspense snatched by the dolls from the world of sleeping humans.

The ability to sustain the roles in exact relation to musical notation indicates their surrender to the idea or image presented. It might have been this quality that John Galsworthy sensed when he came to visit a class. The stage had been turned over to the children's group so that they were free to abandon themselves to its space. Later we found Galsworthy's comment in the Guest Book: "The House where magic has come to stay."

CHAPTER NINE

GUEST CONTRIBUTORS

Although some of the participants on both sides of the footlights were associated in various ways with the Settlement, the Neighborhood Playhouse as it developed could not be looked upon as a continuation of the Settlement's club and class work, since the productions, in spite of being amateur, held to a standard that was not suitable for club members interested primarily in social values. In fact, the Playhouse appealed to the unusual person, not necessarily in regard to that ambiguous word "talent," but unusual in being possessed by an urge profound enough to overcome the fantastic hopes of the stage-struck. Association with the Playhouse was, in fact, a dubious privilege because of an unwritten decree: Abandon hope all ye who seek an outlet for personal ambitions.

Those of us relatively responsible for the direction and development of the program, feeding the productions individually and as a group, the corps of workers, many of them professionals in their fields yet serving the Playhouse as "learners" for the thrill of theatre, all were gripped by an image that could not be explained, but which exacted the tribute of devotion. In this sense, the Playhouse was more a fate than a choice.

The festivals, the plays, the motion pictures, and the children's productions formed the ground plan of the Playhouse for the first several years. Though the Festival Dancers and the Neighborhood Players were independent groups, many productions called for an interchange of personnel, made possible because the training was adapted to both forms. In fact the essential requirement for participation was to qualify in both types of training.

Audiences did not clamor at first for admission, but gathered gradually from here, there, anywhere—neighbors, inhabitants of limousines, Negroes barred at that time from the orchestra in other theatres. The motion picture program served the purpose of attracting an audience to whom theatre and dance had previously been totally alien. Soon our audiences were sharing another new experience in the occasional guest performances that brought us into widened contact with the international brotherhood of the arts.

The first guest offering was in celebration of Shakespeare's birthday, on April 23, 1915. This was not anticipated, but was one of those happy accidents often repeated, which never became a rule.

Oddly, the agent of this event was Dr. John Kingsbury, the Commissioner of Public Welfare in New York. Though his office did not include the public's welfare as related to Shakespeare, he had a lifelong devotion to Ellen Terry. One evening at a performance in which Phyllis Nielson Terry was making her debut in New York, he glanced up from his seat at the back of the balcony and noticed a woman standing nearby, her head swathed in veiling. Her outline and carriage suggested Ellen Terry. Yet, could it actually be she, he wondered, as he offered her his seat. During the intermission, he asked her. "Yes," Miss Terry answered, "but don't tell anybody, for nobody knows I am here. I just slipped in to see my niece in her new role."

Before the last curtain, she had confided to him that she

wanted to give a recital to. people who had never read
Shakespeare, foreigners perhaps, and those who could not
afford uptown prices. Could he find her such an audience?
That night, Dr. Kingsbury telephoned to Miss Wald. Could
she help him? "Of course we will find the audience," was
the enthusiastic response. A week later the posterboard on
Grand Street framed the announcement that the Neighborhood Playhouse had the honor to present Ellen Terry in
readings from Shakespeare. Word was quickly spread by the
mothers, accustomed to sun their babies in front of the
building, that a friend of Shakespeare was coming that night
to the Playhouse.

When Ellen Terry came to a lighting rehearsal the afternoon preceding the performance, the first thing that caught
her eye was the bulletin board in front of the building
stating the price of admission, twenty-five cents. She turned
to us with her beguiling smile, pointing to the board: "Far
too much for Ellen Terry, but very modest for William
Shakespeare."

The greater part of the afternoon was devoted to exploiting
the resources of the lighting board for just the right nuance,
as a recent operation on her eyes had made her acutely sensitive to light. The desired effect was finally achieved by one
amber bulb at the extreme end of the footlights, and a suspicion of glow from the overhead. After hours of working
for the effect she had in mind, we realized there was no such
thing as fatigue where Shakespeare was concerned.

The evening of the performance, while the audience was
assembling, a message from Ellen Terry! Would I come to
the dressing room? When I hurried to the door with some
anxiety, she was completing the ritual of making up, but
no costume was visible. She pointed to the couch where yards
and yards of rich, flame-colored silk lay in a heap. Gathering

it up in her arms, she said: "My son Gordon [Craig] designed it for me; I thought you might like to see it grow into a gown." Then she began to fasten it, fold upon fold, with safety pins, until she was encircled in its wine-colored sumptuousness. When, later, she sailed across the stage as the curtains parted, one felt as if all the joyous heroines accompanied her.

How lucky to carry the memory of such feminine grace flowing from every gesture—inflection, poise, all anticipated in that sweep of her presence across the stage. In her acknowledgment to the audience she was her inimitable self, gracious and intimate, interspersing her reading with delightful spontaneous comment, gathering us all into her confidence. Whether or not they understood her, there was no doubt that even the foreigners that night left with a loving sense of Shakespeare. And, in turn, Ellen Terry was enchanted with the naïve response of an audience that caught and reflected her mood.

The next guest to offer a program was Sarah Cowell Le Moyne; the occasion, to honor the anniversary of Robert Browning's birth, on May 7, 1915. The evening was devoted to readings from the poet, a hazardous adventure judging by the attendance at her former readings on Broadway. But Grand Street lent a receptive ear. Students, friends, members of the Playhouse groups filled the house in appreciation of the honored "teacher."

Mrs. Le Moyne held that audience solely by the force of her interpretive spirit, and something more—her capacity to sound the overtones of the poet's feelings so that the inflexible word became accompaniment to the image. We were carried that night into those intricate byways of the soul which Robert Browning penetrated and expressed with poignancy. For example, "The Bishop Orders his Tomb" was a monologue carrying the essence of the earth, so ingrained in that old prelate of the Renaissance that the quality of the marble to support his body, as well as each detail of his tomb, had a sensuous delight for him. Mrs. Le Moyne, with a few bold strokes, brought the Bishop's personality to life in presenting a masterly portrait characteristic of the Renaissance, that is, the rediscovery of earth as the divine value to be immortalized.

Soon after these birthday celebrations came the first of Yvette Guilbert's unforgettable nights of song. Europe in 1915, exhausted by the war, had little place for its artists. Many had wandered to our shores for the first time; for America had not until then been the haven for European artists it has since become. Yvette found her way to the Playhouse through Elinor Fatman, later Mrs. Henry Morgenthau, Jr., who was directing a children's production. The eagerness and appeal of the children, the atmosphere of the Playhouse embedded in slums, the searching spirit Yvette found there, were enough to quicken her sympathy. Would the children like to hear her sing French ballads and folk songs of long ago? Thereupon a night in February 1916 was chosen.

Children who had never before come to a night performance appeared proudly escorting a parent, for this was to be their "show." Yvette won instantaneous response. Although few of the audience knew French, still, toward the end of the program, during the infectious "C'est le Mai," they chimed in, encouraged by her evident desire to have them sing with her. This was the prelude to Yvette's devotion to the Playhouse and the neighborhood's love for her.

These three unique personalities, Ellen Terry, Sarah Cowell Le Moyne, Yvette Guilbert, stand out as monumental figures, each in her way a signpost in the annals of the theatre of yesterday. Each expressed that quality in woman which cannot be defined and therefore belongs to her secret. Each of them, though a child of earth, was held by a tie which transcended it, giving her creativeness its essential quality. Mrs. Le Moyne was wedded to the spirit of Robert Browning, not in an abstract way, but as a beloved companion and guide. Ellen Terry was, in this sense, the bride of William Shakespeare who dominated her life, not as the fleshless bard, but as a potent, loving presence, so much so that his idiom and rhythm flowed through her voice even over the telephone. This was not an affectation, but simply because Shakespeare was the kernel of her life.

In Yvette one felt the fire and verve of the troubadours, as if she carried and released the heights and depths of the Middle Ages, their mystical flights and kaleidoscopic shadows. Whatever life held for or denied to the personal nature of each seems in retrospect of comparative indifference because of the passionate creative image to which each was dedicated. Each lived life largely, each enacted and mirrored back her uniqueness.

Another guest offering was Ethel Barrymore's performance of *The Shadow* in which she was starring on Broadway. This was again an unsolicited occasion, suggested, this time, by Charles Frohman. We had not been aware that he knew of the existence of the Playhouse until he telephoned one day in 1915 to confide a plan he had in mind, to send his stars and companies for an occasional Sunday night performance to the Neighborhood Playhouse if our schedule permitted. But before the program could be arranged he had sailed for Europe on the *Lusitania's* tragic voyage. Miss Barrymore, who knew of the offer, gallantly responded after his death by bringing her company, as he had desired. This generous gesture, the warmth of her personality and glamorous presence won her audience completely.

We had little notice of her coming. The signboard was placed in front of the theatre Saturday evening, and before Sunday noon another notice appeared—"All sold out." During the afternoon, the littlest tots swung themselves up to the narrow window grating in the foyer, shouting: "Has Ethel come yet?" After the final curtain that evening, there was a storm of applause. And later, when Miss Barrymore appeared at the stage door, shouts and cheers reverberated through the street: "Hurrah for Ethel Barrymore of Grand Street."

Tagore was another memorable figure who made the pilgrimage to Grand Street, wearing his customary dust-colored robe. The patriarchal beard, which accentuated his venerable carriage, was a conspicuous event in any city street. His other-worldliness may have been emphasized because of his tendency to retire behind the philosopher's mask. Those who had the opportunity to hear his lecture on the philosophical background of India were moved not only by the interpretation of a poet but by the sage who brought the spirit of the Vedas to us in the beauty of his chant. This spirit was sensed even by a child who had crept in unobserved from the street and, tucking herself beside Miss Wald in the back of the auditorium, whispered in awe:

"Is that God?"

"No," Miss Wald whispered back, "but a friend of His."

A fragment of India was brought to us in another way by Roshanara, a young and lovely Englishwoman, born in India and brought up by her ayah, through whom she had been immersed in its folk culture. Her gesture, body, face reflected the exotic grace of a Hindu woman's impersonalized femininity. Her creative quality lay in conveying through dance what she had deeply experienced. Roshi, as we called her, adopted the Playhouse as her family; it provided a root which she had lost and could find nowhere else in the West. Her early death was a shock to us all.

The Duncan Dancers, Isadora's "children," were the delight of the Playhouse audiences, and brought a freshness and spontaneity that was so beguiling that one did not stop to consider whether the Greek form or the romantic quality of Schumann's music dominated. These dancers were adored by the Playhouse students who literally served as claque whenever they appeared uptown.

There was an increasing influx of foreign groups during those years, and the Playhouse naturally welcomed these strolling players. For example, the Irish Theatre of America appeared in a series of Lancaster folk plays. After its premature demise, the flavor of its Celtic wit and whimsy lived on with us in the person of Whitford Kane, who became a devoted friend and playing member of the Playhouse family. Augustin Duncan was another guest, in Charles Vildrac's *S.S. Tenacity*.

For a short season, over several years, the Workingman's Circle, a Yiddish organization, presented plays by Hirschbein, Asch, and Pinski, as well as translations from Hauptmann and Sudermann. The plays were competently handled by these studious amateurs, and the East-Side workers were their loyal supporters.

Jacob Ben-Ami came into our midst from tormented Russia. He asked permission to present a group of plays by Perez, the Yiddish poet who had just died. Ben-Ami's modesty, his fervor and dignity, were so convincing that the barrier of language—for he had not yet attempted to learn English—was no hindrance to our immediate accord and understanding. His able production and quality as an actor anticipated his later career.

Emanuel Reicher was a seasoned German actor who now belonged to the wandering artists seeking refuge in New York. He laid before us his dreams of theatre rooted in the romantic and classic traditions of the German stage. For he felt the need of heroic stature in the theatre, as well as romantic love. The Playhouse appealed to him as a possible opportunity to transplant the European tradition upon American soil.

Many plots and hopes knocked at the door and we were often torn by the appeals of creative personalities, such as Reicher's, with much to offer, yet having little chance of a foothold in America; artists who thought hopefully of the Playhouse as a medium to carry on their experience. Again and again, we had to weigh values of the traditionally perfected theatre with the as-yet potential image of the Playhouse, shaping its own reality, even though the goal was not defined. Reicher's production of Ibsen's *Rosmersholm* at the Playhouse, and his own impressive performance, showed us the cleavage between his theatre world, now of the past, and ours, still in its infancy, yet demanding its own right to "become."

This assortment of guest performances was only a part of those in the schedule, which included, for example, Edith Wynne Matthison's *Everyman;* and Walter Hampden's tabloid version of *Macbeth,* which was planned as a "tryout" to launch his long and successful repertory in Shakespeare.

The Wisconsin Players from the University of Wisconsin, much heralded for their playing, presented a program. A self-made play and production by a group of colored actors from Washington was one of the first attempts of the Negroes to express their values in the theatre.

The Gurgieff group, though not of the theatre, should not be omitted from the record. Their demonstrations, seen from the angle of performance, suggested a super form of acrobatics. Whether arresting the body in mid-air to a sudden command of the master, or reading the mind of a person chosen at random from the audience, they were equally startling. It was surprising to find many English and American students giving themselves to this form of occultism, developed under the hypnotic spell of a master whose magic attracted not only seekers of a new pattern but the intellectually elite. A heterogeneous audience packed the Playhouse for this demonstration: superintellectuals, artists, and cranks of every description. Yet the only notice of the performance was an abbreviated statement on a post card announcing the hour and address. This may serve to indicate how the intellectual and rational attitude seeks compensatory channels. Gurgieff was one of the quickly rising and setting stars of that epoch, decidedly on the side of the dark magician whose spell remained mysterious.

Ruth Draper appeared in one of her first programs, at Miss Wald's suggestion, long before her unique gift captivated Broadway. But I feel sure that she never had a more enthusiastic ovation than at that first performance. I remember, too, how her sensitive expressiveness won Yvette's heart.

The most purely American of all the American offerings was that of a group of Indian chiefs in a program of ceremonial dances. In New York following a visit to Washington, where they had gone to plead for the right to continue their ritual dances, they were brought to the Playhouse by John Collier, later head of the Indian Bureau. Their ritual dances in ceremonial dress were not performed for an audience, but our inner circle was allowed to be present. The one secular touch was the Lincoln canes they carried,[1] secular to us, but to them full of divine power. These chieftains were

---

[1] An offering from the President after the Civil War.

adept in the art of magic. Above all, they could conjure up the intangible world of primordial images by a simplicity which held us spellbound. Of all the performances, this brought us closest to the feeling of a religious mystery.

This chain of variegated offerings, however inadequately reviewed, may indicate something of the warmth and relationship between these guest artists and the privileged audiences. All of these programs were voluntarily offered—for the joy of the experience. Although this tuned in with the original image of the Playhouse as a center of interchange between students, audience, and creative artists, nothing was done to bring it about; it just happened. Was it possibly because of the artist's instinctive urge to share his gift where there is no emphasis upon the "press," no goal of self-advertisement on either side? To us it also had meaning by showing how the spirit of the amateur is a natural impulse when practical considerations are eliminated.

One can hardly think of these first offerings in the traditional sense of theatre, for there was an atmosphere of intimacy between audience and stage difficult to convey. The performer was in every respect the honored guest, while the audience played the role of host, and an interchange of warmth glowed between. It is, alas, impossible to recapture the essence of these experiences in which the creative spirit and the response to it were so intimately united that no line could be drawn between the stage and the audience. In retrospect, it suggests a kind of prism in which brilliant colors, drawn from the four quarters, were reflected. However diversified the experience brought by these guests, the link which bound us was the instinct of creative play, our common language.

CHAPTER TEN

SHAW AND DUNSANY

A Night at an Inn, included in a bill of four one-act plays in the season of 1915–16, had proved to be a thriller under Agnes Morgan's direction, and won for Lord Dunsany an immediate vogue in New York. This was the second Dunsany play at the Neighborhood Playhouse; the first, *The Glittering Gate,* had appeared in 1915, also under Agnes Morgan's direction.

Then during the summer of 1916 Dunsany sent us the script of *The Queen's Enemies,* which held further promise. Its drama lay in the tension, yet assumed relaxation, of a dinner party given for her stalwart enemies by a queen of ancient Egypt. For these royal personalities from neighboring countries to attend a banquet given by the Queen of Egypt, though an obvious honor, is not unmitigated joy. The feast takes place in a tomb under the Nile, the one attendant is a grotesquely evil-looking guardian of this underwater chamber. In the foreground, a table is lavishly spread with exotic foods and wines. The huge, dark visitors are greeted by the timid little Queen, whose obvious fear of her enemies is flattering, if not entirely disarming.

To find the right companion piece for this exotic fantasy was a problem, until Helen Arthur suggested inviting Gertrude Kingston, well known in England as the founder of the Little Theatre in London and an actress of distinction, to play *Great Catherine,* which George Bernard Shaw had written for her and in which she had appeared in London in 1913. Apparently it appealed to her adventurous spirit to play in a wholly unknown little theatre with problematical outlook. For us, it was also an adventurous collaboration. Everything about Miss Kingston, in contrast to Ellen Terry, savored of the theatre of sophistication and intellectuality. But Miss Kingston's interest in the production problems and her cooperative spirit gradually warmed us into friendship, while her slant on theatre and her brillant wit were stimulating.

The appeal of *Great Catherine* lay in the sophisticated treatment of its title role. There could have been no greater contrast than the personalities of Shaw's and Dunsany's Queens, each exceedingly effective in presenting the dark side in woman's nature. Catherine, as Shaw and Gertrude Kingston conceived her, played her game boisterously and with sangfroid; while Dunsany's unhistorical Queen emerged, one might say, out of a subhuman area, intimately related to the serpent in its remoteness to human warmth and the effectiveness of its sting.

These contrasting qualities applied also to the technical problems of the two plays. The spirited burlesque treatment of *Great Catherine* was colorfully brought out in Warren Dahler's setting and costumes, while *The Queen's Enemies* provided far greater complications. The fantasy of an archaic setting, a tomb under the Nile, a scene of drowning war lords had somehow to be related to authentic details in costume, color, and properties, as well as setting. As designer Howard Kretz-Coluzzi, versed in this background archeologically and philologically, was admirable in simplifying the basic Egyptian values, while Warren Dahler brought his designs into theatre idiom.

This collaboration on the décor was fortunate, for some days before the dress rehearsal, Kretz-Coluzzi mysteriously disappeared. Though well supplied with name and erudition, this genius of a sort had no address. One of the Playhouse's devotees volunteered to survey the doorstep of the lodging house that he was supposed to inhabit on occasion, but with no success for her vigil; for he had neither entered nor left the building for several days. We had, therefore, to plunge in and reconstruct the unfinished work as best we could.

The day of the dress rehearsal, he quietly appeared.

"Where in heaven's name have you been—no excuse—even if dying," and so forth.

In a quiet monotone, "I had a shock. My favorite tree on my mother's estate was cut down. I couldn't work."

"But where were you?"

"I went to the obelisk in the park"—then, in response to an incredulous glance—"I took a bag of grapes with me and meditated."

This was the way Howard functioned. Still, this uncertain source contributed a spark to the family spirit and was as indefatigable in work as in mourning.

In retrospect, the effort to stylize the movement and playing in the Egyptian mode was not wholly satisfying; on the one hand, it constrained imagery, yet on the other, it gave an exotic definition to the images. How difficult to gauge in advance that happy union in which tangible reality can be subtilized and imagery defined!

Unfortunately I never had a chance to see *Great Catherine* in its finished state, because of the arduous make-up and wholly other mood needed for my performance in the role of the Egyptian Queen. But the peals of laughter that reached my dressing room on the third floor indicated that the Shavian verve was brilliantly handled, even though *Great Catherine* does not rank with Shaw at his best.

The underlying tension in *The Queen's Enemies,* combined with the fascination of Shaw's wit, and Gertrude Kingston's mondaine characterization and authoritative performance in the title role, attracted audiences from the highways and byways to delight in riotous laughter and the thrill of a petit grand guignol. As the response induced an extended run, not possible at the Playhouse because of the next bill, the production was transferred to the Maxine Elliott Theatre. This Broadway adventure was also stimulated by an unwritten obligation to Miss Kingston, whose fee at the Playhouse was nominal. As a matter of fact, all of the professionals in the Playhouse productions received their slender weekly envelopes in the spirit of an honorarium, proving again and again that the actor in those days was seeking something Broadway could not offer him.

The call to the "white lights," seemingly so authentic, proved how misleading full houses on Grand Street could be. Only disappointment was in store when these plays were transplanted upon foreign soil. This Broadway misadventure was a timely reminder that our way was not along the thoroughfares, but in lonely bypaths, coping with the many-faceted problems knocking at our door.

The spirited quality in both productions was largely due to Agnes Morgan's skillful direction. Perhaps *Great Catherine* was paving the way to her gift in handling burlesque, which was later to create an infectious vogue on Grand Street and Broadway through the *Follies.*

It was of course exciting that the correspondence over *The Queen's Enemies* between Dunsany at the front and myself in Grand Street should consummate in his sudden announcement at the close of the war in 1918 that he was about to visit the Neighborhood Playhouse, which had "harbored his waifs," with the hope of seeing *A Night at an Inn* and *The Queen's Enemies* come to life on the stage.

From the letters and stage instructions, we had gleaned how foreign the technical world of the theatre was to him. This unexpected plan to revive the two plays on a twin bill was a thrilling but anxious occasion for us, for there was a dubious element in a performance concentrated in and upon the author, and besides we should never have chosen these two plays as companions on a program. Even for the author it might prove an overdose of caviar. So an entirely home-brewed production by the Festival Dancers was served between the two plays. *A Russian Wedding,* spirited and colorful in its folk atmosphere, was accompanied by the Balalaika orchestra, manned by the Playhouse students under the direction of Sunia Samuels. As this zither-like music, zealously practiced by the Festival Dancers, had a spirited appeal, we hoped it would add a "fantasy relief" to the plays.

Meanwhile Dunsany was being hailed by the theatre world of America as a princely lion to be baited with lecture tours, meetings, luncheons, parlor entertainments, wined and dined because of his sudden rise to fame; so that Grand Street's part was, after all, a modest and personal incident, with the questionable privilege of introducing parent and offspring. Would they appeal at first sight? His letters were the only gauge we had to his personality. I still see before me the bold strokes of the quill pen, the envelopes sealed with the ancestral crest and, in contrast, the winning informality of their text, combining episodes of the soldier's world with the fantasy of the poet. With one stroke of the pen, some whimsical allusion to the play; with the next, the technique of delousing after the strain of trench warfare.

The first meeting with the soldier-poet-lord was at our home the afternoon of the performance; whatever anticipation I had harbored was held in check by the perpendicularity of Dunsany's form. From headquarters far above came the voice of the soldier, brusque, impetuous, to the point. "Have you a copy of *The Queen's Enemies?*" A challenge lay in his tone. It was quite obvious that no time was to be lost in diplomatic courtesies. The objective of the visit was to instruct me in the reading of the Queen's prayer to the Nile at the end of the play. Realizing that there was no way to avoid the soldier's tactics, my proportions shrank to an invisible point, for the only copy was my acting version with its surgical incisions at the very spot he wished to examine. The unanticipated fatal moment had to be survived, knowing that the criminal offense of cutting could not be lived down and that no tactical innuendo could intervene, not even the arrival of tea.

The perpendicular form collapsed in the low cushioned sofa, while the voice of the master emerged out of the depths in monotone. The prayer, in and of itself passionately stirring, was reduced to a mournful wail. The catechism continued:

"This is of course the way you will offer the prayer?"

What could be said but: "Why not wait for the performance? After all, an actress can only inadequately express what the poet perceives." For me the command performance had already taken place, its doom sealed.

The hour of performance was approaching. Dunsany made no attempt to disguise his role of bridegroom waiting for the bride, counting off the minutes by striding up and down the foyer, or again graciously committing his characteristic signature to the storm of programs thrust upon him by a circle of devotees. For authors were rarities at Playhouse productions at that time, and what could be more romantically stimulating than this unique chance to encounter a poet-soldier-lord towering in the center of an ever-expanding circle.

From my dressing room on the third floor I gathered that the spell of *A Night at an Inn* had not failed to bedevil each "able-bodied seaman." When peals of "author, author" could be heard through the volley of applause, Dunsany slowly emerged from the hard wood seat and admitted the baffling effect of the play upon him: "I had no idea that I could be so held by what I have considered a poor play." A charming admission.

This positive response belonged to the first part of the bill. Would the gods be kind and allow us, the cast of *The Queen's Enemies,* to overcome the mutilations of the script? Could the fine line between the author's emphasis upon poetic color and the director's responsibility to the dramatic tension be reconciled? This intricate problem of values developed into acute suspense before the rise of the curtain.

The Queen's Enemies proved to be a stab in the back to Dunsany's Celtic imagery. He had to suffer the loss of precious phrases in the Queen's apostrophe to the Nile, thereby sacrificing poetic feeling for the pull of dramatic tension, climaxed in the Queen's diabolic plot to destroy her enemies by committing them as a sacrifice to the Nile. Another criminal offense lay in the restraint of that scene, played in a darkness punctuated only by blood-curdling shrieks of the drowning war lords, while the Queen, at the top of the stair, covers their voices in her worshipful prayer offering them to the Nile. Then, with swaying movement, she comments with a yawn: "Tonight I shall sleep sweetly."

Alas, I never discovered how the duel between the poet,

tormented by the desecration of his poetic meter, and the soldier, robbed of the satisfaction of seeing the enemy war lords cunningly trapped in the dark waters by a simple device of the Queen, finally ended. For these are living but unrealized conflicts out of which creative images are shaped.

As a matter of fact, quite apart from the deliberate restraint of playing a gory scene in the dark, our simple lighting system could never have measured up to anything but a blackout, in spite of the elaborate stage instructions offered by the author. Alas, Dunsany was to realize a still further disappointment in the suspicion of stylized movement and gesture, especially on the part of the little Queen. Seen in perspective his reaction may have been justified. On the other hand, the exotic quality of the play and its elusive borderline between inner and outer reality seemed to call for the convention.

In the theatre the sins of omission and commission linger on as shades in the underworld, taunting us with inadequacies in the lives of the dramatis personae, as if they, the characters, stepped out of the tomb to show us how to deal with the problem we could not solve at the time. At any rate the command performance served as another testing of the way. But I have asked myself if the poet who retires to the realm of fairy tale is not attempting to protect his dream children from the definition of the here and now. To mutilate an image in order to mold it as flesh and blood is a sacrifice which we have again and again to make on the stage. That Dunsany shunned its seeming crudity and retired to the realm of fantasy was a loss to theatre. Actually the difference in approach to *The Queen's Enemies* even at the time was trivial, compared to Dunsany's creative imagination and the sensitivity he brought to the excavation of this archaic fantasy.

CHAPTER ELEVEN

A PRODUCTION
IN MEMORY OF
MRS. LE MOYNE

During the first years, Mrs. Le Moyne was guide, friend, and consultant, offering helpful criticism and unfailing encouragement. Toward the end of the season of 1914–15, her health began to decline and during the summer 1915 she died. In Mrs. Le Moyne's death the theatre world lost a distinguished actress and interpreter of Browning, and we lost our guide and teacher.

Pippa Passes was chosen as a memorial to Mrs. Le Moyne, for the opening of the 1917–18 season. The cast was entirely composed of members of the Neighborhood Players with the exception of Rollo Peters in the role of Sebald. He came to us as a young amateur with a flair for theatre design, but became more interested in playing. Later he was one of the founders of the Theatre Guild. Everyone who took part in *Pippa Passes,* those who had known Mrs. Le Moyne and those who had not, felt the impress of her personality. It was she who had established a standard of speech at the Playhouse, and through her we had learned to evaluate the spoken word as an art.

This production underwent a natural inversion from Henry Miller's some years before, the production which Mrs. Le Moyne had inspired and in which she herself had achieved such distinction in the part of the Monseigneur. Now every bit of ingenuity had to be contrived to compensate for the missing solo. The most loving care and effort were placed upon each detail to enhance the atmosphere, to give color, to restrain where previously rococo had invaded, to convey the simplicity of reality where obvious symbolism had once been injected. The Monseigneur was played by William Rothschild, a member of the group previously schooled under Mrs. Le Moyne's direction in other parts. His performance had a directness and sincerity that would have been encouraging to her. My own memories of having played in the Broadway production seemed to grow more vivid with each rehearsal. In this production, Irene played the role of Phene, I that of Pippa.

The settings were designed with charming simplicity by Warren Dahler. The problem was to emphasize the quick passage of time, as the three scenes, prologue, and epilogue take place within twenty-four hours. The black velvet proscenium curtains served as permanent background as Pippa moved on her way between prologue and epilogue. A feature of the production was the interpolation of a scene of the girls on the steps in which Pippa is being enticed through them by Bluphocks. This additional scene, written in by Agnes Morgan in a Commedia dell' Arte manner, gave the color and atmosphere of an Italian town during the early nineteenth century. In the original Broadway production, music for Pippa's songs had been composed by William Furst. At the Playhouse, the songs were unaccompanied, treated more as though a child were humming to herself.

Quite apart from its being a memorial to Mrs. Le Moyne, the production of *Pippa Passes* was of inestimable value to the group, not only because it demanded meticulous regard for English but because the problem of Browning's verse was exacting.

In spite of all the difficulties attending this venturesome

PPER: *Great Catherine* by G. B. Shaw, 1915–16. Catherine, Gertrude King
lady with the tiara, Cathleen Nesbitt.

6. LOWER: *The Queen's Enemies* by Lord Dunsany, 1916–17.
The Little Queen at right, Alice Lewisohn; kneeling, George Abbott.

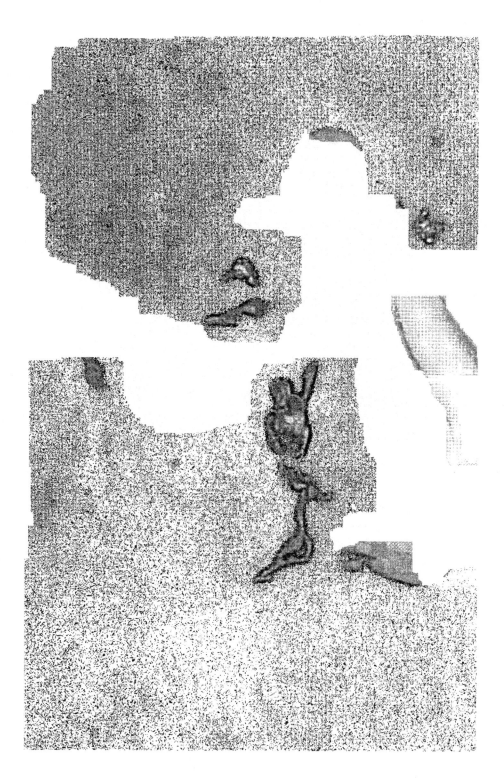

uı a, Japanese Noh play by Zeami, in the Fenollosa-Pound translation, 191

UPPER: Masked Waki, a Priest, Irene Lewisohn; Shite, a Sweeper, Michio I

ER: Priest and the Sweeper, now transformed into ghost of Tamura, in the

at left and back, chorus and musicians.

production, and most of all in spite of the missing dynamo of Mrs. Le Moyne, the ten scheduled performances were played to capacity, and toward the end, "standing room only" reached its zenith. What had happened during the years between the tepid reception of the original Henry Miller production on Broadway, screened to popular taste, and the warm response to this modest memorial offering on Grand Street? Browning was as unfamiliar to our audiences as he was to Broadway. Could the positive reaction possibly indicate the value of a trained audience? An interrelation between stage and public which had developed the creative dynamis often referred to as the spirit of the Neighborhood Playhouse, a spirit lovingly guarded by the searching need of the amateur?

This interplay, or marriage, between the play, the players, the concerted emphasis behind the curtain—the support of the entire group, directly or indirectly participating—and the receptively critical audience strikes me today as one of the happiest links of the Neighborhood Playhouse School with its ancestral parent.

To withdraw *Pippa Passes* while it was a "going concern" would have seemed a poor acknowledgment to the response had it not been for the engrossing problems of the oncoming adventure, *Tamura*. This experiment in the Noh drama was to attempt a translation into Western theatre idiom of an exotic, mystical experience. I do not think it would have occurred to us to consider the strain we might inflict upon the imagination of the audience had we not been wholly beguiled by this fugitive, ancestral soul of Japan.

CHAPTER TWELVE

THE PLAYHOUSE FAMILY AT HOME AND AT WORK

From the moment of its conception the Play-house building was thought of as a more flexible structure than its static brick wall suggested as home for the varying operations in the transforming process of production. In fact its dimensions seemed constrained before the building was completed. The production of plays and lyric programs was like the Roman hearth, the center from which the different functions radiated—workshops for the construction of scenes and costumes, provision for rehearsals and classrooms, office, kitchenette, washrooms, as well as dressing space for the large groups taking part in the lyric programs. This was the technical equipment for theatre conceived of as an organic whole. As such a building had not yet an analogy in the American professional theatre, its shaping and technical needs required searching consideration and planning.

But these intensive operations were like a façade behind which lurked the most persistent image, not tangible enough however for discussion. Might not our cooperative effort be linked to a wider cultural experience? For example, the relation between our group, carrying on whatever work was exacted for production, and individual artists who might find in such a dynamic center a stimulating response to the values they held? Cooperation for a creative idea or image had been tested again and again in the past; one had only to think of the contribution of nameless craftsmen to the cathedrals of old under the inspiration of the master's vision. Or a parallel in our time might be the concentrated relation between a musical director and orchestra to the score, each fulfilling his part, yet united in realizing the part as an element of the whole. Could not a theatre serve also to release values through the impact of relationship, wider yet more intensified than the values fostered by competitive commercial standards, offering an opportunity for those eager to absorb from those who carry the traditions of matured experience?

Though this was merely a dream for some future unfolding, it came to pass in actuality, as a dream frequently does, if the image it holds is grasped and made conscious. The humming eagerness for the work of production was not only spirited behind the scenes but contagious in its effect upon the audience sharing the unpredictable currents of the adventure. In the same way a magnetic link was forged between gifted artists and this Playhouse family indefatigably laboring for the thrill of experiencing, without an apparent or purposeful effort. This relationship has been partially indicated in the chapter on Guest Contributors; it will again be referred to in the interplay between seasoned actors and the student amateurs. A sense of partnership behind and in front of the curtain became the vital impetus fanning the hearth of production.

Perhaps something in the nature of a Cook's Tour through the building may present a glimpse of its atmosphere and the activities it harbored during and after 1918.

Turning back in memory to a typical Monday night reserved for stage rehearsal, we enter the building through its

green door and pass the box office. Then, on through the foyer
with its cork floor and parchment-tinted walls, spacious
enough to serve as a gathering place during intermissions.
Facing the doors, an Elizabethan refectory table is bare tonight, but during performances it is presided over by Mary
Mowbray Clarke, and serves as a bookstall where magazines,
theatre literature, and art books are available. Our relationship with Mary began in the schoolroom, where she was an
enthusiastic teacher of art. A later adventure of hers was
the Sunwise Turn, a bookshop which became the rendezvous
for writers and artists before and during the twenties. She
had also assisted in organizing the Armory Show in 1913.
Her presence at the bookstall is an inviting introduction
to the play, and during the entre-act she is often encircled
by young and old devotees seeking some guidance or judgment. Occasional exhibitions are also held in the foyer. These
innovations win appreciative response at a time when a
personal touch with the audience is almost unknown in the
commercial theatre.

An Elizabethan settle stands against the side wall and
above it hangs a frieze of three dancing figures carved in
marble by Jo Davidson during the summer of 1914. The
frieze is his contribution to the Playhouse, a tribute to the
spirit of the festivals. To us it is a treasured offering from
a distinguished artist whose early years have been lived in
that neighborhood. The frieze has a quality distinct from his
later work, as if in growing out of association with his roots,
it captured a simplicity and lyric feeling not characteristic of
his powerful portraits.

Now we pass through the back swing-doors leading to
the auditorium. Its walls, parchment toned, are paneled
in black. The plain black highly polished wooden seats are
bare of upholstery. From an architectural point of view the

stage, which occupies one third of the building area, is disproportionately large in relation to the auditorium seating three hundred in the orchestra and ninety-nine in the balcony. The emphasis upon the stage rather than audience expresses our individual problem, the variety, scope, and experimental value of production. Mr. Ingalls, the architect, has so successfully met the visual and acoustical problems that all seats are equally satisfactory. The uniform price of fifty cents for the orchestra and twenty-five cents for the balcony is never questioned by the audiences.

The black proscenium arch is proportioned with meticulous care for the correct line of vision, and the stage is minus a fly gallery. Compared to the conventional theatre, it is almost without equipment, except for the plaster wall at the back, concave at either end to suggest a cyclorama. This lends a sense of space and atmosphere when played upon by the simplest of lighting boards.

Monday night the house is dark and reserved for stage rehearsals. If a festival is in the making, Irene is in command, if a play, Agnes Morgan or I, or perhaps two or three of us are officiating to bring the elements of the production into order.

An ungodly smell of sizing comes from the scene dock, where a group is gaily at work painting scenery. Above, on the mezzanine, we hear the click of the typewriter from Helen Arthur's office, where the varying details of the business administration are carried on.

We climb the stairs near the stage and are on the third floor in the domain of the rehearsal, class, and dressing rooms. Dancing classes are in progress, one group following another —beginners, advancing, advanced—under the direction of Irene and her assistant Blanche Talmud, both admired and loved by the group. In the hall, separate practice teams are working. High school pupils, office assistants, stenographers, factory workers, or teachers by day, on these Monday nights all are far from the madding crowd, creating fantasies in rhythm. Young men are working as eagerly as the young women. If we could look forward in time, we might recognize many of these students, such as Anna Sokolow and Sophie Maslow, as well as Blanche herself, pioneering later in the field of the dance and ballet on Broadway.

The rooms on the third floor open into a central hall which serves as Green Room. The bulletin board is placed here for rehearsal calls and other information necessary to the work of the students and actors. A later visit would find photographs on the walls of distinguished players who have participated in Playhouse productions.

The workshop, originally planned for this floor, has moved in 1917 to an adjoining building on Pitt Street. This has released space for additional rehearsal and classrooms for the students, many waiting patiently weeks, sometimes months, for entrance to the classes.

Let us wander over the roof to the top floor of the Pitt Street building, and enter the workshop, the real pulse of the Playhouse, for it registers all the tempi of productions. In a corner at one end are the washtubs, alias dye vats. Long windows open onto the roof where newly made props, or costume materials, just dyed, are hung to dry. Centered in the room is a long straight work table for the volunteer assistants and student apprentices, many busily occupied under the direction of the workshop chiefs, Alice Beer and Polaire Weissman, both of whom, after the closing of the Playhouse, will find their way into the museum field, enriching a curator's knowledge with the experience of theatre. This is also the camping ground of Aline Bernstein's creativeness before and after her adoption by Broadway.

If we stop and talk with some of the assistants, we will find that many of them are skilled craftsmen who devote their spare time to Playhouse productions. Dye vats are sizzling with colors, papier-maché forms are being shellacked; sewing machines are thudding along; yards and yards of oilcloth trail on the floor and costumes in every stage of making lie about; unutterable confusion to the uninitiated, but the accepted way of growth to those who know. No matter how discouraged, even if groans are heard from the stage in the throes of rehearsal, laughter and gaiety are the keynote of the workshop.

Along the corridor on the third floor of the Pitt Street building are rooms occupied by Lily May Hyland, the pianist for the dancing classes and motion pictures. Mrs. Peterkin, the hostess of the Traktir coffee-house, where members of the audience as well as the Playhouse family can dine at small cost, is another resident whose personality is as agreeable as the meals she provides. Anna MacDonald, who translates and adapts plays from French, Spanish, or German for the repertory, and her distinguished cat also live here. She, like Agnes Morgan, is a product of Professor Baker's 47 Workshop at Harvard.

Now the model room hiding from inspection. Here, in miniature on the stage model, problems of lighting, setting, colors, and even plastic composition are studied and technical experiments for the production are tested

On the floor below, we find another classroom and the Le Moyne Clubroom, used as library, study hall, and rehearsal room; it contains Mrs. Le Moyne's books and some of the furniture we have inherited after her death. It is occupied now by the choral group under Mrs. Elliot's direction.

Next we come to the Traktir. In the early days of the Pitt Street building, this room has been a carpenter's shop occupied both day and night by boys from the Henry Street Settlement learning how to hammer, and fashion wood. Howard Kretz-Coluzzi, designer of *The Queen's Enemies,* is their director, a craftsman as well as an artist, who teaches the boys to model as well as to carpenter. Now the carpenter's shop has given way to an expansion of the Traktir coffee-house, with its brightly colored walls, peasant decorations, and hospitable open fire. A long table is reserved for the acting group and staff. The actors "at home" have an additional appeal for the Playhouse patrons.

The roof has a life of its own. In the spring and autumn it serves as a cloister for the study of one's part. Children's performances take place here in the springtime; and during the summer, dances are held on certain nights of the week. In fact, the roof is one of the most popular dancing resorts for the young people of the neighborhood. Later, when the Grand Street *Follies* are playing during the summer, the roof will undergo another transformation as a café where soft drinks are served.

This is just a glimpse into the activities of the "dark" nights when rehearsals took over the stage. On Tuesday, Wednesday, Thursday, and Friday nights the motion pictures in two, sometimes three, nightly programs attracted audiences averaging six to seven hundred people a night. Friday nights exceeded capacity. Saturday mornings and afternoons belonged to the children, with classes and programs planned just for them. The festivals and plays were given Saturday and Sunday nights.

Rehearsals of the Balalaika orchestra, the first of its kind in America, were another event of the weekly program during the first years. The gay and swishing rhythms of this

Russian instrument added a festive note to many of the gatherings and programs.

On the midweek nights, while the motion pictures were in progress, the rehearsal rooms and workshops were alive with work on current productions, for the plays and lyric bills followed one upon the heels of another. Usually two or three months of rehearsing were devoted to each production. Again and again these eager amateurs, after a full day's work, would spend a whole evening working on some characteristic movement, posture, or experiment in choral speech.

Besides the actual production classes, there were the courses related to the arts of the theatre and ritual drama. Robert Edmond Jones, Rollo Peters, Dhan Gopal Mukerji, Mary Mowbray Clarke and others, as well as the directing staff, contributed lectures and informal talks to the students and others interested in theatre craftsmanship. The craft side of production, still in its infancy in the regular theatre, was a significant part of this pioneering schedule; for example, the role of lighting in the development of plot, color in relation to atmosphere and characterization of setting and costume. These values were like a Bill of Rights necessary to the individuality of experimental theatre.

Players and dancers met in monthly sessions. Each group had its informal organization, voiced its problems, claimed its identity, yet both cooperated as one. These meetings, interspersed with much criticism of the productions and performances of the players individually and collectively, ran late into the night. Or the forthcoming play was read, analyzed, discussed. If a festival, the music and scenario were presented. Never were meetings more alive with storm and the urge of youth.

Apprenticeship was perhaps the most charcteristic feature of the Playhouse activity. Work had to be prepared and organized, workers trained to develop theatre craftsmanship; for even such a collective thing as sewing must conform to theatre technique, whose values and proportions vary from those of the everyday world. The problem of scale on the stage was complicated by the fact that each production was a law unto itself, the proportions having to be increased for one costume and diminished for another, even the stitching undergoing changes according to the needed ultimate effect.

Helen Arthur's office was a center of apprenticeship in the mysteries of liaison between house and staff, audience, playwrights, picture exchanges, specialty artists, newspapers, and so on. Here ten or more volunteer assistants were absorbed with her in bulletins, mailing files, posters, their chores enlivened by her gay anecdotes.

Agnes Morgan's apprentices were the stage crew, a neighborhood corps of assistant property boys, scene shifters, and painters. But her technical facility was such that she was everywhere in the theatre, combining a collection of functions the mere mention of which would drive any "self-respecting" member of the theatre union of today into a decline. Skilled as an actor, she played an occasional role; she developed the technical side of lighting, and had an instinctive gift for stage direction, as for the function of stage manager. As an amateur she responded to any production need while pursuing her professional career as playwright.

The scene dock was yet another popular field for apprenticeship. Night after night, devoted assistants, many of them professional artists by day, labored under the direction of Aline Bernstein, Frank Zimmerer, or Warren Dahler. This work had to be carried on after the movie show, for that was the only time the stage was free. And as these activities were extracurriculum for busy professionals, night had to be turned into day by enthusiastic craftsmen donning smocks and splashing on paint, or devising like alchemists of old how to transform common oilcloth into cloth of gold. The profession of stage designer, as we know it today, was in its infancy then. It was our task to develop a point of view toward the coordination of acting, setting, costume, among the group.

Rehearsal was a serious business that often seemed to the uninitiated to be poaching upon the domain of an insane asylum, and yet utterly simple, natural, and matter-of-course to the initiated. I still wonder how this intensive schedule was fitted into the appointed weeks, for the rehearsal chart was like a railroad schedule; we as directors, had to rush our way to the "platform" of the incoming train, ready with our troupe to board it before it was snatched by another. The stage groaned under its uninterrupted pressure.

To say that there were tempests and storms over the conflicting needs of voice, dance, speech groups, the workshop equipment with its schedule of costume rehearsal, the agonized workshop leaders who were waiting patiently to wrest the actors from the indomitable persistence of voice or dance director, would be too restrained. Yet these fires, burning through the night and smoldering by day, were somehow purifying, for only so could the magical potion of the ultimate performance be brewed. In all that tension and intensity the joy of creative experience never lagged.

Up to the time of *Tamura* no production at the
Playhouse had been a more daring attempt.
Stemming from Japan's middle ages, and a product of Zen
Buddhism, the Noh drama had nothing about it that could
tie it to anything the audience might recognize as familiar.
Even the literati could not have been on familiar terms with
the text, for a first translation by Fenollosa and Ezra Pound
had only recently been published. These poetic fragments
unlocked a further source of ritual drama, bewildering
and gripping for us. Could we attempt to express in terms
of Western theatre something of their mystical quality?
And if so, which of the many Noh dramas would lend itself?

The religious or mystery dramas of Japan, called "Noh,"
were a development of ancient religious dances, originally
performed in the temples. They were written by priests during the fourteenth and fifteenth centuries, analogous in
time with many European mystery plays, and were given
in cycles on festival days, the performance lasting from
morning till evening. Each Noh symbolized some human
emotion, experienced by the hero or semi-divine character
of the play.

The choice of *Tamura* was the result of a series of unforeseen circumstances. Our special interest in the Noh had grown
through Irene's visit to Japan with Miss Wald some years

before, as guests of Baron Takahashi, Minister of Finance. In her various contacts with Japanese life, the Noh dramas, their ritual form, and the spirit in which they were performed had impressed Irene deeply. Through her host she had had an opportunity to study with Kongo San, one of the foremost teachers of the Noh and its tradition. He had responded to her interest and desire to work with him on the complicated and subtle rhythms and gestures of these dance dramas, in spite of the taboo of tradition. For, as in all classic cultures, acting was a prerogative of men.

While studying with Kongo San, Irene had lived the life of a Japanese girl with Wakita, Baron Takahashi's daughter, wearing Japanese clothes, eating Japanese food, living a Japanese life in an environment which related her to this ancient culture.

On her return, Irene had danced fragments from the Noh at our home for a group of friends, giving the first insight into this art, then practically unknown outside of Japan. Quite apart from the stylized movement, its swift glides and sudden dramatic turns in varying emotional tempi, the traditional colorful costume, scaled to heroic proportions, required elaborate technique to manipulate. The appropriate mask added the essential character. In watching these fragments authentically presented, one had the sense not of a studied replica of a traditional art but rather of an experience utterly foreign, strange, and beautifully reverential.

Another factor contributing to the production of *Tamura* was Michio Ito's arrival in New York. We had seen him dancing in a tiny theatre in London a year before, so his coming at that time seemed a fortuitous omen for a possible collaboration. When we met Ito in New York, we asked him if he would cooperate in the production of *Tamura*. At first he was wholly uninterested, for his contact with the West, via Dalcroze in Hellerau, had deflected his interest from his native culture. Western art, Western ideals, Western music were firing his imagination. Why did we wish to resurrect the Noh which belonged to feudal Japan and was only occasionally performed there as an exotic experience? We agreed that to achieve an exact reproduction would be impossible, but could not the spirit of the Noh be translated to the stage as sympathetically as it had been treated in the text by Fenollosa and Pound? Then he continued, still resisting, had we realized *Tamura* was the most difficult expression of the Noh? Yes, unfortunately we had.

Finally Ito decided to meet this challenge, to help with *Tamura* and to play the role of the Cherry Sweeper who brushes away the blossoms which have fallen from the trees surrounding the temple of Seisui, that they shall not be crushed by the heels of the wayfarer. The pilgrim monk, or Waki, who recognizes the divine nature of the Cherry Sweeper was to be played by Irene.

The problem in this production was to bring about orchestral values. In Japan as in many theatres of the East and of Europe, the actor not only mimes but dances and intones the lines, the style abstract and depersonalized. In our version of *Tamura* the actors did not speak, but enacted the drama by mime and gesture while the dialogue was carried by voices in the background. Ian Maclaren "voiced" the Waki while I "voiced" the Cherry-Sweeper. We sat in the body of the chorus, masked and traditionally dressed. The chorus which combined vocal and instrumental color, conveyed the mood and described the imagery of the drama much like a Greek chorus. In our production the orchestra consisted of flutes, drums, and bells, which together with the chorus formed the background. Behind the chorus were three dwarf pine trees against a background of gold screens, symbolizing the three levels of reality—earth, heaven, man—expressed in each Noh drama.

In the rehearsals, Laura Elliot and I labored over inflection, rhythm, and the nuances of color necessary to bring out the values that were obscure in the text. Then came the exciting job of synchronizing instruments, movement, voices, as well as the Noh fans used by the chorus and the beat of the drums that punctuated the pauses, all of which served to accentuate the pulse and rhythmic content of the drama.

In a Noh, nothing is left to the individual will of the singer, or dancer, as he is sometimes called. Every step, every gesture, is highly symbolic, prescribed by age-old usage, that the devotional mind may be in accord with the spirit. Through such contemplation, the performer enacts, and yet is acted upon, through forces symbolized by the three levels of reality. These prescribed and conventionalized forms were reflected in the traditional costumes and masks, as well as in the postures of the actors and in each gesture of the chorus.

The translators said of this particular Noh, *Tamura,* that one might look upon it as a ceremonial play for the temple of Tamura.

The Waki, the pilgrim priest, wandering in front of the Seisui temple, meets the spirit of Tamura in the guise of a boy. The Waki asks about the temple and the boy tells him how Tamura founded it in honor of Kwan Yin, the thousand-armed Goddess of Mercy.

The Waki is struck by the spiritual beauty of the boy and asks his name. From the boy's reply, he realizes that he has seen a spirit. The Waki prays all night under the cherry blossoms, and as a reward for his devotion the spirit of Tamura reappears as a warrior. He describes his service to his Emperor in driving out the evil spirits of the land and in bringing peace. The play ends in a prayer of thanksgiving to Kwan Yin.

The battle, which is experienced by the Waki as a vision, is expressed in the scene by a violent storm of sound in which voices, as well as drum beats, clanging cymbals, and other percussion instruments, dramatize the conflict until, over and above the sound of battle, voices resound in devotional praise of Kwan Yin:

How great is the mercy of Kwan Yin!

It is not possible to recover the peculiar mood evoked by the silent but powerfully expressive roles played by Ito and Irene. In each the characterization was reduced to utmost simplicity of human feeling, conveyed with the greatest economy of expression, for the whole value lay in suggestion. This carried through from the moment the drama opened with the entrance of the chorus. In strict accordance with the traditional form of presentation, we strode in in the conventional bifurcated white stockings, the walk itself curiously stylized. Arriving at the stools placed in front of the gold screens and pine trees, we stood for an instant to acknowledge the solemnity of the Noh, then sat in traditional fashion, each holding a Noh fan.

In the foreground the dialogue in movement and gesture took place. At one moment expressing a lyric quality, at the next a majestic power in the heroic gesture, never flamboyant, always quiescently intensified. The Cherry Sweeper revealed in attitude and gesture that he was not only a temple servant but a divine presence, the ethereal quality accentuated by the costume and mask, and in the significance of the measured speech. In the same way, the Waki conveyed his supernatural quality in spite of being a wandering pil-rim.

The emphasis upon the dual nature of experience through gesture and attitude was also a feature of the costumes, architectural in outline and of richest, stiffest brocade. The masks, loaned by Howard Mansfield from his unique collection, added an unbelievable illusion to each expression. How the lacquered mask mirrors every nuance of expression remains its secret. The dialogue, for example, between the Cherry Sweeper and the Waki never for an instant lost its fluidity of individual personality and responsiveness to the partner; and still there was nothing incongruous between the mask, the gesture, and the movement; all was traditional, not least the lyric quality released in the gliding, boat-like stride, the suddenness of the swift yet measured turn. All was as prescribed as the notations of music, and as music the action flowed.

The movement should of course be visualized to be grasped. In the case of *Tamura,* a tribute is due not only to the Cherry Sweeper and Waki but also to the audience who seemed to be drawn into an experience which, with a lapse of concentration on the part of the actors, might easily have broken the spell and produced a sense of the ludicrous.

The scheduled ten performances received sympathetic response, indicating an interplay between the intensified experience of actor and the mood absorbed by the audience who together released the magic of theatre.

CHAPTER FOURTEEN

YVETTE GUILBERT IN
GUIBOUR

After one of the good winds of the war had blown Yvette Guilbert to America, she soon began to apply herself to teaching. With the help of American friends, she started a school through which she could pass on to students something of her art, her attitude toward theatre. Among her students were one or two members of the Playhouse classes, now privileged to have this unique experience. In spite of Yvette's inspirational qualities, teaching was not her forte. For how could that creative spirit inject itself into students unprepared to translate her gift into terms of their own personality? Yvette considered these students in the light of a playing group who would later assist her in presenting programs out of a repertory of medieval material she was collecting, a source which fired her imagination.

Yvette, the great diseuse of the prewar years, had been an insurgent element in the French theatre twenty-five years before, acclaimed by the painters and poets of the earlier era. Her uniqueness had been the foil of innumerable brilliant caricatures, among them a famous painting by Toulouse-Lautrec, slim waisted, fiery haired, green gowned, black gloved, towering in its daring above the mass. Here we see her as the chanteuse of the Boulevard, yet something more—revealing in its grotesqueries, with inimitable genius.

Whether she sang in the vernacular of her beloved Quartier Latin, or, as later, in legends and tales of the Middle Ages, she tapped a source of understanding that reached from the depths to the heights, from the heights again to the inmost kernel of the heart.

One day in 1918, in a burst of enthusiasm—for with her an idea became an immediate reality—she startled us with the question, "Would you like to make a collaboration?" She had in her possession the manuscript of *Guibour*, a French Mystery play of the fourteenth century. Would we read it, and if we approved, consider its presentation at the Playhouse? She to play the part of Guibour and the Playhouse group the supporting parts? It was not only startling but altogether thrilling to consider an association with Yvette. For her it was exceptional to play a role, and this was to be her première in the English language.

Preparing for *Guibour* was an exciting experience. The manuscript had been transposed from the original text into quasi-modern French. Its garbled dress was transformed by Anna MacDonald who probed back into medieval sources and types of expression and gradually evolved, with the help of Agnes Morgan, an admirable acting version, satisfying even to Yvette's critical eye.

We were accustomed naturally to versions of English mysteries and moralities but the French type had an engaging naïveté. To murder your son-in-law and then transform the act into a divine gesture had a breath of refreshing paganism linking it to the background of Mediteranean culture with its emphasis on the cult of the Great Mother.

Meanwhile the plans for production were being shaped. A cast was selected from among the Neighborhood Players and the Festival Dancers, with the addition of Rollo Peters. After a few performances, Rollo withdrew to accept a professional engagement and was succeeded by Kenneth MacKenna, then a young amateur eager for experience. Irene played the part of the Virgin who officiates as a statue in a niche of the cathedral; and I was the suffering wife of the murdered son-in-law.

Having Yvette in our midst was like a reflowering of the spirit of Mrs. Le Moyne. With unquenchable vitality, completely immersed in what was to be created, Yvette was wholly unaware of fatigue. Never for a moment did her interest flag, nor was the production treated as a frame for her expression. On the contrary, there was no detail too insignificant to be noted by her. Often, needle in hand, she would indicate her skill as a seamstress, refashioning a headdress or reinforcing a girdle. One moment she was brimming with buoyant gaiety that was younger than the youngest, and the next insistently demanding the utmost in untiring concentration. I recall her battle with torturing English words she found cramped and limited, while for us the problem was not to allow the elaboration of French emotion to appear exaggerated in our English idiom.

Under combined efforts *Guibour* eventually assumed a form that was neither a replica of the original, produced with the scrupulous exactness of a facsimile, nor yet a free interpretation. Yvette was not one to examine microscopically, or to look out from another age to sort and transpose medieval values. With her, emotion became the instrument and life the melody. With life for her theme, she must play its harmonies, sound its fundamental chords. Seizing her role, as Casals his instrument, she made it vibrate with immense tonality. *Guibour* was no longer a figure seen through the mists of the Middle Ages, a symbol created through the church, but to our Anglicized eyes and ears a gigantic tour de force leaping beyond the bounds of the picture.

Robert Edmond Jones, whose setting for *The Man Who Married a Dumb Wife* on Broadway had created a milestone in theatre design, undertook the setting and costumes for *Guibour* in spite of his many commissions. He entered into the production with keen enthusiasm, stimulated by his admiration for Yvette. For him as for her the cooperation was con amore.

I am sure no designs were ever carried out with more devoted care than that lavished upon them by Aline Bernstein, Ethel Frankau, and the workshop staff. Even the most critical theatregoers would have been startled to discover that the sumptuous robes of the Virgin and her angels were of oilcloth gilded and so formed to give the illusion of sculptured wood.

Irene, as Our Lady, and her angel messengers, careful representations of the gilded statues of the early Renaissance, were unforgettable as they stood in niches of the cathedral's portal. Irene's part was more than exacting, not only because she must carry the voice of Our Lady in her chanted speech but also because she had to remain motionless during a scene of fifty-five minutes. This feat made its protest one night when, in the midst of the scene in which I hear the news of my husband's murder, I saw Our Lady suddenly fall from the niche, prone onto the stage. Irene had fainted. Fortunately, the alert stage manager drew the curtain at an appropriate moment to avoid alarming the audience. The success of this maneuver was evidenced by the city fireman on duty that night, who bursting with pride for the Playhouse rushed backstage: "Gee! A great act! On Broadway she'd get fifty dollars a night for that fall!"

Guibour was distinguished for an interpolation of the Mass done in the characteristic style of the period, selected from Yvette's own library of some of the oldest of the Gregorian chants. Also for a remarkable "conversation" with Our

Lady written by Yvette, absolutely naïve and of the period, yet inimitably human and enacted as only she herself could express it. Guibour's coquetry is so irresistibly feminine that the Virgin in her niche is moved to grant her pardon for the sin.

This miracle was elaborately supplied with religious incidents, through its Mass, church rituals, processionals leading to the pyre where Guibour is to be burned, the threatening flames, the pleadings for and against the evildoer, and finally the voice of the Virgin granting pardon, the awe of the crowd, the religious ecstasy.

In spite of its artificiality as vehicle of the church, *Guibour* had a delightfully sympathetic touch in voicing the miracle of mercy over and beyond justice. For us the significance of *Guibour* lay in the association with Yvette, her wholehearted warmth and the inspiration of her creative spirit.

CHAPTER FIFTEEN

FROM AMATEUR
TO PROFESSIONAL

It is sometimes asked how players at the Neighborhood Playhouse were chosen. There was no rule; it just happened, much as membership in the Neighborhood Playhouse School happens today. But it was recognized that the Neighborhood player must first and foremost be a person whose interest and belief in theatre, whose desire for expression, was not confined to a personal desire to play. Though no formal examination was required, there was much testing through preliminary trials. Admission to classes in dance, singing, diction, provided further steps toward the desired goal. In short, to play a role meant that one had not merely qualified for the part but anticipated readiness also to serve for any function behind the scenes. For all were practically indentured to production. Names of individual players did not appear on the playbills during the early years, merely information about the production. And curtain calls, at first taboo, were only reluctantly introduced later on as a concession to professional needs. The Festival Dancers continued to be distinguished by the absence of curtain calls, and Yvette Guilbert gladly conformed to this omission in the production of *Guibour*.

The Playhouse had grown out of an intensive urge of the amateur to realize an image of theatre which could not be found at that time along highways and byways of the professional stage. I used the word "amateur" in its original sense, as one who loves his craft unconditioned by any personal gain or self-exploitation. Therefore, as a term for an instinctive creative urge; as, for example, the craftsmanship of primitive peoples, or their rituals worked out with meticulous care; or as the origin of classic drama of Greece, from the Dionysian cults, or the Eleusinian Mysteries; or again, the folk festivals of Europe—to mention only a few examples of culture unfolding out of creative instinct. For primitive or original art mirrors the throbbing pulse of nature. An interesting piece of research might be done about the creative contribution of the amateur to art at a time when the amateur has fallen into disrepute, a situation which always confronts us when technique, in and of itself, is glorified, and the will to power has overridden the instinct of relatedness. Nothing could be a healthier symptom of our present time than the little bands of theatre groups again emerging throughout the country and the renewed interest in theatre and its craftsmanship as an avocation.

Yet the amateur approach carries its own burden of difficulties. As the work and standards for production increased at the Playhouse, we were faced with a double-edged problem: How to keep pace with these developing standards and yet meet the stern realities of the situation? During the first five years, so crowded with experiment, we had gone beyond the horizon of the original vision, although the productions, up to this point, had been scaled to the experience of the amateur. Excellent as the work of the amateur was, fresh and vigorous for certain characterizations, as for example in *A Night at an Inn*, we were limited and hampered in the selection of plays that depended on maturity and finesse and the careful interweaving of motifs that comes of prolonged rehearsal. But how could a professional attitude toward work be reconciled with the need of our players and backstage workers to earn a living and meet the obligations of daily life? Rehearsals presented increasing complications, for Sunday was the only day we were assured of full attendance by our amateur dancers and players. As our demands increased, the elusive goal seemed farther and farther beyond reach.

Little by little, it became apparent that the strain of the dual effort to combine practical necessities with the life of the theatre was too great. Were we being driven after all toward professionalism and the pay envelope, which could so easily undermine the natural, spontaneous experience? Yet, under the conditions confronting us, how was it possible to do otherwise? Had we reached an impasse? After weeks and months of the most searching thought and questioning, the decision was finally made in 1920. A small professional company, prepared to give full time, would be installed. The announcement that the motion pictures were to be abandoned followed this decision.

Sport has long been recognized for its value in developing individual leadership and group loyalty, but I question if there is any game that demands more sportsmanship or personal equilibrium than theatre. This testing was now lying in wait for the student body in the announcement that a professional company would enable the Playhouse to present a continuous repertory. However carefully presented, this statement served as a bomb; for they saw, at first, only their beloved home invaded by an enemy, its informality threatened by a new regime, and they themselves exiled in a certain sense. Instinctively they realized the end of an epoch which required the greatest fortitude to accept.

Actually, the decision to incorporate a professional company did not materially change the organization. It indicated, rather, a daring experiment in uniting the lyric program, still to be manned by amateurs, with a mixed professional and student dramatic group, available for a more exacting repertory than we had heretofore been able to develop.

The stimulus of an ardent student body seemed to us as important as the equipment of a professional. If it could be made to work, just this combination might give the essential impetus needed for further growth. It was obvious that the roots of the Playhouse were embedded in the festivals, and that the student body, including the children, belonged root and branch to its development. The Playhouse had grown in the spirit of a family, with its quarrels, devotions, loyalties, and conflicts, and that family spirit had to be maintained at all costs.

The transition from the amateur period to professionalism was not achieved without growing pains on the part of the student players and the sacrifice of optimistic expectations by the directors. This was to be expected; we were familiar enough with the limitations of the students as well as our own inadequacies as directors. But we were totally unprepared for what the ensuing skirmish for a professional company was to reveal.

The rank and file of Broadway actors who applied, though they responded with enthusiasm to the idea, were trained to exploit obvious stage types rather than individuality of character. Their technique was based upon theatrical effect rather than upon relationship to the inner experience. This was a time when the star system dominated, and any other approach was not only foreign but as a rule unwelcome. To find professional players willing to search behind the obvious form and character of the part—in short, to enter into rapport with the orchestral values of a production—soon seemed like a quest for the Golden Fleece. The situation was exaggerated of course by our own lack of professional contacts and the difficulty of translating the values we held into the usual theatre idiom.

We were also to observe the Broadway system at closer range. In those days, when David Belasco's star rode high, the stage designer was still a pioneer, just beginning to blaze a trail on Broadway, where scenery had been produced en gros with meticulous regard to photographic exactness, and costumes were bought or hired from one of those remarkable caravanseries, the theatrical costumer. It was rare to find a play in which costume and setting were looked upon as a creative part of production.

A few schools of acting existed in New York where conventional technique could be acquired. But stock companies were the primary training for the beginner who, if gifted, had a chance to develop memory, observation, repertory, and alas above all, the banality of theatricalism. Except for Professor Baker's 47 Workshop at Harvard, there was no center of training for all the related crafts of the theatre.

This was the era of specialization and glorification of technique, spoils of the West, inherited from World War I. Collectivism was supplanting the old image of personal values; the human claims of the individual had little chance. Industry's attempt to reap the spoils of a universal market had resulted in mass production and mass control, and theatre as an industry was naturally influenced by the collective standard.

It was out of the urge to realize a new dimension in theatre, freed from this tarnish of conventionalism, that a triangle of insurgent theatre groups had emerged almost simultaneously out of several corners of Manhattan. All manned by amateurs, and unknown to one another, they had begun their independent careers, not in a revolutionary attempt to upset the existing order, but merely to voice another image of theatre. Confronting the Goliath of Broadway, they were as unprotected as the boy David with his sling. But what a sense of freedom there was, unshackled by "what ought to be," unconscious of anything but the image that moved us. The Washington Square Players, with their intellectual outlook and interest in glittering innovations, were a bubbling fountain of enthusiasm for the word, as well as for translating it into terms of theatre. The Provincetown Players, dedicated to authorship, were a source of inspiration to personalities such as Eugene O'Neill and Susan Glaspell, their outlook a kind of reformation in theatre, suggestive of a Quaker meeting house—austere, purposeful in pursuing their essential values.

And there we were, the third corner of the triangle, in the lower depths of Grand Street, experimenting toward a synthesis of expression. The theatre, we believed, was neither a place for the intellect alone, nor for the presentation of the shams and foibles of the day, nor just a laboratory in experimental drama. We were searching for a root, or, one might say, a trail to blaze to that inner world of reality which is the source of drama. We held the value and need of the lyric form, in and of itself, as a stimulus to imagination, as well as in guiding us to mythological values as, for example, through the early religious festivals and the Noh or later the *Salut au Monde* and *The Dybbuk*. Our task seemed to lie in developing forms not of the traditional theatre, which might be released with simplicity of means. Another characteristic form that had possibilities was the spontaneous burlesque, growing out of the Playhouse experience; this was later to develop into *The Grand Street Follies*. These were potentialities which belonged to the function of theatre, a never-ending round, nor could one side be divorced from the other, isolated or developed alone.

Theatre meant to us a kind of pilgrimage into various dimensions, strata, or areas of life, and an attempt to capture something of the mood and atmosphere of each. We visualized it in the round, with all its many-sidedness and interests; and if our experiments were slow of growth, they were not unlike the baffling conflicts that life itself presents.

In acknowledging ourselves first and foremost amateurs, we had naturally to submit to the suspicions of the public and the patronizing tolerance of the professional world. On the other hand, we had gained a direct experience in technical factors of theatre which could hardly have been acquired by specialized courses or university degrees, even had such providential direction existed at the time.

And now another epoch was approaching which required the intensity of nightly performances with a professional company, yet without any deviation in direction. To continue to create, to sense the need of each day, to experiment with faulty material and methods, but always with the need to probe inner forces—that was our reality. However naïve or ineffective the attempt, behind it there was the desire to reach deeper levels of experience. Heaven knows how often we were plunged into confusion, how often the battle raged between outer needs and inner values. And yet it was only at such times, when we persisted in following an impulse regardless of rational consideration, that we realized something of the thrill in creative effort.

LAUNCHING UPON A
PROFESSIONAL CAREER

By the beginning of the 1920–21 season we were definitely committed to a professional company. In the plans now adopted plays would be presented each night of the week, while the Festival Dancers would continue the lyric programs on weekends. The constant adjustment in schedule to the available time of the student players was now to be a thing of the past. The anticipation of a professional company promising the dawn of a golden age was, however, soon to present its quota of drawbacks.

The student players' inexperience and immaturity had been compensated by a tremendous eagerness to learn. Now we were confronted by the inflexibility of the professional's technique which forced him into a mold by the demand of the commercial theatre. Working with actors who though personally sympathetic were geared to the needs of Broadway made us increasingly conscious of the cleavage between their theatre and ours. How could this gulf be bridged? We were in search of a technique to release the inner experience so that the mood or atmosphere might come through. The student players had learned to subordinate personal desire to play a role to the values of the whole, that is, to accept themselves as members of an orchestra. But this approach could naturally not be expected of actors engaged for a "part."

Never was this deep-seated feeling for the experience over and above self-interest tested as it was through *The Mob* which opened the season of 1920–21 and initiated the professional company supported by the Neighborhood Players in nightly performances. We had appealed to John Galsworthy for the rights some years before, but he had refused his consent while the war was in progress. Now that the problem in the play—the conflict of an individual attitude *vs.* the collective stream of patriotism—was no longer taboo, we felt free to ask for his permission again, and received it.

The rehearsals for *The Mob* were launched amid "Sturm und Drang," for the student players were still suffering from the invasion of the professionals. Our hope of a reconciliation between the two groups, each having their contribution to make, each the chance to learn from the other, merely added fuel to the fires. But their irresistible feeling for the Playhouse and desire to play gradually overcame a surging resistance to the new system. As a matter of fact the title role of The Mob, characterized by the student players, came through with an explosive vitality that challenged the professionals. It was apparent to us that the drama taking place behind the scenes contributed to the heightened tension and fervor in the playing. So in the end *The Mob* offered a unique opportunity not only to initiate a professional course but also to reconcile amateur and professional in their relation to the Playhouse.

In contrast with the undisciplined outbursts of The Mob, the main characters of the play were typical of a sophisticated stratum of English society, an exacting study even for English actors. The play characterized these opposite values with Galsworthy's meticulous sense of balance. Stephen More the hero, of conservative tradition, is a member of Parliament. As pacifist he struggles to maintain his opposition to the government's stand at the outbreak of a colonial war. He is treated as a renegade by his colleagues, family, and wife, and ultimately becomes a victim of the hysteria of public opinion. In its structure *The Mob* was reminiscent of a dialogue between the protagonist and the chorus in Greek drama. Here the conflict lies between the destiny of the individual asserting his image and the passion of the mob to which he is sacrificed.

With the steel edge of irony Galsworthy presents an "aftermath" at the end of the play:

Several years later: A spring morning in London. A square is indicated, in the center of which a pedestal is visible bearing the inscription:

ERECTED TO THE MEMORY OF
STEPHEN MORE
FAITHFUL TO HIS IDEAL.

The play, directed by Agnes Morgan and myself, was a tour de force in the management of the mob scenes. Agnes was as skillful as indefatigable in dealing with The Mob. Although no attempt was made to impersonate a British crowd, the temper of the scenes was so sincere that the British flavor was not missed.

Ian Maclaren, who played the role of Stephen More, was to be an associate of the Playhouse through the years. He had adopted the Playhouse as "home," feeling a link through it with the little theatre world of England where he had been leading man with Miss Horniman and closely identified with

Granville-Barker's productions. At the Playhouse he was confronted with roles in unexplored fields, and rose to each new demand with a readiness to cooperate whatever the test. I think, for example, of the transformation from the "voice" in the wholly mystical Noh drama, seated on a low stool with other members of the chorus, to the role of Stephen More, with its individual stamp; and again of the unusual quality he brought to the poet in the *Salut au Monde* the following season, through his rarely fine voice and expressive reading of the verse, and his lifelike portraiture of Walt Whitman. His feeling attitude toward the problems of production was an eloquent indication of the influence of the insurgent theatre in England.

The four weeks of concentrated rehearsals, which at first appeared as a new lease of life, seemed to melt like the surface of an ice pond under the midday sun before the impending opening. As with previous ones, this opening exacted the usual conflict between the play conceived with all the possibilities of orchestral wholeness and the acceptance of its limitations when translated to the stage. The verdict of a critic, even if damning, could but feebly echo the reactions of the directors. However, though each production with us was treated as an end in itself, it was also thought of as a process toward a more complete experience.

The enthusiastic reception of *The Mob* was wholly unexpected. In fact it seemed incredible that it was actually selling out night after night. Just as surprising and encouraging was the esprit de corps developing between the student players and professionals. It was not long before many of the "foreign" group felt and were accepted as part of the Playhouse family. So the worst fears of the amateur were never to be realized. It also became evident that in spite of the drastic change in plan the Playhouse had not abandoned its personality or direction.

The Mob marked still another milestone; for the first time we were being inscribed upon the critics' calendars. Heretofore a friendly visit was occasionally vouchsafed by an individual critic, but none felt the obligation of a review. Now though the circuitous journey from Broadway to Grand Street continued to be commented upon by the press in the lighter vein, the Playhouse appeared more frequently in the theatre news of the day.

Another surprise was in store for *The Mob*. A telephone call for two tickets at the box office.

"Sorry, all sold out," the peremptory reply.

"This is John Galsworthy, can't you possibly find two seats?"

"Aw, quit yer kiddin'," the ticket seller's suspicious answer.

It later became clear this was not a ruse to obtain tickets but John Galsworthy en route, incognito, with his wife to England from Arizona.

Before curtain time the news had spread that the author was in the audience. There was much strolling up and down the aisles to catch a glimpse of him. Behind the curtain those of us who knew of his presence had a sense of acute anxiety. At the final curtain after more than usual applause and an insistent call for "Author, Author!" Galsworthy rose and addressed the audience, remarking that this was the first play of his that had ever been produced without his personal direction; he added that he preferred it to the London production.

I recall his courteous appreciation to the cast and the way he brought some illuminating thought to each character. In a later conversation I asked him about the younger generation in England and what kind of plays we might expect from it. "Why expect plays of young men? A play requires far more maturity and experience than we can hope for from the young generation." He felt that experimenting in all other forms of literature should come first.

The personality of an author seldom conforms with his work. But Galsworthy represented to me the consummation of "gentleman," a wholly finished product.

The first year of our professional career was full of adventure, bringing with it a new responsibility. With all the hazards of theatre and the limited size of the Playhouse the box office receipts could not measure up to the cost of production. At this point we decided to enlist seasonal subscribers instead of depending upon the uncertain response of the usual audience. While some of the productions played to "standing room only," others naturally attracted small audiences. The income under these circumstances was inadequate to carry the cost of production, even though the overhead was guaranteed.

Subscribers proved both an advantage and a curb. They were a stimulus in adding another branch to the Playhouse family, yet a hindrance too, for they necessitated committing ourselves in advance to a specific schedule. This meant that we had often to close a production during its successful run in order to hold to the promised program. Started as an experiment, the subscription audience continued through the years, for its loyalty and interest far outweighed the inconveniences of additional work and the rigidity of a promised schedule.

If the subscribers were a constructive element in further-

ing an experimental program, how can one measure the contribution in devotion, support, loyalty, energy, creativeness,
given unstintingly by the staff, the voluntary assistants, the
student players, and numberless others, many of them unknown?

CHAPTER SEVENTEEN

SUCCESSES AND
FAILURES

Again and again, we were forced to observe the discrepancies in the evaluations of Grand Street and Broadway. Why did the productions that played to packed houses at the Playhouse fail to win a glimmer of interest on Broadway? Or again, we had to face up to blunders in the choice of a play, or in the failure to bring it to life. If these "mis"-productions could have appeared at the time as humorously constructive as they do in retrospect, the life of the directors and actors would have been a long paean of rejoicing.

The Whispering Well ranks in the category of "mis"-productions. It was suggested by Iden Paine during the first year of the professional company, as a folk divertissement to follow *The Mob,* and also as an excellent vehicle for Whitford Kane, who had been active with the Playhouse from the days when the delightful troupe of Irish players presented their repertory there.

It must have required a great deal of self-hypnotism to consider its production seriously, but, that applied, *The Whispering Well* went sailing on toward a fatal doom from which we struggled to rescue it. First, we tried deleting the obvious symbolism, and boiling it down to simplest terms. Thus and so was tried and discarded. The more we tampered, the worse it seemed to grow. Why was it resisting every effort toward salvage?

The dreaded doom of its opening was steadily approaching. How face the ignominy? In all the days of amateurism, I had never plumbed such woeful dullness, nor could the most skilled or gifted of actors endow it with any reason for existence. Perhaps something positive would have emerged had Iden Paine, versed in English and Celtic folklore, fathered the production. But as it was, there was only one possible respite; a reception so shattering that it would topple into its grave the opening night. But even that release was denied, and we were forced to face the trial of its tolerable reception.

There is a certain exhilaration in an honorable failure. One has done his best and in the end the play, the audience, or the production fails; of course always with the haunting question in pursuit: Where? Why? But to be guilty of sheer banality, by adding complacency to artificial simplicity, cannot be forgotten or forgiven.

This failure was more than compensated during the same season by Granville-Barker's *The Harlequinade*—hardly a play, rather a series of scenes linked together as a fantasy to convey the eternal spirit of youth as mirrored in the theatre through Harlequin, its playboy. With the deftness of his wand, he conjures up the image of theatre as it is transformed through the mask of different epochs. This fantasy had a refreshing quality at a time when problematical social values occupied the playwright. The audience listens in to the sequence of episodes by way of a commentary between Uncle Edward and his niece Alice, present as eye witnesses, and seated at the side of the proscenium. Whitford Kane and Joanna Roos were delightful as these observers, while Albert Carroll brought distinction and style to the Greek and restoration scenes. The incidental dances were also arranged by him.

The appeal of *The Harlequinade* to continuously growing audiences forced us again to consider an extension of the run. *The Queen's Enemies* and *Great Catherine* had journeyed to Broadway and failed; but the flattering response to *The Harlequinade* several years later tempted us once more to follow the sign post to Broadway. So *The Harlequinade* was packed and sent to the Punch and Judy Theatre, only, or perhaps quite naturally, to be ignored in the confusion and glamour of the "Great White Way."

How explain to ourselves why the magic which had lured crowds to Grand Street drew but a handful of wayfarers to its admirable setting on Broadway? A rational answer might have reminded us that all productions were scaled to the dimensions of the Playhouse. Still Gertrude Kingston's vivid personality, combined with Shaw's wit in *Great Catherine*—surely strong enough to carry on Broadway—had not won response there either.

Should we have read into this repeated experience the absence of the spiritus loci? At the Playhouse the whole building pulsed with a dynamic feeling and a sense of relatedness shared by the audience. The theatres of Broadway, even the charm of the Punch and Judy, were merely houses or caravanseries for selling their wares, while the audience, to a large extent transient comers, had no relationship to distinctive values. Although this fundamental difference was obvious from the start, it had apparently to be tested again and again to actually "take"; and so a similar fate was in store for Granville-Barker's *The Madras House* which opened the season of 1921–22.

The Madras House is a couturier establishment. Victorian morals at home and in the shop skirmish through satire in settings unutterably drab and amusingly modish. Equivalent fashions in mentality and morals are also exhibited. It was quite to the point that much study and dissection during production revolved around the workshop's handling of these attitudes. Though always a vital center it soon became the plumaged abode of the play, offering blanched mid-Victorian and futurist mode in extraordinary combination.

The curtain rose upon a scene so diabolically drab that it provoked wild laughter. As daughter after daughter appeared, the Victorian prototypes of the Seven Foolish Virgins, the audience could barely contain itself. Today as I think of *The Madras House,* it is the opening scene that has lived on, with its seven daughters moving in and out of what appeared a vault of Victorian chastity.

Scene followed scene with varied but mounting approval from the audience. Albert Carroll's listless enthusiasm as the purveyor of fashion provoked flashes of delight. Aline MacMahon and Esther Mitchell distinguished themselves as the chaste daughters of the Victorian home, emerging in the third act as flaming moths of the twentieth century. This was the first association of these two actresses with the Playhouse, a collaboration that, in Esther's case, continued for several years, while Aline, who left the Playhouse in 1924 for Broadway, nevertheless kept her link with Grand Street and in later years became a unique inheritance of the Neighborhood Playhouse School.

Whitford Kane's Huxtable, proprietor of the house and of his seven daughters, was invested with that actor's usual charm, and if old Hux was more winning than the author intended, one gladly forgave him. The leading lady, crippled through a fall from the stage, had missed the crucial last rehearsals, but even her sketchy relation to the dreaded final scene was unable to destroy the mood already evoked. The play drops lamentably in the last act and with all our efforts to overcome a scene that was obviously a mere makeshift we could not resuscitate the theme, or preserve the sparkle and witty penetration Barker had written into the earlier acts.

Still the popularity of *The Madras House* threatened to swamp the Playhouse. After playing to packed houses through the weeks devoted to subscription audiences we again decided to brave the lions on Broadway in order to·clear the decks for the next play. Again our fate was sealed, and after a tepid reception at the National Theatre we watched *The Madras House* give up its Broadway ghost. The bones and tattered relics were penitently and solemnly collected and removed to Grand Street as a sacred warning never again to stray from the native heath.

Another question-mark failure during the same season was *The Green Ring,* a translation from Russian by Zinaida Hippius, wife of the famous novelist Merejkovsky and herself a distinguished writer and editor of the *Mercure.* The dramatis personae consisted of children groping through the mists of adolescence in conflict with the unstable relationships of the grown-up world, an experience which had universal validity at that time. Although the meager audience which ventured to come were gripped by the poignancy of the children, sensitively played by Joanna Roos, Esther Mitchell, and Albert Carroll, the play failed to stimulate a mildly interested response. It anticipated a later epoch however, when playwright and actor were moved to dramatize the searching needs of youth.

CHAPTER EIGHTEEN

THE GRAND STREET FOLLIES

Our subscribers were the actual cause of the accident of *The Grand Street Follies*. Toward the close of the season of 1921–22 we were sitting gloomily one night around the dining table of the Traktir wondering how in thunder to conjure the special invitation production promised to the subscribers. Rashly we had agreed to supplement the season with an experimental play, but no manuscript of sufficient interest had so far presented itself. Suddenly, a brain wave: "Why not," I asked, "invite the subscribers to our annual burlesque? Why not include them in our family party?"

The suggestion caught fire, though at first it seemed doubtful that we could develop into a more or less impersonal form what had been a purely personal entertainment. Heretofore the family party had been the creation and inspiration of Agnes Morgan and Helen Arthur, who were the playwrights, producers, and performers of the inimitably clever burlesque of the year's productions, planned exclusively for the Playhouse group. All the amusing incidents and anecdotes of a season, by others completely forgotten, lodged themselves somehow in their fertile brains, to be gathered up at the end of the season into a delightful and often brilliant satire which, until now, only we had enjoyed.

The Chauve Souris had made its bow in New York a few

months before, and echoes of its whimsical naïve character were often heard at the Playhouse. Balieff was an excellent subject for Helen's wit, and within ten days *The Grand Street Follies of 1922,* christened by Helen, bubbled fresh, crisp, and sparkling.

Apparently skeptical of the homemade brew, the subscribers for whom it was given gratuitously responded at first in small numbers. But the infectious delight of those who came blazed a trail for *The Follies* from one end of the city to the other. The two succeeding performances originally scheduled created almost a panic of excitement. I had never before heard the walls echo with such robust applause. The spontaneity of the playing reached out, capturing the spectators until they too entered into the performance, sharing in the refrains of some of the songs as though the theatre contained one large family of players.

Suddenly, from all over the city, people who had never heard of the Neighborhood Playhouse flocked to Grand Street. They stormed the doors to gain admission; tried even the subterfuge of pretending they had been subscribers, in order to attend one of the ten additional performances now scheduled. *The Follies* might have continued to play to packed houses during the entire summer, but the engagements and the holidays for the staff made it necessary to close. Now once and for all, the ghost of any future season's closing performance for our subscribers was laid. However little response there might be to the productions during the year, we felt sure that at least the final bill would retrieve the heart and coffer.

From then on—after a year's enforced intermission—*The Follies* became a silent partner of all that took place at the Playhouse. We began to meet informally for the sake of exchanging and discussing incidents that might offer amusing possibilities, and in this way the mood of *The Follies* bubbled in moments snatched from more serious productions. The impression created by the first one naturally inspired considerable anxiety in developing the second edition, till Agnes Morgan presented the script. Then it was clear that her genius for brilliant satire had flowered overnight. All the enthusiasm of the combined audiences which later acclaimed it could not equal the instantaneous and warm reception of the Playhouse group at its first reading.

With Lily May Hyland's contribution of the score, *The Grand Street Follies of 1924* achieved a Gilbert and Sullivan quality. In *Hamlet—Who Killed the Ghost?*, the inimitable all-star Barrymore-Hopkins-Jones production for which Robert Edmond Jones had originally designed a wholly individual, subjectively treated setting, was spoofed in the spirit of high comedy. Albert Carroll, who had so often delighted us with his unique improvisations at our family parties, for one of which he recreated the unforgettable Pavlowa swan dance, now evidenced the richness of his talent for subtle imitations of distinguished personalities. Although a copy of another's interpretation, his playing of John Barrymore as Hamlet came through in a masterly way. It had all the qualities of the performance to which he brought an astounding characterization perceived with his own penetrating sensitivity.

In another memorable sketch Aline MacMahon produced a vignette of Gertrude Lawrence—with a beguiling lyric written expressly for her by Anna MacDonald in an ultramodern comedy key.

Notwithstanding these satirical slants on outside productions, *The Follies* continued to fire its wit upon the Playhouse as well, seeing itself "as ithers see it," though preserving a spontaneous, homemade quality. The effect on the audience was even more infectious than before. *The Follies* had now become an event ńot merely of local interest; it was received by the satiated critic and Broadway audiences as an innovation which neither the long pilgrimage to Grand Street nor the sweltering heat could mar. The roof, which in other summers had been used for neighborhood dances, was now commandeered for *The Follies* as an informal café during the entr'actes.

From the standpoint of the company, *The Follies* was one of the most refreshing and releasing experiences of each year, relieving by the bubbling delight of its preparation whatever intensity and strain the repertory might have exacted. All departments, lyric, dramatic, classes, and staff, were called upon to participate. From a practical angle it enabled us to keep the company intact, for with *The Follies* running all summer there was no longer any anxiety on the part of the actors to secure other engagements. The realization of a long-cherished desire for a permanent company ensconced for the full year might now be possible. But this new development of a summer program involved changes in organization. To carry on the whole of the year was impossible without a careful holiday schedule, necessary for the actors as well as for the rest of the staff; but this had the disadvantage of introducing a foreign element into the company while the original members of the cast were holidaying.

One of the charms of the earlier editions of *The Follies* lay in the fact that everything was subordinated to the spirit of play. The whole impromptu informality of costume and setting, the emphasis upon the group or individual quality, rather than the exploitation of personality, contributed to its special nature of naïve and contagious gaiety. Now that it was accepted as an indigenous part of the schedule, how retain that informality and at the same time acquire just enough technique for its growth as a recognized expression? What was to be the trend of the new venture? Unless a revue can maintain its individual character there is danger that it will become identified with the very standards and attitudes it is lampooning.

Somehow the later editions tended to lose the perspective which contributed the sparkle to the earlier brilliant satire. Any form, no matter how slight in itself, has its own integrity, and in the natural course of its growth can either remain free to evolve its unique character, or else bit by bit it begins to compete with its own achievement and, through imitation, to lose the original thrust of the idea. And this, it seemed to me, was the serio-comic fate of *The Grand Street Follies,* although they remained in each season's repertory of the Playhouse until its close.

CHAPTER NINETEEN

SALUT AU MONDE

The *Salut au Monde* preceded the first *Follies* in 1921–22. A weekend festival production, it was inspired by a feeling of at-oneness that swept from land to land at the end of World War I. Walt Whitman's poem seemed to us a fitting expression to commemorate a moment for which no journey upon uncharted seas was too adventurous, no discouragement too depressive. Our hope was to convey the vision which Whitman expressed at the end of the Civil War in a form adapted to presentation on the stage. The appeal of the poem lay in his concept of America not only as a harbor but as a unifying influence for peoples of the world. In it Whitman saluted the new spirit of enfranchisement for all nationalities composing America, a burning problem at that time, and he envisaged a way to such liberation through his perception of a widened consciousness. As poet, Whitman penetrated beyond principles and ideologies and appealed to the heart to voice itself in eternal images out of which expressions of freedom and brotherhood have sprung.

Salut au Monde, salutation to the world, demands awareness of the cultures of the world and the possibility of their enrichment to the individual and, through him, in Whitman's spirit, to a feeling of brotherhood. In this sense, his image can never be called "outworn." The *Salut au Monde* still holds for us the vision of unity formed out of diversity, a wholly different concept from that pressed into the rubber-stamp slogan of freedom; for it involves the acceptance of that which is other, strange, even questionable.

His apostrophe to unity includes light and darkness, earth and spirit, the acknowledgment of all opposites, on a human and cosmic plane; such awareness was, for him, the guidepost to a social structure based upon relationship. This vision re-emerged in 1918, but its voice was too often drowned by the heavy thud of the machine and the promise of an efficient collectivism.

When *Salut au Monde* was written, its prophetic appeal to America reflected the goal of a triumphant spirit. Half a century later at the close of the first World War, the triumphant spirit had been drenched in the holocaust of war.

Had the poem been wholly directed to rationally conscious values, it would have found little echo in the deeper areas of our nature. But Whitman's reverie included acknowledgment to the religions of the world, and their appeal to universal images which are the heritage of mankind:

> Each of us inevitable
> Each of us allowed the eternal
>   purports of the earth.

The instinctive need of communion with deity as envisaged in the poem was suggested in five inner scenes, or veiled fragments of one scene.

The first scenario grew from a year's study of the poem in translation to the stage by the Festival Dancers. A first rough sketch, hardly more than a mere statement of the poem, was presented in June 1919 following the Armistice, purely as a student affair to which the public was not invited. Notwithstanding its lacks, something of Whitman's fire "took."

This gave the necessary impetus to reshape and develop its ultimate form. But that it would require three more years of experiment was not realized at the time.

The original text had naturally to be cut and some lines transposed for its adaptation to the stage. Ultimately the *Salut au Monde* consisted of three episodes: the darkened side of the cosmic sphere; its lighted side; the apostrophe to the peoples of the world passing in procession under one banner. Following these were five inner scenes, related to Whitman's acknowledgment to religious culture through spiritual communion.

The first of these scenes presented the Brahmin in meditation chanting an age-old prayer from the Vedas, intoned in Sanskrit by Basanta Koomar Roy. The Hebrew scene conveyed through priestly ritual and chant from the Torah, the sacred Scrolls, man's affirmation of the law as declared in the name of the God of Israel. The Greek scene, a fragment of the worship of Dionysus, was suggested through movement as a passionate release to deity, yet it too was veiled as an instant caught in a faraway image. The Islamic ritual, in measured circling movement around an invisible point, symbolized man's at-oneness with Allah through the cult of the Dervish. In the Christian evocation, a personal relation to deity was suggested in a group of medieval pilgrims on their way to a shrine, pausing for meditation, murmured in penance, then in praise of the Saviour, "the beautiful God, the Christ."

The music for these scenes was drawn from authentic sources, voiced either as solo or as faraway chorale. The setting, a circular frame within a wider circle, symbolized two levels of reality, or the inner world within the greater whole. A sense of depth, remoteness yet intensity, was produced through the use of the double circle.

As preparation for the religious background, all taking part in the production were invited to a series of lectures at the Playhouse one night each week. We were fortunate in having unusual guides for this comparative study, among whom were Coomaraswamy, the distinguished Sanskritist, later director of Eastern Art at the Boston Museum; Dhan Gopal Mukerji, a passionate interpreter of India to the West, whose readings from the Vedas were an unforgettable experience, for he brought us their mood and feeling as well as interpreting the texts. Kahlil Gibran, the Syrian poet, introduced us to the spirit of Islamic cults as well as to the Koran. Arthur Pope, the authority on Persian art and later director of the Iranian Institute, presented the historical background of Islamic culture. Alas, the excursions into the Old and New Testaments had necessarily to be abbreviated because of the heavy program of immediate work. The lectures were given con amore as an offering to this undertaking.

The musical composition for the *Salut* was entrusted after deep consideration to Charles Griffes, a young American composer who had written the score for *The Kairn of Koridwen,* a dance drama based on a Celtic legend from which we had prepared a scenario and developed the choreography for a production in 1917. Griffes was not only interested in the plan but inspired by its musical possibilities. Irene worked with him through a busy summer, till sound and movement, unfolding from the images of the poem, gradually became synchronized. As the tone color of strings did not lend itself to the plan, women's voices were substituted for the strings, while the basic composition was carried by woodwinds.

In the midst of the development of the musical and dramatic structure, we were called to England because of a family tragedy. While crossing the ocean word reached us of

Griffes' dangerous illness, and soon after our return he died. For a time it seemed as if the *Salut* would have to be abandoned; for to continue without that vital association and basic support was unthinkable. The score was in sketchlike form, the orchestration but slightly indicated. On the other hand we felt the obligation to go on; Griffes had poured his soul into the composition which, even uncompleted, held the promise of a work of rare quality, if not genius. Irene then set to work with Edmund Rickett's help to decipher the musical text, which Mr. Rickett later orchestrated.[1]

From that moment the Playhouse was precipitated into a production which seemed to present every known and unknown problem. Each day the synthesizing of its design became more bewildering, and yet in spite of incredible obstacles the *Salut* never lost its grip or fascination. For example, problems of synchronizing the speaking chorus, which voiced parts of the text in dialogue with the poet, and the movement, related to the darkened and lighted spheres; the women's chorus impersonating the missing strings fitted to the orchestra. Each element had not only to be integrated but to respond to the baton of Georges Barrère, the enthusiastic conductor of this multiple orchestra.[2] Combined with these elements, treated also as part of the orchestration, was the play of light and color upon the greater sphere symbolizing the cosmic whole, dark and light. These changing moods were played by Thomas Wilfred on his color organ as an introduction to the darkened and lighted spheres.[3] This flood of color was expressive of a world in the making.

---

[1] Rickett had been accompanist for Yvette Guilbert and collaborated in the research for her medieval programs.

[2] Barrère, foremost in his field as flutist, was equally valued for his unique chamber music ensemble.

[3] Wilfred had created an instrument, related to the notation of color as an organ is to musical notation. His silent color compositions were deeply impressive.

Perhaps the most surprising and heartening factor through these unending experiments was the attitude of the cast. During the years of the *Salut's* gradual development there was no sign of waning interest or discouragement. Each member was so electrically charged by the poem that details or repetition never became routine or stale.

As the pit was barely large enough to hold the small ensemble orchestra, the chorus required careful training to shift back and forth in time for cues, one group moving out into the cellar for another to take its place in the body of the orchestra. Or again the "voices" traveled to different parts of the building to give the illusion of echoes sounding and resounding from far and near, all orchestrated under Barrère's baton.

Although the burden of the production fell on the Festival Dancers, the professional players appearing in the midweek production lent themselves wholeheartedly to walk-on parts for the inspiration of the experience. In the role of the poet, Ian Maclaren's reading of the verse was admirably tuned to the orchestral color. The musicians, usually a foreign body, were peculiarly infected by the appeal of the *Salut*. In fact the whole corps of workers were indentured to the vision that grew from darkness to light, from chaos to form. And the tiny tots who heightened the "Lighted Part of the Sphere" with their bounding rhythms of play were also under the influence of a creative experience. Perhaps *Salut au Monde* more nearly achieved the atmosphere of festival than any offering before or after it at the Playhouse, though it was neither the first nor the last production to inspire in the company the fervor of a religious ritual. If such tension is the stuff of drama, then the drama behind the scenes was the very stuff and substance of the *Salut au Monde*.

Though we were conscious that this hybrid production

was threatening to a creative form, its raison d'être was to commemorate a situation which was profoundly significant to us collectively and individually; so that its content and image overruled the form.

I shall never lose the memory of that hushed moment on the opening night when Georges Barrère raised his baton; for we realized that the *Salut* would either release the spirit we felt contained in it, or prove a complete failure. Yet there was the faint hope that something that had gripped us so intensely, had survived so many obstacles and difficulties, had contained life for so many people, could not fail.

As the indefinable chords sounded the first notes of awakening from chaos, every head behind the scenes was bowed, each player involuntarily breathless. The opening theme played by the horns touched the inner chord that had sustained the *Salut* through the long pilgrimage of its creation and made it vibrate almost unbearably. Every member of the company, amateur and professional, waited his turn under the spell.

There was Ian Maclaren standing silently, looking like an idealized resurrected image of Walt Whitman. In the passage stood Basanta Koomar Roy in Yogi garment, intensely concentrated upon the chanting of his Sanskrit prayer. Further on, the Persian medical student who was to intone the Mohammedan ritual was standing as if already he were some distant muezzin calling the worshipers to prayer: "Allah, il Allah." Still further along the passage, waiting for their cue, the Greek priests in their white robes and black beards were concentrating upon their "Evoe."

The curtain rises upon the darkness of the void. Forms but dimly distinguishable struggle blindly to release themselves from the torment of chaos. Out of the darkness sounds of ploughmen and cries of fisherfolk are heard, merging into a radiant whirl. The rift of joy as the children leap into the scene, the golden light, the falling petals, the voices, the bells, the major tones, all for a moment contrive to shake off any shackles that ever bound theatre.

In the third episode we follow the poet's vision of man's social destiny, from the symbol of the totem through successive stages of kinship, to the sweeping banner enfolding all races, colors, peoples, and "at last his spirit having passed in compassion and determination around the whole earth," he cries out, "Salut au Monde!" His salutation is carried on in chiming reverberations and echoing voices.

VOICES

Whom do you see, Walt Whitman?
Who are they you salute, and who
   one after another salute you?

THE POET

I see ranks, colors, barbarisms, civilizations.
   I go among them, I mix indiscriminately,
And I salute all the inhabitants of the earth.
You whoever you are!

All you continentals of Asia, Africa, Europe, Australia,
   indifferent of place!

All you on the numberless islands of the archipelagoes
  of the sea!
And you of centuries hence when you listen to me!
And you each and everywhere whom I specify not,
  but include just the same!
Health to you! Good will to you all, from me and
  America sent!

VOICES

Each of us inevitable,
Each of us limitless—each of us with his or her
  right upon the earth,
Each of us allowed the eternal purports of the
  earth,
Each of us here as divinely as any is here.

THE POET

My spirit has passed in compassion and determination
  around the whole earth,
I have looked for equals and lovers and found them
  ready for me in all lands,
I think some divine rapport has equalized me with them.
You vapors! I think I have risen with you, moved
  away to distant continents, and fallen down
  there, for reasons.
I think I have blown with you, you winds!
You waters I have fingered every shore with you.
I have run through what any river or strait of the
  globe has run through.
I have taken my stand on the bases of peninsulas
  and on the high embedded rocks, to cry thence:
Salut au Monde!

VOICES

Salut au Monde!

THE POET

What cities the light or warmth penetrates
  I penetrate those cities myself,

All islands to which birds wing their way
I wing my way myself.
Toward you all, in America's name,
I raise high the perpendicular hand, I make
the signal,
To remain after me in sight forever,
For all the haunts and homes of men.

VOICES

Salut au Monde!

The five inner scenes were evolved from the lines: "I see the temples of the deaths of the bodies of Gods." There passes before the poet a vision of five manifestations of the divine message as revealed in religious ritual: the formalized, ethical, social teaching of the Jew; the mystic concentration of the Hindu; the pagan rites, woven by the lyric spirit of Greece; the Mohammedan abandonment to Allah; the passionate faith kindled by the "divine life and bloody death of the beautiful God, the Christ"; all picturing man's longing for spiritual freedom through the transforming light of communion.

There was no way of gauging in advance if the *Salut* could steer through the impedimenta of production and still retain a semblance of unity. This question remained in the air after the final words, "Salut au Monde," resounded from above, below, left, and right, and the final curtain closed in darkness. As the house lights slowly appeared, there was unbroken silence, not even a rustle of audible response. But we behind, still under the spell, were peculiarly moved by the apparently frigid reception, for how could we have ventured to assume that this wholly unknown quantity would be received as a religious experience?

As each performance was followed by the same response,

we asked ourselves what really carried over the footlights? We knew that it was not the actual factors of material or production, but that the drama lay in the heart and that the heart of the audience had caught fire. Those playing and those played upon were held in the spell of a common reality. Musically, the *Salut au Monde* had significance; but had the spirit of the whole not been so intensely felt, the scales could easily have tipped in favor of a banal representation.

I have entered upon these details, dwelt even upon that extra quality which escapes the reasonable, because the *Salut*, in spite of all shortcomings, which to us were legion, approximated in a sense the intention of festival and distinguished it from other forms of production during those first years.

The silent audiences soon registered their reactions; we were appealed to by various organizations to increase the number of performances. That was not possible because of the scheduled oncoming production: a play by a Harvard student, highly praised by the faculty. The break in the *Salut* performances was particularly distressing since the heralded play proved to be wholly inferior. We were appealed to by public-spirited citizens to send the *Salut* on tour throughout the country, a fund to be guaranteed for what they considered the most adequate expression of the spiritual values of the time. But such offers were not as alluring as they appeared when we considered how an individual experience would inevitably suffer under a blast of organized propaganda, however well intended. This does not mean that we were invulnerable to the temptation of such offers, but that experience was finally prevailing. Several times we had been lured to Broadway and returned to Grand Street with burnt fingers and singed tails. Had we not to realize that the Playhouse had its individual way, subject to trial and error, the fruits of an uncharted course?

In spite of being more remote in time and space from the affairs of the world in those days when we plodded our way without loudspeakers and radios, television, air mail, and all the marvels of existence made to stimulate and saturate, we seemed somehow more aware of our own reactions to world events, or perhaps we sensed more and speculated less. An awareness of an approaching end of an epoch and a new beginning was apparent in many directions. For example, the International Art Show at the Armory in 1913 had served as dynamite to erupt form, for Picasso had already intuited the abdication of the object as such. He was peering behind the walls of form, anticipating the destruction of matter as a thing in itself. In the same years, Freud was discovering a new borderline to consciousness in challenging the illusions of the ego personality. It was not surprising that the changing face of the world was touching us all, at least below the surface of consciousness. In our faraway corner we too were gripped by the need to find a new-old route behind the threadbare pattern the theatre reflected.

The *Salut* had brought certain values, not least a feeling of unitedness in the group, growing through the wider vision and the focus upon the lyric form. Still the need of a new impetus and time for reflection was greater than ever. Theatre as such seemed barren of content, its new breath could not be anticipated from intellectual sources. Irene and I felt that a new impulse might reveal itself out of the depths, out of that which had always been and still existed in primitive form. This was the need that soon carried us to the East, an urge that overruled all rational considerations.

CHAPTER TWENTY

THE SABBATICAL YEAR

During its seven years the Playhouse had been plunged in the maelstrom of growing up. We had developed the lyric form up to a certain point. We had given a series of productions in which the drama of immediate reality, as interpreted by Shaw, Galsworthy, Granville-Barker and others, played a leading role, not to mention values communicated by actors from the United States and abroad, who had generously contributed to the guest performances, or had collaborated with us in productions.

The audience had also become an established part of the Playhouse family, responding as subscribers to the varied program. And a sympathetic relation with the neighborhood had grown through the years. Activity behind the curtain had increased immeasurably. Through the evening classes geared to production needs, the children's work and their programs, the technical organization, the growing needs of the workshop, all had assumed an unforeseen intensity. Notwithstanding the increasing tempo resulting from this expansion, we had grown equally aware of the as-yet missing elements. The image was there, and the structure, but what of the inner pattern? Irene and I faced and pondered over this situation after the *Salut*. How approach those roots out of which theatre emerged? What was the trend of the Playhouse which had grown out of some such impulse?

Suddenly, all we were doing appeared in patches like a grandmother's quilt, joined together with bits from a bag of old remnants. The design for the moment might be pleasing, but it failed to satisfy fully. Forms, even the best in our modern world, lacked undertone. To go on repeating the gestures, stemming from forms grown threadbare and tarnished, seemed hopeless. How find a way to those roots which, we felt, could alone answer the need of theatre of our day? The *Salut* had released not only a call to primal beginnings but the desire to contact, if just for a moment, the atmosphere of the East which had given birth to ritual art. And further, the desire to relate to the flow of life, carried as it ever was in symbols eternally valid. This need, though not actually clarified, was insistent.

The first mention of a suggested pause in the cycle of production was greeted at the Playhouse with dubious looks. And quite naturally, for to close shop for a year, just at the time when the Playhouse was getting its second wind, was preposterous. Our colleagues pointed to all the complications of reviving interest, especially on the part of the subscribers, after a "dark" season.

In spite of the hazards and limitations, however, there were arguments in support of the proposed leave. For example, our organization needed pruning and direction. The changing repertory allowed too little time to absorb a play requiring atmosphere and research. For some time we had had in mind a production of *The Little Clay Cart,* a Sanskrit drama, but it was impossible without a long period of preparation. The workshop chiefs, though already overburdened, were champing at the bit to carry on further experiments in research for the anticipated production.

The irrational way was chosen. It offered the staff, student groups, and collaborators the chance to pursue whatever

theatre adventure appealed to them; and for those who desired it, the opportunity to cooperate in the research work
preparatory for *The Little Clay Cart.* The children's classes
and productions were to be continued as usual.

The sabbatical year meant that the house and stage would
remain dark, but that behind the curtain, whether near or
far, a new light might be kindled. This, at least, was the urge
behind the closing. Once we were on our way the Playhouse,
instead of receding with all its problems, traveled along; its
pulsing reality somehow increasing as Grand Street receded.

CHAPTER TWENTY-ONE

THEATRE OF THE
EAST—EGYPT

How curiously devoid of theatre New York appeared as we approached the shores of Egypt where theatre revealed itself in the light, the color, the form, the pageantry of each hour! How could we really catch the spinning rhythms of our West until we had sensed the gentle, swinging glide of its cradle? After all, we were but the searchers after the pattern, the ebb and flow of the life-stream of theatre.

Egypt! The horizontal planes of golden earth and sapphire sky, bound together by palm trees or the upright pillar of the temple. The moving pageantry of caravan, misting its silent way along the horizon or the border of the river. The distant chant or call of the muezzin; the prayer at noon, as simple and unrestrained as the midday meal-rest of our Western harvesters. The bared limbs of bronzed bodies like those chiseled by the makers of the tombs. Camels moving proudly as though a link with some forgotten past, yet seeming, even in an enforced servitude, to mark the pace. All an unending stream moving silently, steadily on—into an eternity as silent and assured.

Cairo offered many anachronisms. Here the meeting of East and West seemed a sorry business, and at first sight a crushing blow to the idealism of the *Salut au Monde;* for now we beheld the unsalubrious effect of the Oriental flaunting an ill-fitting, Western-mannered superiority, and the occidental a decadent, effete sophistication.

Farther on, the bazaar presented another scene even more fantastic in its color and sound. All our senses and sensibilities were so simultaneously assailed that at first it was hardly possible to be aware of the setting—streets so old and crippled that one wondered how they could support that stream of human energy, pressing, crowding, hawking and yelling, working and praying in continuous succession.

Cobblers and brass menders, weavers of rugs, makers of sweetmeats and aromatic coffee, callings too specialized to enumerate; donkeys navigating through loitering crowds, and now and again a cart bearing its black-robed harem burden —here was the bewildering effect of past and future, enlaced in a zigzag Mohammedan pattern. What strange irony to think of escaping for a brief space the hectic movement of the West so that we might find in the East a silent understanding, and then to find ourselves hurled, body and soul, into deafening confusion!

For a while, monuments and forms seemed to slide away under the pressure of human drama. There loomed one respite, the desert, and that called so persistently that every other interest disappeared. A donkey gallop through desert sands to the tombs of Sakkara and all the monuments of the past, temples, statues, political propaganda, the orthodox teaching of the Koran, the confused values of East and West —all were swept into nothingness. Day by day as we ambled through the sands, our tiny tribe of ten Arabs, one dromedary, two camels, two donkeys, seemed more and more to complete the new proportion of our heritage.

With that ever-widening space carrying us further away from the oasis, the personnel and activities of the tribe became more and more absorbing, and the world outside seemed to disappear like a ship on a distant horizon.

The theatre, as we had known it, seemed pathetically limp and lifeless compared to the stirring work of each day and the varied humors of our tribesmen, like children at play, one moment freely expressing themselves in verse or legend, dance or song, and at other moments suggesting the dignity of an age-old freedom. Barefooted, white-robed, heads outlined by the graceful lines of the keffiyeh, they became the lords and hosts of the desert, dispensing hospitality with an eloquent gesture.

In our tent, we could feel the greeting of the dawn and hear our tribe responding in prayer. Then there was a warming process around the brazier while a dark muddy substance was brewed under the pseudonym of coffee. And while we gulped it to the accompaniment of bread and treacle, the tribe, or as we soon fancied them, our traveling troupe, prepared for our day's journey. Tent pegs were pulled up and kits of paraphernalia tossed on the backs of the unwilling camels. Then the day's march began, and on we journeyed toward the objective of the evening camp.

To find a housing ground; to foregather each night and share the simple comforts; to make some new discovery of line, of light, of color in the sky; to prepare for the evening meal and, when the night winds seemed too treacherous, to find welcoming cheer within the tent whose sides were covered with the holy but happy script of the Koran—what could more perfectly express the mood or meaning of ritual? There in the desert, even the simplest action is enhanced with meaning. The function of the home each day becomes a symbol, and during the brief night expresses the image that the next day calls forth.

All the courtesy and charm, invention and discovery of

which the Arab is capable is somehow stimulated by the nightly dedication and blessing of his home. It welcomes any passerby for a night. We found ourselves at times playing hostess to travelers from neighboring oases and, in return, were entertained the night long with song and ballad, dance and sword play.

In these nightly gatherings at the tent flap with our Arab comrades, the tabl'a never ceased its syncopated rhythm. The repertory of songs and ballads seemed unending, and the bodies of the dancers tuned themselves to every nuance of thought and expression. Never had we sensed the flavor of such intimate theatre, effervescing with spontaneous energy.

As our minds traveled back to the theatre of the West, we wondered if upon our return we could recapture the sparkle and the joy, the sheer lyric delight that theatre might offer if freed of all its trappings and its static formalism. For, in the desert, theatre lives in and with the individual, who carries it as the troubadour, in tale, song, and legend. The rhythms, all the expressions of his ancestors, he translates into his own experience.

One night a fearsome guest came to our tent. At first it was thought he was a bloody enemy to one of our comrades, but later, when he professed friendship and gave assurance that he was on his way to see his love in a distant oasis, he was invited to remain. All through the night he sang of her, and our tribe questioned him. In verse, in song and dance, they improvised upon the moment. Next, a mock battle for her hand! With swords they played, and as the combat became more tense, the swords gave way to wrestling, but never for a moment did they lose count of the rhythm of tale or song. Wild ecstasy one moment; the next, romantic love; then humor and grotesque byplay. Then, when all the earthy emotions seemed to have spent themselves, Ali, the donkey boy, was ready to dedicate his last breath in a howling dervish.

Yes, the theatre of the desert has all the charm and fervor and clear, bold freedom of the epic.

The desert has its moods, and to feel their spell, even for a moment, reveals the varied inheritance of the Arab, its child. The calm repose, the sudden tempests, all the combative forces of the elements, the mysterious call leading on and on, the intimate gatherings of family and tribe, all experiencing through its own needs the living theatre! When we finally parted from our tribe after ten days of journeying, I felt as if the world outside the desert line was some disturbed and terrifying dream. For enchantment lay in the briefness of the desert's moods—in the convincing reality of unresisting elements, the burning pressure of sun and blasting whorls of wind, driving the sands in blinding spiral sallies —its changing appearance, yet the infinity of its presence.

The Nile reveals another world from that of the lower, desert Egypt. The form, face, walk, expression, contour of head and body, is as unlike that of the Egyptians of the south as the mode of life and dress. The ebb and flow of the river penetrates the core and rhythm of life along the banks, as it bears the flukah, with its gaily colored Phoenician sails, murmuring the song of the fellahin, to whom it gives its melody and nourishment, its untiringly friendly sky, and the enduring comfort of the palm tree.

And at last its sleeping soul which lives on in the carved pageantry of king and queen, scribe, tiller of the soil, craftsman, and holy man, the proud commanding overlord and humble burden bearer, all linked as one reality—Upper and Lower Egypt—floods and arid wastes, the unending multiple and unitary presence incorporated in the Pharaoh—as manifestation of all. The one who, in death, is acknowledged deity, symbol of an eternally existing presence.

CHAPTER TWENTY-TWO

THEATRE OF THE EAST—INDIA

We had gone to India aware that we could touch only a fragment of the paradox in its creative vision. Innumerable impressions of temples and caves, of landscapes and peoples, of tropical fauna and snowy summits, of jazz blaring from gramophones, pressed on all sides. Woman suffrage was being widely discussed under the leadership of the Hindu poet, Madame Naidu, whose alert swiftness and energized remarks were in strange contrast to the languorous curves of her body. In continued contrast, ever-present murmurs of heterogeneous religious sects sounded from temples, while the tambourines and brasses of the Salvation Army vied with the music of the sacred shrines.

Where, how, find a footprint of India's ancient pattern? In the midst of our bewilderment, we were unresistingly snatched from the hotel by that enchanting wizard and one of the first town planners, Patrick Geddes, at the time guest professor at the University of Bombay. Taken to his home in the Scottish compound, we were pulverized under the dynamis of his knowledge. But India was a far journey from the Scottish compound of Bombay.

Fortunately, through him we were soon invited by Hindu friends to see *The Little Clay Cart*. No performance could have been more opportune, for our colleagues at home were already at work on Ryder's translation for possible production at the Playhouse later on. When we arrived the play was an hour or so under way, for to our hosts time was a timeless reality and, as we soon learned, played a soothing but somewhat confusing role in India.

The theatre was large, reminiscent of the type fashionable in England a century before, its gold and plush decorations encrusted with neglected dust, giving an air of decaying pride. As we entered we were conscious of dark, impenetrable eyes and scantily clothed bodies, covered heads and naked feet, all enveloped in silence. Here and there, texts were being studied. We gathered that many in the audience were comparing the Mahratti, the colloquial language of Bombay, with the original Sanskrit. Apparently, all social strata were present, in various admixtures of European dress and bearing. Writers, statesmen, barristers were pointed out to us, and side by side with them were women, serene, curiously unaware, many of whom gave the impression of having escaped for an hour or two from purdah, to return again to their traditional seclusion. Their poise and stillness were more suggestive of the plant or forest world than of the human, for the Indian exudes silence as the Westerner does action.

Out of the stillness, the play continued. To call it "play" is hardly correct, yet opera would be equally misleading. The text was chanted in a rasping falsetto, something totally new to us, and untrained as we were in the convention of Hindu tone production, we found it impossible to gauge values. Tradition was strictly adhered to, and all parts were played by men, exquisitely drawn characterizations providing, for us at least, the real interest of the evening.

No attempt had been made to costume the characters fittingly. The producers, the actors, despite all their knowledge of custom, had completely garbled any significance in color and costume, and the worst of the so-called "modern" elements in Hindu dress was blatantly evident. Yet the performance was apparently completely satisfying to the audience, indicating that the play was an inner experience, its outer dress negligible.

We became more and more aware that with the Hindu, theatre is primarily an experience of the ear. Gesture, singing, or rather a highly stylized form of speech, were indissolubly united. Throughout the four hours of our stay, nothing seemed reminiscent of Ryder's translation, consisting of forty-two acts, that we had read in New York. It may be that portions more familiar to us had not yet been presented, for when we left at midnight *The Little Clay Cart* was still in active operation, the actors giving the impression of merely tuning up for the actual performance.

From the moment we touched the shores of India, we had been hoping for some evidence of a festival shrine that would show us the worship of people whose daily life is a ritual of prayer. At last we were to find it in the Siva festival at Benares, where thousands of pilgrims greet the dawn of springtide beside their sacred river, the Ganges. All day long pilgrims with bags and bundles jostled themselves through crowded station platforms and into the congested carriages of the train. Wide-eyed children solemnly trudged along under the weight of tin traveling boxes or rolls of gay bedding. Finally the train lurched into Benares and we got out amidst crowds of buzzing coolies, the sun-helmeted, white-suited Briton, the barefooted native, and mongrel-dressed Eurasian, and were driven in silence through narrow, dark lanes of the holy city. We must wait, we were told, for the sun to rise upon the sacred rite of bathing in the Ganges. So we returned to the cheerless hotel and tumbled into bed. Before dawn, a lighted candle, a refreshing bath, a swallow of tea, then a chase with the sun to the river.

A muddy bank, a strange little boat up which we climbed to sit on its roof, and then off we were rowed, slowly, quietly, with the sun still crouching over the horizon. Already the ghats were full of bathers, hundreds mingling their prayers with the rite of the bath, the washing of garments, their salutation to dawn and the welcome approach of springtide. There was a spell of silent concentration, each individual performing his own rite without the slightest intimation that he was not isolated.

This was the Ganges—long streaks of orange, misty blue of sky, ghats, river, bathers, ritual! No dream could challenge the drama of the holy river; and how reveal that chant, that morning prayer, so utterly simple and as illusive as the shimmering dawn itself. Soon the sun was warningly aggressive, and in need of bodily refreshment we returned to shore.

Then, the adventure of the night. We followed a young Brahmin host through the circuitous streets of Benares which gradually narrowed into passageways winding into darkened alleys, silently drab. Now and again we could hear the accent of a tambour issuing from behind closed shutters. We turned a dingy corner hidden even by day from the slightest fleck of sun, then climbed steps whose angle suggested an Egyptian tomb.

We paused at a door. Our host tapped. A scurry of movement within; the door opened cautiously, and an old stump of a woman, seemingly square from top to middle, appeared bearing a lighted candle. The face, at first inert, gradually showed signs of life, and shrewd, expectant eyes blinked with obsequious courtesy before our host. From the paddling gait to the shrill, hawking voice, the figure greeting us was the perfected type of the professional madam. We were ushered into a bare room and invited to sit on the floor.

Presently a tiny, delicate figure in white appeared. The curious late-Victorian patterns of her sari enhanced the dark skin glowing like soft, rich earth. Her black hair was tightly drawn, Indian fashion, accenting the oval lines of her face. As she moved toward us, it seemed extraordinary that so much grace could flow from so tiny a center. Nor was it at first possible to tell whether youth or age dwelt in her deeply curved eyes, for she shared with other Hindu women these marks of ancient lineage.

As the visit was planned by our guide for a chance to see the so-called nautch, the beating of the tambours soon accompanied the tuning up of her exquisite body. These thudding drums were like echoes from which she wove her melody. Rhythm coursed through her body until, reaching her toes, it seemed to spin itself into imperceptible threads. As a tiny leaf caught by a breeze communicates its rhythm until the whole tree is in motion, so did the pulse of her song. Beginning with almost expressionless eyes, and a mere gesture of her hand, the rhythm of her song possessed her until every center of her being throbbed its melody. She had extracted the essence of rhythm, playing upon our sensibilities until we ourselves seemed to become instruments accompanying her.

We had met the engaging young Hindu who was our guide to this experience through the courtesy of Patrick Geddes; and he attached himself to us during our stay in Benares. We soon learned that he was as efficient as he was eager to direct us to any bypaths of the Holy City that might contribute to our insight into ritual patterns.

The first time he called at the hotel in his starched English clothes he was obviously on dress parade for sightseeing foreigners. But the starchiness gradually dissolved in con-

versation aimed at getting behind a suspicious fear of patron-
age one often felt in this ancient race. The next day when he
called he had doffed the Western shirt for the Hindu shawl.
After that, all Englishism disappeared from his dress, he had
become wholly himself, and we were permitted access to his
world of reality without any formalities. Not only was our
young host wonderfully perceptive in grasping the direction
of our interest in bypaths of Indian culture but his resourcefulness and the mercurial speed with which he functioned was astonishing. He had guided us to the taboo
quarter of Benares to see the enchanting dancer, and now
he made it possible for us to see native folk rituals by gathering together the retainers on his family's estate.

There was a feudal atmosphere in this Brahmin household.
The uncle of our host was a distinguished philosopher. A
maternal uncle was an ardent follower of Gandhi, wearing
the Gandhi cap and homespun suit. The young sister
whom we met at tea—a girl perhaps twelve—was an exquisite
and touching figure, a child widow who, through the death
of her affianced husband, was cut off from the world of a
Hindu woman. Her life was now devoted to poetry, for
which, they indicated, she showed marked talent.

We were taken into an immense courtyard where different groups had come to enact their ritual dances for two
strangers, a mark of courtesy and consideration for our interest in their native culture. These dark-skinned men with
patient eyes were divided into groups according to their oc-
cupations: tillers of the soil who enacted rituals of sowing
and reaping; the herdsmen; the cartwrights and wheelwrights,
craftsmen or menders of that most unique Hindu vehicle,
the cart with its beautifully carved wheels; and many more
occupational groups. After these traditionally observed rites,
expressive of the daily life of the folk, we were asked to

join the family at tea. We wandered through a wide, open, gracefully colonnaded corridor leading from the court to the main house. En route we passed through the chapel, an inner sanctum where every devout Hindu spends an hour or more each day in meditation. Along one of these passages the sacred cow was ambling with self-evident poise, not even regarding the intruders. We recall her mythological ancestry from Vac, consort of Prajapati, creator of the world, and as Vac she lives on in the family group as symbol of the Great Mother.

Tea was not a ritual in our sense, but obviously a courteous gesture for the guests. Ceremonial etiquette forbade the Brahmin to break bread with any but his caste. Our young host, however, disregarded the observance by sharing in the meal. Whether he had doffed such orthodox customs, or did it this day out of his meticulous yet spontaneous courtesy, we could not tell. But we realized the dishes used by the guests were contaminated and could not be used again in a Brahmin household.

The traditional background, as we glimpsed it, seemed like a continual prayer to the Mother of Life, so much so that each little girl in India is perceived as the potentially creative nature of the Great Mother, the dominating principle in India. Personal relationship is profoundly influenced by the traditional attitude: for example, the wife is modeled upon the epic figure of Sita in the Ramayana, trained for centuries in an attitude of devotion. This was the only way to explain the immense families living together harmoniously, quietly accepting their differences while pursuing individual interests. It seemed as if, in spite of the unsavory surface aspects of teeming life, in spite of eyes saddened by centuries of deprivation, in spite of the silent, gliding, ghostlike forms, so marked in British India where the cleavage between cultural standards confronted one everywhere, each had his or her inviolable identity.

We sometimes asked ourselves if the caste system, however undemocratic to Western sensibility, was not in a measure responsible for the regard for differences and the tolerance of differences. Did it not also give rise to an inner sense of security, as a sort of boundary, without which one would be lost in the chaos of the mass? Had it not been for our charming and perceptive young host, and another Hindu, Boshi Sen, a scientist who combined in a rare way Western and Eastern culture, we should hardly have had the chance to feel into the Indian way of life, which at that time at least was guarded from Western intrusion.

Other memories of our stay in India vividly recall a Buddhist festival at Darjeeling. Pilgrims began assembling in early morning, slowly making their way up the mountain, some moving in strange contortions of penance. The scene above on the crest of the high slope supporting the temple was one of scintillating gaiety. Families wandered in and out of the temple, decking it with festoons of blossoms. Incense poured out in pungent waves upon the icy atmosphere. Rice grains sparkled between the knees or gathered in clumps around the toes of a benign Buddha sitting enshrined, listening to the prayers, extending his blessing with the promise of a plentiful season. Shaven priests in saffron robes, also garlanded, chanted from the inner depth of the temple, while bells in constant pealing marked off each prayer.

When the rites were over, happy people in family groups settled down to bless the year with sweetened cakes and yak tea, a concoction made of rancid butter and swallowed necessarily in gulps as a ritual of the pious. We were initiated into the Buddhist ceremony by partaking of this hospitality and receiving the blessing of the priest. When that gay company had drunk of the warming brew and feasted upon the confections piled in conical mounds all about them, they leapt into a tribal dance, the privilege of the men, who marked most complicated accents with a force that was breathtaking. The long-sleeved Tibetan garments, with their linings of sapphire, flew out like brilliant wings. The long black queues played a counter rhythm as they followed the movement of the vigorous forms, accenting the energetic play with dramatic feeling. The Russian ballet, which we had previously seen in England, seemed crude and anaemic beside this Mongolian Buddhist ecstasy. In this polyandrous group the men assume the feminine role, and are guardians of the children, while the Amazonian women carry on the business of the community. The dress and features of both men and women have a Mongolian stamp, but most characteristic are the stencilled markings on the face. We wondered at the time when this mode would be imported by Western women.

Though it was not the season for the rites of the Devil Dancers, these accommodating and lively tribesmen, after due consultation, said that for a consideration they would enact the ritual for us. The Devils, of course, were creatures of the night, and we had to protect ourselves from the night frost as far as possible in order to witness the ceremony which they performed before the inn where we lodged. Strange, guttural sounds and shrieks broke the silence, not with the staccato notes of the West, but as a polyphony of elemental cries. Grotesque figures appeared, and heads of beasts gesticulated upon forms naïvely disguised. Monsters, varying in degree and order, succeeded one another in feats, contortions, and weird vocal utterances. The costumes, masks, and prop-

erties were made by the tribe and treasured by them as heir-
looms. Finally, discarding the Devil masks, the dancers re-
appeared, happy, calm, and courteously reposeful.

In strange contrast to this old tradition was the Buddhist
temple ritual service in the monastery at Goon. At the morning ritual of the brotherhood, one by one each took his place
in the open court. Seated on low stools, suggestive of the
Japanese Noh, each priest became a member of the ritual
orchestra, each voice mingling with the bells and drums.
And most startling of all, the great trumpets, held to the right
and left of the group, were face down on the ground so
that the tone could descend into the earth and mount
again. At first muffled, all that underworld of sound rushed
like a torrent through unbounded space until, the service
ended, the priests rose solemnly and put their instruments
away.

In Calcutta we were invited through Boshi Sen for an early
morning visit to the Tagore home. In India formal visits
begin any time after sunrise. Here was Rabindranath Tagore
in his own setting, a long spacious room like a baronial hall,
leading out to porticos and gardens. On the walls hung delicate paintings by Abindranath Tagore, brother of the poet,
whose art, Eastern in concept, was influenced by Western
technique. The painter appeared quite informally in his
morning gown and pantoufles, while Tagore, the poet, although majestic as ever in his dust-colored robe and flowing
beard, had doffed the oracular manner associated with him
in the West, to become spontaneously human, radiant in the
beauty of his traditional background.

On his earlier visit to the Playhouse, Tagore, the poet, had
familiarized us with his prophet-like aspect. To see him at

home in Calcutta was startling enough. But we were in no way prepared to watch the venerable figure taking part later on in a lyric performance, in rhythmic movement that flowed into almost Bacchic ecstasy as he sang. In this Spring Festival, given by the students of his school, he made an attempt to re-assemble and interpret ancient traditional themes in modern terms of stage decor and lighting. His power to release the ancient spirit of song, to find its note in the modern rhythm, to unite the wisdom and delicate flavor of India's past, gave us an insight into the Tagore not evident in the West. Here we realized that the philosopher and teacher reflected the mediating values of his personality, but that the poet was its source and substance.

CHAPTER TWENTY-THREE

PWÉ IN BURMA

Our introduction to Burma was through a magnificent fiesta at Rangoon, the occasion being the obsequies of a distinguished punghi or priest, whose last journey was being witnessed by thousands as a splendid spectacle. Festal areas had been ingeniously transformed into what appeared like a luminous bridge. A gliding burial barge set afloat on the river bore the remains of the much-loved punghi. At first a shadow on the evening tides, it burst suddenly into a flaming torch; then, like a pennant of fire, it sailed on and on till it disappeared in the saffron vestment of the setting sun. No sign of grief or mourning accompanied this majestic drama. The burial rites of the punghi, starting before sundown, continued in an ascending scale of magnificence and fantastic beauty until dawn.

The ritual of the pwé commemorates the major themes of life—birth, adolescence, marriage, death. And between these modes, innumerable significant events are also memorialized by the pwé, such as a pwé for a journey; for entrance into a new profession; for building a house, or honoring some noble deed; for the ear-boring of an adolescent girl, or a boy's entrance into a monastery, the seat of all education.

Being vulgar foreigners, we were not aware that one must be invited to participate in one of the many ceremonies dedicated to the occasion. This day we had strolled into a huge marquee where a pwé was being held; we soon found that we were guests of a retired merchant, guests though un-invited and unannounced. Presently, we were being greeted by our venerable massive host, his long black hair coiled upon his head. He sat, or rather reclined, in a Burmese chair, con-structed so as to afford the comfort of a bed without the necessity of retiring.

Our host's charming young wife, in traditional dress—the sarong and short jacket—her lovely hair coiffed with blossoms, her arms and throat gleaming with rare jewels, glided over to welcome us. After they had served us with native wine and sweets towering in pagoda-like forms, we were ushered to formal chairs placed for us, as foreigners, along the margin of the enclosure. The center was freed of any encumbering furniture.

Presently families arrived in swarms. The very old, the sedately mature, the quietly young, filed in, all uniformly dressed, the only difference in costume the fillet of pink silk worn on the head of a man, and the tiny garland of blos-soms which distinguished the dress of a woman. Each group was followed by a caravansery of provisions, utensils, and bedding. It was surprising how quietly and unobtrusively that large space gradually became occupied. What seemed unpreparedness on the part of the host was of course the acme of courtesy, for it permitted each guest to express his own taste and habits in the assortment of personal household equipment he carried in anticipation of a considerable stay.

From that perspective, our Western attitude seemed curi-ously stiff: to sit in the theatre for a couple of hours in formal rows to receive (perhaps) some intellectual or emotional impression, then to hurry away, turn off the current labeled entertainment and turn on another called occupation. Small

wonder that theatre with us acquires more and more a clip-
ping beat and tempo! As we sat there in Burma, our Western
pigeon-holed attention seemed strangely unreal compared
to this preparation to absorb, to give oneself completely to
an experience. For here all "assist," that the performance
from nightfall to sunrise may proceed uninterruptedly.

At a pwé, if you are not prepared to sit the night through
without refreshment, you simply sleep for a while; or if
prepared, you fortify yourself by cooking where you are
seated, without in any way disturbing the actors. This does
not signify a casual attitude; on the contrary, in this land of
the pwé—a generic term for dance, song, mime, comedy,
tragedy—the performer is not only esteemed but is often so
in demand that he travels back and forth with his company
from one end of the country to the other, receiving such
flattering remuneration that he has no need to leave his native
soil.

We soon forgot everything but a fluttering, winged,
lilting sound, more the tuning of sound than sound itself.
We could observe it in the process of growing, tapped from
exquisite boat-shaped instruments, the bathala, delicately
plied by earnest musicians. The tones seemed quickly to
detach themselves from human control, and to leap and mix
with the beat of the tambour. Then, suddenly, the very essence of that sound was translated into visual form, as four
exquisitely dainty beings appeared. The dark, rich curves
of the torso could be seen through the crisp whiteness of
finely woven muslin jackets. The limbs were encased from
thigh to ankle in a skirt drawn so taut that movement below
the waist seemed impossible. Yet that very limitation served
to develop and enhance the dexterous movements of agile
limbs, the fantastic whirls and frothing flight seemed to dis-

engage themselves from the body, as the essence of tone from the bathala.

Yes, "it" was here, flowering in its ancestrally cultivated form and rhythm, as the perfected expression of a traditional art. The inflection of each movement, the twist of the wrist, the curve of the finger tips, poise of the head, glance of the eyes, were bred during centuries of another era, and had been tended not as goals in themselves, but as passing gestures. Originally valued for its symbolic significance, this highly cultivated expression had no doubt migrated through eras of changing forms until, caught in a web of tradition, it had assumed a classical and mannered consciousness. Nevertheless the pwé, as it revealed itself through every scintillating gesture of the body, unlocked a creative fervor that, for a moment at least, released us into the pulse of an eternal rhythm.

The classical quality of the prelude relaxed with the night. It was followed by more and more robust entertainment. Interlocutors in spirited dialogue delighted the audience, preparing them for the mood of each succeeding scene. The forms of these episodes were strictly traditional; the characters, based upon mythological forms, lent themselves to any period; but the material used had local flavor, and to a large extent was improvised. An actor then lives in the true sense of living. He is part of the current of his time, he catches its foibles, its characteristics; he molds, translates, reshapes it through his own individuality, then carries it where he is bidden. As he recreates the events of his day in terms of his understanding and temperamental qualities, so too is he at liberty to freely translate traditional and classical modes of drama.

Later we met Po' San, honored at that time as the most

creative pwé artist of Burma, a tiny man neatly wrapped into his native dress, with ends of the inevitable pink chiffon pennant floating about his head. It is impossible to describe the quality of his performance. The drama we were told was a yen pwé—that is, it had a traditionally epic character— yet as his medium was essentially comedy, he reclothed the material in terms of his particular slant, yet did not alter the form, scale, or proportion of the original structure, merely invested it with the colors of comedy. Not understanding a word, we had naturally to gather this interpretation. At the time, it made a deep impression that comedy and tragedy were accepted branches of the same tree, perceived as moods of nature. Po' San was as renowned in his land as Charlie Chaplin in ours, with but this difference—that Po' San's art is based upon an aristocratic tradition, while Charlie Chaplin's is the outgrowth of collective experience.

The memory of those days teems with color, for Burma seemed dressed for a perpetual pwé. As we wandered with the quietly moving throngs among the festive highways of booths decorated with fantastic sweets, strolling bards with their companies of puppets performed here, there, and everywhere. Interspersed were improvised stages which harbored various orders of strolling pwé. These were the village companies, on carts with wheels gaily decorated; operations of dressing and undressing, as well as the intricacies of make-up, taking place in full view of the audience. Still other forms of dance pwé were performed on more limited areas, but always the same beguiling dancers created rhythmical patterns on the cart stages.

Buddhist wisdom in this land of fée is tinged with fantasy and austerity. With naked feet and shaven head, their saffron garments subdued under a sunshade, the brotherhood was symbolically dedicated to perpetual wandering for truth.

They pursued their uninterrupted way, silently affirming, through the black-lacquered begging bowl, their negation of the personal ego in a pursuit of the eternal self. Over sun-baked valleys, winding streams, and wild mountains, the punghi silently continues his pilgrimage.

During our stay in Burma, officials of the British East India exposition were combing the native states for material to show at the London intercolonial exhibits the following year. A trial performance of various Burmese rites and rituals gathered from remote corners of Burma was being staged at Rangoon, from which the exhibition material was to be chosen. Thus we had the good fortune to catch a glimpse of Burmese culture as it flowered in faraway spots, including even the Shan State with its tribal culture as it ever was.

We found the Burmese piano beguiling to eye as well as ear. The player, seated in a circle of engaging-looking drums, which he manipulated as if they were a unified keyboard, plied wrists and hands with a skill and abandon that seemed difficult to achieve in a lifetime, and he was only a boy, for youth seemed to be a requisite for suppleness of wrist. A liquid tone was tossed into the air, to be followed by other tones brilliantly whirling in an eddy of joy.

While we still marveled at the musician's art, the animal dancers of the Shan State were announced. We had heard that these primitive men had been persuaded with great difficulty to leave their native tribes, and were being guarded in the building to prevent their escape. In fact, it was the first time such a daring experiment had been made. We were anticipating something aggressively daring when a bird appeared on the improvised stage, an extraordinarily beautiful creation, sensitively taut as if hunted, a creature whose proud plumage suggested its link to the forest foliage. Every detail of the performance had been so carefully told by the dancer that it became neither a representation nor impression, but a kind of communication and translation of the essential qualities of the bird. Such subtlety and finesse of expression could be achieved only through the highest gifts of perception.

After the performance we had the privilege of seeing these "savage tribesmen," who proved to be dark, gentle beings with haunted eyes, paralyzed with fear by the mobs of people in the hall and the unfamiliar sights and sounds of the city.

Physically, pictorially, dramatically, Burma continued to reveal fascinating reflections of a culture which had evolved out of its rocks, trees, streams, and mountain tops. Fantastic unreality constantly played through this mélange of the primitive and the aesthetic, the exotic and the diabolic. Had it not been that we still held to a definite image of our journey, who knows but that we too might have been sucked into the Burmese fantasy! But spring and Palestine, with its cycle of rituals, beckoned. In spite of the urge to pursue the sun to its rising, we turned toward Jerusalem.

THE DRAMA OF
EASTER IN PALESTINE

It was the Easter season when we arrived in Palestine. At the Jaffa Gate, that all-inclusive mart of travel with its drama and its pictures, Arab shepherds, crook in hand, paused to exchange news of the road, while their flocks strayed away, bleating in chorus. Pilgrims came and went, priests of Rome, Greek fathers hearkening back to Byzantium, with patriarchal beard and sweeping ivory gown; noble Africans from Abyssinia, mantled Moroccan Jews, and bearded brothers of Eastern Europe with ghetto marks still stamped upon them, remote, aloof, seemingly wandering along some path to Zion.

British officialdom was on hand, sportively carrying the keys of office; and caravans of Arab merchants carefully guiding camels undistracted in their ageless calm; women of Bethlehem in gowns of black festally embroidered, their forms and headdress made familiar from Crusader days, and other women of Ramullah in unbleached linen patterned with scarlet stitches; and donkey boys goading on their animated carriers of Jaffa oranges, banked high in towering mounds.

No collective mass of unidentified humanity this, but more like a reflex of some distant radiant prism, variant colors of one whole; or like notes of a symphony, distinct, wandering

159

into variations, yet held together by some intangible theme. Easter with its beautiful sights, its ritual dress, its echoing bells, burst in a fantasy of color so emotionally stirring that we found ourselves swung almost literally into the arena of religious ritual.

Through the offices of a friend, we were invited to the Seder service on the eve of Passover, at the home of the Bokhara Rabbi. We had hoped to find the family in their Bokhara dress, but as the Passover commemorates the shedding of the old and innovation of the new, for this occasion the pious had exchanged their colorful traditional dress for stiff, quasi-modern substitutes. Fortunately the traditional courtesy was not doffed with the clothes, and we were invited, as the prescribed strangers, to partake of the ritual meal, still repeated in Jewish homes the world over.

A quiet, almost hushed moment while the mother lighted the candles, anticipated the meal. Perhaps we can read in this the mother's relation to the hearth and the spirit of the home. Suddenly the Rabbi stood among us, a tall, aged slender figure in a robe of gold and crimson stripes, the noble head covered by a brilliant cap towering upwards, accenting the patriarchal beard, a veritable brother of Abraham.

We sat on low chairs, while the family reclined on cushions at a long, low table, upon which dishes of the traditional ritual food were served—the bitter herbs, to indicate the hardships of Egypt; a bone of the lamb, unleavened bread, and a roasted egg, symbolizing the sacrifice of the lamb, the manna eaten during the hasty flight from Pharaoh's yoke, and the renewal of life. These symbolic dishes were eaten at intervals during the service read by the Rabbi, while at more frequent intervals a glass of wine was offered and drunk to the dregs, and blessed with the unleavened bread. An empty place at the table and a goblet of wine awaited Elijah, the prophet who returns mysteriously through the house door opened to receive him.

At the end of the service, the youngest child asks the four traditional questions: What is it that distinguishes this night from all others? Why, on other nights, do we sit, but this night lean? And so on. Do these questions, asked by the youngest to recall the past, emphasize the significance of spiritual freedom shared by old and young alike? We must recall the background of nomadic life out of which this ritual grew, when the home, however transient, was the sacred precinct of a folk dedicated to Jahve.

The most vivid memory is that of the Rabbi seated cross-legged on his cushion chanting the ancient ritual; he appeared to flow with it into the past, not merely to partake of the ceremony but to reach through it into communion with the brotherhood of Israel, drawing to himself its heritage of grandeur and suffering. Aloof, remote, unmindful of the human, simple scene, undisturbed by crying infant or presence of the family, he sat among his children's children, among them yet not of them, their symbol, as Israel itself.

* * * * *

The Mohammedan offering to the shrine of Easter is the Nebbi Mussah, the procession to the tomb of Moses. High in the bleakness of arid hills it stands, that isolated shrine held sacred to Moses, revered by the Mohammedan as prophet. On this day of rejoicing in Allah, encampments thousands strong were massed about the tomb, and the worshippers, dancing off the still outpouring ecstasy, came and went in ceaseless tides, like the sands blown hillward for a moment, to be scattered once again.

Nothing that we had heard, seen, or imagined, not even the ceremony of the Holy Fire, had prepared us for an emotional feast so overwhelming. All night long the devotees of Allah marched, entering Jerusalem at every portal. At first the procession moved joyously, freely, yet in ordered waves toward its goal beyond the gates of Jerusalem, the tomb itself. But gradually what had at first the semblance of a march was translated into an orgy of wild movement, the rhythm mounting as though inspired by the presence of the prophet himself. Whirling figures danced along, keffiyeh and abayah streaming like colored wings to lend them speed. Scimitars flashed, swords were brandished, and the faithful leaped upon each other, dancing over the heads of that human column. Those of the traditional past mixed with those infected with the new order, stamped with a veneered pattern of political radicalism—until, with one accord, all were swept like a whirlwind, in the name of Allah.

*   *   *   *   *

Another impression of dramatic fervor surrounded the Abyssinian ritual, celebrated in the courtyard of the church. The service combined regal simplicity with the aesthetic beauty of the embroidered vestments, dress, and kingly bearing of these African bishops and priests. Magnificent vessels and mitres of silver and brass were carried in the procession and suddenly a tribal mood followed, when the procession ceased and the participants seated themselves on the ground, African fashion, chanting their services to the accompaniment of the syncopated, rhythmic beat of drums. In some mysterious way, this curious mélange of African-Byzantine linked an ancient past with our own.

*   *   *   *   *

The Roman church, with its regal splendor, burst into the sumptuous Easter Mass, whose brilliance seemed to overshadow its mystical inheritance. Processions dedicated to the Stations of the Cross, monks and nuns of various orders, cowled and shrouded, were followed by penitent pilgrims, all treading with humility in the steps of the Saviour. Services of the orders dedicated to perpetual prayer for the redemption of the world were held by veiled virgins who raised their voices unceasingly in misted chant, like pale ghosts of the Middle Ages.

*   *   *   *   *

Following Selim, the faithful Arab dragoman, son, too, of the holy Greek Church, we were swept with the zealous worshipers into the body of the Holy Sepulchre—a seething mass, magnified as one, straining after a miracle! Up we clambered, higher and higher, to reach the gallery. There was a whirlwind of life below, above, and around us. Finally the movement of the wedged mob ceased. A pause, full of suspense! Then the aged Patriarch, in vestments, with flowing snowy beard, entered. Although supported on either side by stalwart dignitaries of the church, he too was swept along by the crowd toward the centered sepulchre. No one had eyes or ears for priests or choir swinging censers, or for other signs of the Mass. In those orgiac moments even its brilliance was submerged.

The Patriarch descended into the "Tomb," where the inexhaustible flame is buried. From this flame he lighted the torch through which the miracle of Spring blazes into being. Outriders from each See of the embracing church, each holding a torch, were the first to receive the light of the rekindled flame. Instantly, his torch lighted, each outrider pushed his way through the mob, brandishing its yet un-lighted tapers. The entrance once gained, these riders mounted waiting horses and galloped off to the distant Sees with the tidings of Resurrection. Whether the light was literally carried by horse to Russia or Greece I do not know, but the Greek Church the world over is yearly renewed from that buried flame.

Meanwhile the Holy Sepulchre rocked with the mob straining and struggling for a spark from the torch. Like a cloudburst of fire, the lighted tapers, swung high and low, deluged the church with flaming tongues. Then scimitars and swords flashed from the hands of worshipers who, climbing on the shoulders of others, began to dance on this human bridge. Madly swinging sword and torch, they shouted in chorus that drowned the refrain of the Mass, "Death to the Jews!" All about us the lighted tapers flashed, a sea of light adored by the congregation, who swayed with them in ecstasy, pressed them as nurslings to head and breast, played them as melody upon fingers, hair, and face, sucked the flame into vital organs. Thus to these children of the Greek Church the miracle of fire, light, life was proclaimed.

Notwithstanding the centuries of acknowledged acceptance of Christ as Saviour, the instinctual nature of the Chris-tianized Arab has remained undomesticated, reflecting light and shade in vivid contrast. This could explain his vul-nerability to political demagogy, rampant at the time, yet met by the governing body of Palestine in what seemed to us, as observers, a further challenge to conflict, the presence of the machine guns lining the streets during such Easter festivities.

*   *   *   *   *

Protestant services, simple and severe, were also in the Easter cycle. When the chimes had mellowed their pealing, the fragrance of spring played on in the multicolored fields where the abundance of new life showed itself in clustered scarlet, gold, and blue. Over purpling slopes and through verdant valleys, the call of the shepherd, answered by a startled bleat of an infant lamb, echoed the same refrain.

CHAPTER TWENTY-FIVE

A FAR-REACHING QUESTION

A tomblike inanimation clung to the solid walls of our Austrian hostel in Jerusalem, where we seemed so removed from the turbulent life of the old bazaar quarter. Yet, one step into the garden, another out of the gate, and we were hemmed within ancient Jerusalem, winding in and out of medieval archways, losing ourselves in the human stream which, dammed up by centuries of walled-off brooding, burst with equal zeal into excited barter or murmured prayer.

It was but a short route over those ancient cobblestones to the Mosque of Omar. Suddenly, like a mirage, the Mosque spread its welcoming spaciousness before us, domed, pinnacled, glistening. At some distance down the slope, a waning olive tree reared itself, oblivious of the comings and goings of the Arab pilgrims devoting themselves to secret communings.

As we rested in the shade of that olive tree, the Playhouse seemed even closer, more real, calling persistently for more life as the vast procession of the centuries spread itself before us in a gamut of color. How could we help but intuit a wider scope, possibilities that might grow out of the urge which had given the Playhouse birth?

In this contact with the East, one question pursued us.

What is it that lives on so tenaciously in ritual, reveals itself as mystic communion? That, whatever its name, has not perished. It might still breathe through the poet, vibrate into melodic forms, flame into images, light and shadowed. The glimpse of life revealed by the East revitalized the urge to feel into creative values rooted in rituals.

Shielded by the olive tree in the quiet evening, it was easy and natural to build a dream castle, but to feed that vision with substance was quite another story. How sound through the modern medium those depths that link the individual to the mystery of nature; sense, as original man, his union with the Great All as a transpersonal experience?

The painter was already undergoing a transition. And in the theatre, thanks to pioneer scene designers, photographic representation was being doomed. What then of the stage director? Even if, for a time, the theme of a play remained transient, the situation transparent, could the content not be revealed through the characters instead of the characters serving as mouthpieces for the author's ideas—as in the problem play of the period? Such an approach would naturally require a psychological attitude on the part of the director and the willingness of the actor to search behind the word, feel into and reveal that which is unspoken. In other words, the emphasis would be placed upon the experience itself rather than upon its representation. The significant meaning, however transient and devious the situation, would then be carried through the inner dynamis of the play.

Some of these reflections concerning our immediate problem were written to our colleagues at home, with suggestions for the coming year's program. Crossing our letters was an enthusiastic report of the Moscow Art Theatre productions which were then overwhelming the theatre world of New York. From the account we gathered that audiences had been powerfully gripped by the Moscow Art method, identified with its great actor-director, Stanislavski. Another letter followed, telling of Richard Boleslavsky, director of the Moscow Art Theatre studio (the beginners' training course), who was trying out their method with a small group in New York. The suggestion was that a similar experiment might be tried with a group of Playhouse students. If these young actors were willing to study with Boleslavsky, and sufficient funds could be secured by them for such training during the summer, would we agree to the plan and also to having a production of this experimental group open the new season at the Playhouse?

This suggestion was not only startling but, we felt, raised a far-reaching question. In itself, the idea of a studio group working continuously under direction had an appeal. But such a plan depended upon the approach of the director. Still, even if Boleslavsky's method reflected the type of realism more familiar in Russian literature than in our own, it might, if wisely handled, serve as a technical foundation for our actors. This could be a heaven-sent plan to develop the purely dramatic programs with a well-tried technique. So cables were exchanged, the die was cast, our agreement was made, with the proviso, however, that the choice of play and production should be, in our judgment, adequate for the opening of the new season.

We found the group, upon our return from the East, established in a happy entourage at Pleasantville, New York, skillfully housed and enthusiastically at work. But we were now to confront a serious and determining decision which would inevitably affect the future of the Playhouse.

Boleslavsky's vivid personality appealed enormously to the group. But we were soon aware that to break down the American inhibitions and to try and build up a quasi-

Russian foundation would certainly be a process of years, if it could be accomplished at all. It might be effected in an individual case, just as occasionally one finds in the West an artist whose work indicates some intuitional or inherited Eastern tendency, or a singer with some extraordinary flair for the Hindu or Arab idiom. But, as a system, to graft one culture onto another in a season, even in a span of years, appeared a questionable adventure. Would it, moreover, be desirable, even if, through some hothouse method, it could actually be done?

In the Moscow Art Theatre, the grotesque often became the foil for detail developed to the nth degree. The explosive energy of the Russian, so long repressed, tended to thrust itself below the surface. This meant that what was a normal, facile theatre characterization for a Russian would be exaggerated and forced in an American, unless the values of each could be maintained and then expressed with the finesse of an artist. To find a common denominator, to exercise a sense of proportion, understanding, acceptance, and evaluation is always the problem of translator and student. In this case, the attempt to develop free emotional expression on the one hand and, on the other, to mold this into a form characteristic of our Western idiom seemed less and less possible. Though the rehearsals reflected Stanislavski's method, the coordination necessary for performance was not, and could not be, demonstrated.

So we were faced with the immediate problem of whether or not to give this production the right of way in its obviously chrysalis state. To interfere with the completion of an experiment was a serious matter, especially when directors and actors had given themselves to it with all the zeal of a new discovery and were so imbued that they were unable to realize its limitations. Yet to open the Playhouse after a year of silence called for a production significant in material and quality. Since both were lacking, we felt that the Boleslavsky experiment, whose value lay in the preparatory training for the actor, should be considered in the light of a studio presentation; but how could this be indicated to the audience eager for the re-opening? The situation was crucial, for it involved far more than differences in judgment, or even the possibility of an opening that did not fulfill its promise.

Up to that moment, there had been an informal understanding within the directing staff of the Playhouse. Plays and policies had been discussed and agreed upon without any apparent imposition of leadership, no one quite knew how. But now a prayerful, objective attitude was needed to deal with a cleavage which had suddenly assumed threatening proportions. Still we reasoned—more correctly, we anguished—perhaps unwisely, that the one chance of restoring equilibrium was to see the experiment through.

The double bill, which reopened the Playhouse in 1923–24, was George Bernard Shaw's *The Shewing Up of Blanco Posnet* and *The Player Queen* by William Butler Yeats. Objectively viewed, the production fell between the attempt at heightened characterization, each actor trying to realize his full stature, and the submergence of the personality through a foreign stylized direction. The plays selected were an unfortunate choice for a Russian director; as for the cast, they were frankly not up to the problems of characterization demanded of them.

Blanco Posnet was written in 1909, and belongs to Shaw's early period. Actually the only excuse for its staging would have been an historical one, as Shaw himself declared it "a religious tract in dramatic form." It was written as an answer to the censorship law discussed in Parliament a year before, and was intended to shock the self-complacent re-

spectability of a contemporary British audience. One could hardly have expected even a mild interest to be evoked for it by our rather special audience in our time and place. *The Player Queen*, on the other hand, would have exacted far more finished and subtle playing by actors versed in the Celtic idiom to give it stature.

These obvious deductions were unfortunately confirmed by the lukewarm response of audiences awaiting a stimulating experience at the reopening of the theatre. There was however a positive side. Boleslavsky had induced a fine esprit de corps among the student actors, as well as enthusiasm for continued technical preparation and study distinct from rehearsal. Heretofore, the evening classes had necessarily had to be an adjunct of rehearsal; so this concentration was in itself a valuable opportunity for an individual relation to, and appreciation of, technical training.

In spite of differences in view, a heightened intensity and energy in organization and direction, as well as a more impersonal, objective relation to production, were undoubtedly fostered by the new tension. What may have been missing in the way of the old, informal cameraderie was perhaps gained in a more detached evaluation of our attitudes and ultimate goal. The development of lyric forms, and of drama lending itself to a more than three-dimensional treatment, was insistently urgent, stimulated no doubt by the year in the East.

If a conclusion is to be drawn at a safe distance, this experience can point to the dangers attending a new way or epoch in the growth of a group as well as in that of an individual; and the need to sacrifice the personal value for a widened outlook. Here it meant a conscious acceptance of an unsatisfactory, alien experiment in order to avert a schism in the group as in the values of production.

CHAPTER TWENTY-SIX

A PERMANENT COMPANY

The plan for a permanent company whose nucleus would be drawn from our own groups was put into effect after the run of the Boleslavsky bill. The company consisted of ten members, freed through a minimum yearly salary to take whatever role was offered. Among the group were Albert Carroll, Blanche Talmud, Paula Trueman, and Lily Lubell, who had for years taken part in the lyric programs and, with the exception of Carroll, had been members of the dancing classes from the beginning. The opportunity for further training in both forms in the alternating schedule was now to be initiated. Ian Maclaren was adopted into the company because of his long association and readiness to conform to the needs of this dual program. Dorothy Sands and Marc Loebell, who first appeared at the Playhouse in the *Follies* of 1924, were also accepted as members of this permanent troupe. Whitford Kane, though not a member, was always ready and happy to join the playing group.

Few actors would have seen the value for themselves in the combined exacting schedule; so it was much to the credit of these players that they realized the need and significance of the intensive program. Each day began early with technical work in voice and movement, then a pause for lunch, followed by rehearsals for the new production and very often follow-up work on the current bill as well as work on some specialized problem, for the productions always required an individual touch in speech, song, language, or racial idiom.

Strenuous as the year was, the group thrived on it, nor had there ever been a better esprit de corps. Something electrical evolved out of that daily experience. In fact we began to ask ourselves if the image that had emerged under the olive tree in faraway Jerusalem was not beginning to take form. This new impulse and sense of coordination had undoubtedly also been stimulated by the experiment in Pleasantville.

Nothing could have led us back to our home roots with more assurance, after the foreign excursion by way of Boleslavsky, than *This Fine-Pretty World,* which followed early in 1924. Percy MacKaye was inspired to write this folk play during a sojourn among the Kentucky mountain folk. Even so, this altogether American production had to be studied as if it were in a foreign language, because of its unfamiliar dialect. Its idiom, so strange to us, was, the author explained, a relic of Elizabethan speech. These mountaineers, rooted in the vigor and traditions of their ancestors, had so long been shut away in their hills that the stream of American life and language had passed them by.

Percy MacKaye brought us types, language, atmosphere of this remote folk, seen through the imagination of a poet. These men and women of the hills were drawn as vivid products of their soil, stalwart as their forest trees, expressing themselves in language robust and direct, in sharply contrasting matter-of-factness and flights of fantasy. Perhaps one could draw an analogy between MacKaye's rediscovered leaves out of the pages of American folkways and Yeats's recapturing of the Celtic spirit.

To assimilate the language as if it were a natural expression was, in itself, a task. Then to attempt to mold it so that it would not seem unfamiliar to the audience was a goal which we might, perhaps, have achieved after months of playing. That we were en route to such interrelation of type and idiom was evidenced in the reviews of critics and discerning observers. "Mr. MacKaye's microcosm of the men and moods of the Kentucky mountains," wrote Glenn Frank, then editor of the *Century* magazine, "gave me unalloyed delight. All along, I felt that a hundred mountaineers and a hundred conversations were brought together in each character, so that, although no single mountaineer may be as rich and colorful as these men and women, the effect is more real than realism, for a whole race speaks through each character. The play has the feel of authenticity and the smell of the soil."

To us behind the curtain the characters of the play were an unending source of interest. We found ourselves carried into their world so that the idiom of their speech lived on with us. Even yet I find a word like "unbeknown" clinging to my vocabulary.

As is often the case in folk drama, the story of *This Fine-Pretty World* was a foil for the characters who lived the earth as its children. This interplay between life rooted in the soil and sudden outbursts of poetic imagery was not only a task to interpret but a refreshing privilege for the cast and directors. That we succeeded in conveying a fraction of the quality of the play might be accounted for by the influence of the material which drew us into just that which we needed and could therefore respond to. Definitely the helpful spirit and guiding hand of the author were factors. Another factor was the virility and freshness of characterization, due to the intensive program of work which the company was carrying on in conjunction with rehearsals. We were at last able to concentrate on spadework, voice, movement, improvisation. None of it done as a "chore" or "must be," but as if the natural way for a pioneer group, for whom the intensive extra work was also a refreshment. Aline MacMahon's characterization of May Maggot, in its simplicity, naturalness, and native flavor, was an outstanding achievement. In fact, the whole cast showed the influence of working and playing together as a unit.

Although *This Fine-Pretty World* won considerable admiration from many distinguished individuals, the audience response was negligible, hinting that the confidence of the general public in the Neighborhood Playhouse had yet to be restored.

The first season after reopening also saw the production of Lenormand's *Time Is a Dream*, translated from the French by Winifred Katzin. The drama is expressed through characters seeking a release from an inner darkness, so gripped by subjective imagery that they are unrelated to immediate reality. This type of expression was following the new trend at that time, in which the object was being depotentiated for subjective values. Although the play had little significance and surely not as production, still it was interesting as a new attempt in theatre, a turning inward toward psychological values, presenting moods that lurk behind the exterior walls of reason.

REHEARSALS

These reminiscences of the Playhouse in the days of its maturity would be inadequate without some reference to the rehearsals. For naturally they were the magnet which drew and, in turn, radiated the varying currents, as source, process, and ultimate experience.

I used to think of rehearsals as an alchemistic laboratory in which we labored to extract the essential values buried at first in an undifferentiated lump. Each element clinging to this lump had to be separated, clarified, then reunited. The dross we sensed in the confusion of reactions, in exaggeration, in over- or under-emphasis, or in the grotesque or skeleton-like appearance of the characters before they came to life.

Each rehearsal was an endless source of adventure and discovery, held in check by the terrifying date of opening, an unalterable decree, hanging over us like the sword of Damocles. After four, five, six, ten, or even twelve weeks, the vein of gold, though visible, had to undergo the process of refining, or, with us, of refinding the essential element. No form of spiritual torture was spared to bring about the needed "shock" to release the living substance.

For the lay person characterization appears to spring fully blown out of the creative perception of the actor; but in reality the process of realizing and then becoming at one with the character teaches us something of the way man must originally have domesticated the beasts of the field: his tact, patience and skill to draw, cajole, or urge them to do his bidding. Yet in the development of a part, we hardly know if the domestication applies to the role, or if the process is not directed to the untractable elements in the actor himself. Nor is it easy for one, as actor, to gauge whether the character is undergoing a transforming experience or if that experience is a reflection of what has been taking place in oneself. We can think of it perhaps as a mutual growth, the influence or stamp of the material, the part, or play, upon us, who then become the vessel or medium.

It is an illusion to assume that we create the role; rather we are the modest carriers. In this connection I think of the Zuni Halako ritual. The gods, giantesque figures, walk through the night, powerfully vivid as they tower far beyond the stature of ordinary humans—then suddenly, at the brink of dawn the masks and majestic attire are removed, and the dancers, now reduced to their simple ordinary selves, offer their prayer to the new day. In this sense they are carriers of divine power, but with the instinct of original man they know it is not their power, but that they are the instrument. Rehearsal was for us a form of rite d'entrée toward some such experience.

The convention of the modern stage interferes to a large extent with an adequate blend of the "here and now" of tangible reality and that which escapes its rational values. Painting is rooted in the tradition of uniting human and transpersonal reality through the symbol, as for example, in the treasured inheritance of the Middle Ages; or in a canvas of Brueghel's, centered in genre activities gay or somber, yet allowing one to peer behind the obvious scene to discover an intensity or dynamis hitherto foreign to genre expression. But the modern theatre resists attempts to bring the two dimensions into focus, although an effort to convey suprapersonal in terms of personal experience can be found on the screen in productions of Cocteau and in drama through T. S. Eliot and the fantasy of Thornton Wilder.

In other forms of expression the artist has his tools, paints, canvas, stone, chisel, or his musical instrument, each of which serves as an intermediary between him and his material or image. But the actor's tools are his body and that subtlest of instruments, the human voice. These two elements, body and voice, though the common and obvious possession of mankind, represent for the actor magical power. With these tools he can conjure to life a ghost, produce a demon, reveal a hero. In each attempt he transcends his own limited personality. Though the character to be portrayed takes possession of his conscious personality, not unlike a medium in a trance, there is a center which knows and directs, even though the actor may not be aware of who or what is directing.

Relation to the unknown character is an indescribable adventure which can easily lead the actor beyond his depth. Anyone who may have seen Nijinski or read his biography will recall how his whole personality was swept away in that godlike leap in "Le Spectre de la Rose." It required a masseur and restoratives always waiting in the wings to bring him back to this planet. The creative daemon is a glorified term for the devil if one yields to it unconditionally. Nijinski's tragic fate is reminiscent of Nietzsche in his flight from his nature. Nijinski impersonated the figure of Christ while Nietzsche identified with the superman.

To distinguish between the creative force and his personality requires lifelong vigilance on the part of anyone influenced by the creative instinct. For he is merely "listening in" to a mysterious reality, not in possession of it. One thinks in this connection of the attitude of the initiated toward the mysteries in antiquity as a secret never to be divulged. In other words the personal and suprapersonal were distinct values which, if confused, could be disastrous, an offense against the gods.

No one doubts the privilege of being favored by the gods, but how many realize the dark cloud also hovering over an experience rooted in tradition and myth? The hero is the original term for an individual singled out through trial and testing for a higher degree of consciousness than the group. Any distinctive gift involves a corresponding dearth. The more developed one aspect of the personality is, the more infantile or unconscious the other. We are apt to forget that overprivileged and underprivileged elements exist side by side in the individual and that these extremes require adjustment first in ourselves. Unless a degree of awareness exists and an attitude compensatory to a one-sided drive for technique as goal in itself, how expect that balance that is the stamp of culture?

In an epoch like ours, in which so much depends upon the quick response to immediate reality with its intensive pressures, counterbalanced by demonstrations of flagrant sensationalism, the cultivation of imagination becomes a restricted privilege. Instead of developing fantasy, the potential artist is tied to his personal illusions and whims. His tendency is to impersonate a waif, or to become infected with exaggerated notions of his importance. This importance misplaced is due in a measure to the little recognized need of society to find a channel for the eternal child buried in each being. The creative germ in the individual has little chance to develop where rational values dominate, unless in the perverted form of adult childishness, a wholly different phenomenon. In primitive societies as in myth the child commands a reverent attitude, even awe, because it forms a close link with an eternal past as well as containing the seed of the future. It is natural that the image which characterizes the creative nature of the child should be personified in and carried by the artist who exemplifies the spontaneity and instinct for creative play that qualifies the child.

Coupled with this gift to evoke and transform are the compensatory characteristics of the child in the artist, its unpredictable moods, its helplessness, dependence upon the object, parent, nature, toy, its wholly irrational demands or fantasy. In the adult artist these tendencies appear in his inability to adjust to conditions, his dubious or irregular behavior that does not conform with social standards, yet fascinates as it irritates public opinion. Virtuosity, which is reminiscent of a precocious child, is acclaimed rather than simplicity, an expression of maturity as well as of the potential nature of the child. The analogy in the creative attitude of the child and artist is touched upon because a degree of awareness is needed by the actor to realize his relation to production.

Although personality in the student actor should be guarded, theatre demands its subordination to the scene, the entourage, yes, to the production as a whole. Modesty is the role to be courted. At the Playhouse we rather avoided the term "artist" and its specialized significance in relation to theatre. The word "craftsman" conformed more to such experience, and also provided a link with the traditions of the English stage. For the term "playwright" has analogy with wheelwright or cartwright as related crafts. And till comparatively recent days the actor belonged modestly to the tribe of the gypsy, a form of vagabond.

A characteristic of the actor's craft lies in the fact that the role or the values of the drama are not conveyed to the audience directly. As a vicarious experience they mirror the effect upon the actor. This is true of music, painting, and the allied arts as well. The actor, however, is not only translator and interpreter of the image but characterizes it while unfolding the subjective experience. This demands a heightening of reality, something more than a threefold dimension, for it can only be conveyed through the intensity of the effect upon him. His problem is not only to feed life to the role but to withdraw the ego from it. Not only to realize the character but to see that it reaches the multiheaded monster, the audience.

The audience is the force which goads, fascinates, terrifies—the unknown partner. It has the power to give and destroy. Anyone who has had anything to do with an audience knows that it is not only a keyboard instrument to be played upon but that he who addresses it is equally played. Through contact with an audience some additional force is released as an unseen presence, the many losing their identity become one, a singular ungraspable being. This interplay between the audience and the one who plays is rooted in the depths of inherited experience. One thinks of the chanted word of ancient hymns, the relation between priest or bard and listeners, the one evoking the image, the other serving as vessel out of which the images are drawn.

In the theatre today we have of course only a corrupted remnant of the relationship. Yet I have had the impression of such interplay through dramas of which I could not understand a single word—in Burma and India for example, where the drama is the outgrowth of tradition; and in New York, through a performance of *The Golem* presented in Hebrew to a purely Hebrew-speaking audience. The effect was like unphrased music, as if the emotion on the stage was the treble, the audience the bass of the score; one could hardly tell where the acting began, where it ended. The actors seemed merely to reflect what was being experienced in the crowd. I realized then what the Greek drama must have meant when the myth was a living reality to playwright, actors, and audience. The intellectual approach of a modern audience, on the other hand, is an obstacle to be overcome by the stage director by emphasizing the irrational, the un-expected.

Acting is a peculiar kind of meditation; much depends upon the external personality, the actor's mask, and yet un-less the ego withdraws, the image is wholly unconvincing. In fact rehearsal is a form of ritual primarily devised to over-come the restraint of the conscious personality. Were we honest we might say to the audience: "We don't in the least expect you to believe what you see and hear but we want you to fall a prey to it." Not, however, in the technical sense of the motion picture, where all devices are focused upon sensation and one feels foully assaulted. In the regular thea-tre, statement, clarity, data, have no distinct value unless treated in the play as innuendo—the images or thoughts as a confidence, a secret which the audience is sharing. As the drama conforms to a personal adventure, the audience wants the privilege of making its own discovery, not of being told, for the whole experience is taking place behind the veil sym-bolized in the proscenium curtains.

The actor's role is not unlike that of the priest, yet one which conveys experience without defining it. Unlike the priest, the actor is commandeered by the unwritten laws of nature. Whether sympathetic or not, whether hero or villain, it is his function for the time being to realize all that he can of this role, this foreign being, to discover its light and its dark nature, plead for and expose it with the guile of a added stature.

During the first stages of rehearsal, the dramatis personae presents a collection of stiff and hollow figures, who gradually come to life as they are fed with the actor's own flesh and blood, for these unknown beings are devourers. The very briefness of their existence demands intensity, a heightening of every value. Nevertheless the characters do not want to masquerade reality, they demand the fullness of nature and something more, to cross the borderland of the everyday world in order to participate in an ever-existing reality; that is, to transcend the momentary, the transient, and to approach that scale of reality which belongs to all time, to reach the essence in the character as the seed in the heart of a flower.

The ever-present snare of the actor lies in the word, which can affect him as opium. The director's task is to rob the word of its compulsion and at the same time to realize and release the melodic values or undertone of the scene.

The passion of the actor to mold a personality is commensurable with the thirst for alcohol or a drug. His personal existence is gladly pawned for a part, the intervals between roles are like reefs on the gloomy shores of Hades. Though the character emerges through the conflicts, trials, and errors of rehearsal, the real union with it does not take place till the opening. A première at the Playhouse had the feeling of a marriage ritual behind the scenes; a festive atmosphere of indescribable suspense; the thrill of adventure in the release of experiencing for the first time "oneness" with the unseen partner; and—the compensatory fear, that never-to-be-forsaken stagefright. Indeed, many elements of primitive magic linger on in theatre—most obviously in the so-called superstitions, all those little devices to check dark spirits or propitiate the fate of production. In the old days at the Playhouse, not only the actors but the whole staff, including stage crew, responded emotionally to the highly charged spell of an opening. In fact the life or death of the drama was registered in the intensity of a united experience.

The director is no more master of his material than the actor of his role. He is often confronted with half-baked plays, banal texts; but just there lies his task. He must clothe a skeleton with substance, endow the text with the breath of life, then strive to give it a certain transparency so that a fantastic light may play upon it, infusing it with something greater or smaller than that which is visible to the naked eye. But when the curtains close, the mysterious intermingling of here and there has dissolved, the stage upon which the divine and demonic beings have spun their web has become an impoverished shoddy affair; nothing remains but a bag of bones.

What is more ghostlike than the play's wardrobe exposed to the light of day! Jewels have lost their luster, silk its sheen, the garden wall is a limp piece of canvas. Yes, theatre is a shoddy affair, pretentious, vulgarly cheap, for nothing has any value in itself. Can its fascination lie in just that? The most precious object is mere bagatelle, paste, make-believe, yet its cheap pretense contains magic. I know that I am holding a paste diamond in my hand, yet it evokes all the excitement of a secret theft. It can save my life or destroy it, still it is nothing but a piece of glass. So all the contents of the stage consist of rubbish for the dustbin, not even a bone for the dog is real. But under the spell of the night the rags and bottles of the day world carry on their mysterious life. They lead us to enchantment and disenchantment, to an apparent escape from reality, yet on the quest of an experience that can pierce the veil of the tangible world, give space, form, substance to the reality of the image.

Because of this secret goal every object on the stage is filled with magic, each insignificant prop at rehearsal commands respect. If you handle a cup or cigarette, it is not a cup or a cigarette but *the* cup that ever was and ever is. The handling of a cigarette, what a commonplace gesture, yet think of the secrets it can reveal! The same is true of the characters. The fisherman Jones may be mending his nets like hundreds of others, but a real actor will bring into play an essence of the eternal fisher in him, the mystery of the sea, the grandeur in his contact with the elements, in other words, that which is not visible to the naked eye. Just so a love scene: What can be more obvious, more ridiculously sentimental to the observer, how easy to travesty or make it trite, unless behind the personal screen you perceive a conflict brewing that belongs to all time, or feel the hushed wonder or magical light hovering over the lovers whether they are aware of it or not.

But naturally such an atmosphere cannot be made, it can only grow to life by dint of perceptive feeling which penetrates the core of experience. La Duse had the gift of chiseling an eternal woman out of a mere façade. Such experience lives on as memory in the touch of her hand, in a deeply drawn sigh, in the profundity of a silent glance, as well as in the magic of voice or utterance of word. And Yvette Guilbert, in her songs of the Boulevard, could endow a vagrant soul with the power and conviction of elemental nature. An artist of these dimensions releases what she must contain in some corner of her being, yet the creative gift is never hers, it transcends the woman's grasp. The woman, however, reflects a trace of the universal in so far as she touches the essence of reality on different levels of experience.

More specific problems of rehearsal have been referred to in the production of the *Salut au Monde,* in which the complicated elements in material and image had to be brought into focus. In the chapter on *The Dybbuk* we will find the problem of coping with daemonic nature in relation to the utterly human values of the characters. Rehearsals for *An Arab Fantasia,* a festival production of the 1923–24 season, offer another slant on the process.

As the name implies, *An Arab Fantasia* suggested moods of the Arab's way of life as Irene and I saw it during our journey in countries where Arab culture dominated. In these "moods" we attempted to reveal something of the movement of life along the shores of the river, a glimpse into that of the desert, the contrasting movement and rhythm of the bazaar, and the mystical values associated with the mountain top, and as expressed through the dervish. This insight into varying modes had gripped us in lands where life was still one with the soil, where morning and evening seemed to grow with it, and where reverence still clung as a ritual.

We entered upon this hazardous production quite conscious that the Arab was either a remote name to the majority of people in our audience or was treated on the stage or in contemporary literature as a figure swathed in an effete romanticism "Garden of Allah-wise." The Arab had not yet made his debut on the front page of the daily newspapers. His demands for self-determining values, though they could be sensed through sympathetic contact, were not yet audible to resistant Western ears.

As this was a project of the Festival Dancers, rehearsals

were carried on to a large extent at night and developed in fragments. For example, the songs had, in a sense, to be dramatized by the chorus eagerly at work in a corner of the rehearsal room, each member acquiring the posture and walk of an Arab woman balancing a water jar on her head, while she sings, during her morning and evening stroll, Rebecca fashion, to the well. To acquire this idyllic feminine passivity required a form of religious devotion on the part of high-heeled inhabitants of New York, accustomed to the jerky rhythm of subway crowds.

In another room, practice in the sword dance occupied the men of the cast under the direction of an Egyptian whose habitat was Manhattan, when he was not in the jungles of Africa collecting animals for Barnum and Bailey. Bistani, whom we had met en route to Egypt, had proved an amusing guide to the unconventional byways of Cairo; it would not have been possible to visit them without a man entitled to wear the fez. The link between us, as he put it, was "the show business"—a reference, of course, to Barnum and Bailey. On his return from the African jungles he became an enthusiastic member of the *Fantasia* corps and, as a skilled sword dancer, a member of the cast.

Another fragment slowly evolving was the dervish ritual dance whose pivotal whirling movement had to be related to the accent and rhythm of the Koran recited by a young Persian student then studying in New York. He too contributed time and enthusiasm to the needs of the *Fantasia*.

Another "mood" slowly coming to life was the off-stage orchestra, an endurance test in sound for the bazaar scene, in which brass and copper smiths, vendors of perfume and other wares are at work; in which snatches of a native cabaret intermingle with the distant prayer of the Koran, or again, with the call of the muezzin; in which bells echoing the gait of donkeys moving in and out of the mass of humans in the narrow street of the bazaar are suggested by the off-stage orchestra, earnestly capturing the interplay of sounds by beating tin cans or pounding chopping boards with mortars, or experimenting in sounding iron rods on brick, and jingling bells while trotting up and down at appointed intervals.

This peripatetic orchestra was the initial form of the score developed by a young Syrian composer, Anis Fuleihan, then studying in Boston. Exploring the archives of his memory for Arab themes, he had supplemented them with others we had gathered in Egypt and Palestine, evolving an admirable "musical" background. To instrumentalize it, we had scoured the Syrian and Arab quarters of New York and with the help of Bistani, our Egyptian friend, succeeded in finding singers, instruments, and players to supplement the Playhouse chorus and musical setting. As the discords gradually accumulated in an impressionistic ensemble, a surprisingly Arab feeling developed, and the *Fantasia* began to bloom with characteristic light and shade. In fact, we felt close to the river folk moving along its shores or gliding upon its waters in the flukah, hearing again the chant of fisherfolk or ferrymen.

The Playhouse had indeed become a hothouse for Arab culture. From foyer to roof its germs were sprouting in the practice of sword play, gesture in ritual movements, the jangle of strange sounds emerging from unexpected quarters.

The first mood was suggested by a flukah gliding past in the sunset. This was indicated by an ambered flukah sail drawn at the rear of the stage in front of the plaster wall. Womenfolk moved along the shore, carrying water jugs en route to the well while singing songs of the river. This scene was followed by that of the desert, the Arab's patriarchal heritage. A Bedouin family is gathered, according to custom, before the tent flap; the women perform their simple, do-men vie with one another in feats of skill, yet with the harmony of a dance, their poise in tune with space, silence, stars.

In contrast to this, the mood of the bazaar scene is suggested, as if in the heart of the city with its masses of humans and discordant sounds. The fourth mood, the mountain top, is indicated by a little band of the faithful on their way to join a pilgrimage to a sacred shrine where those who dream they have heard the voice of the mountain say it sings with serene ecstasy. And at last, there is the dervish, the whirling movement whose chant and dance wind in ecstatic invocation, merging with the distant prayer of praise, "Allah! Il Allah."

There is no doubt that a primitive force was released through the production of *An Arab Fantasia,* and that all the players were responding to something beyond their capacity to understand. Yet it had no story, no dramatic incident upon which to focus attention. Unconsciously the cast seemed actually to be reliving a traditional experience, somehow acquired through the appeal of that which is elemental and ageless. Desert, river, city, even the quality of the dervish were sensed and made to live again as personal experience, not only for the cast but for the audience who, together, evoked it.

One of the rewards for the cast was Kahlil Gibran's visit to a rehearsal and his surprise that people who were not versed in Arabic could produce not only the spirit but such faithful rendering of the diction and rhythm of the songs. This was partly due to our fortune in finding native Arabs at hand to help interpret the spirit of the songs and dances, and to the gift of Anis Fuleihan in translating the original in such a way that the native quality could be preserved; and not least to Laura Elliot who evoked the Arab quality in the singing.

It was not, however, any of these factors that was finally responsible for the *Fantasia.* Rather it was an attitude—the capacity to receive, as an instrument of an orchestra, the spirit of the Arab that his fluctuating moods might be released. To assemble and convey such experience was a labor of months. It would have been surprising had this spirited Arab adventure, entered into with such affectionate sincerity, not received the wholehearted response of the audience.

CHAPTER TWENTY-EIGHT

THE LITTLE CLAY CART

The Little Clay Cart, long considered, was finally scheduled to open the season of 1924–25. Agnes Morgan had prepared an abridged acting version from Arthur William Ryder's sensitive translation of the Sanskrit text. A corps of students, under the direction of Alice Beer, Polaire Weissman, and Esther Peck, had done the necessary research during the sabbatical year and worked on models for design, color, and costumes, which Aline Bernstein later re-created and developed from Rajput sources into a decorative scheme. In color and charm it proved to be utterly beguiling to our untutored Western senses.

Because of the uncertainty of the play's date, Irene and Agnes, the directors, were free in their choice of time and place for its setting. The Rajput setting lent itself admirably to the color and grace of the text. Each moment supplied the senses with some fresh, alluring detail of gesture and movement. The "rags" played upon the seraj and zither by Hindu musicians during and between the scenes were like threads weaving together this decorative pattern. For the magical way that the scenes transformed Rajput paintings into plastic reality, *The Little Clay Cart* would, alone, live on as one of the real events of theatre.

Unlike the Bombay production, the sense of sight was

completely satisfied. Charmingly and naïvely played, *The Little Clay Cart* was welcomed and hailed for its freshness, its human interest and whimsical humor, its emotional flavor, the quality and variety of its characterizations, its aesthetically decorative charm, and the poetry of its philosophy.

The beauty of movement, the rhythm, the colorful atmosphere, and the characteristic gesture were deeply influenced by Irene's perceptive understanding, much of which came through our brief but intensive experiences in India.

Because I was spending a year of enforced absence from New York, I saw *The Little Clay Cart* only in revival some years later and with a somewhat different cast. But the flavor of the original production is preserved in Stark Young's discerning appreciation. His review, which appeared originally in *The New York Times,* was later reprinted in his book *Immortal Shadows.* His commentary is valuable not only in revivifying the production but in proving the significance of the drama critic for the theatre, and the place dramatic criticism can hold as an art. He has generously consented to the use of the following extracts from his review:

". . . the producers of *The Little Clay Cart* must have felt last night when the last curtain fell that they had come off with all their plumage intact. This Hindu comedy as it is done in the Neighborhood is as delightful as the *Grand Street Follies* were and has a fine poetry and wit of its own. The performance is too long perhaps by 20 minutes, otherwise it is remarkably assisted throughout. Aline Bernstein's settings, especially the first scene with the two houses and the beautiful balustrade at the back, are admirable, and the costumes as well. Arthur William Ryder's translation is a fine, free poetic rendering, often in rhyme, and it is good theatrically, fresh and ready to the ear. The acting was now and then a trifle labored, very little so when we consider the remoteness of the piece, but in general, on an excellent level. The verses were well read, especially in the august lines that fell to Mr. Ian Maclaren in the leading role. Miss Kyra Alanova and Miss Dorothy Sands played the courtesan and the maid servant with a loving, flowing delicacy. Albert Carroll played well the shampooer who turns monk, and Mr. Junius Matthews in the role of the scientific and aesthetic thief had the right humor and droll inflection.

"The comedy of *The Little Clay Cart* was written by King Shudraka somewhere between the fifth and tenth centuries A.D. The range of this play extends from poetical comedy to farce, satire, melodrama and a fine, highly formal tradition of the ancient classic. The story of it turns on the love of a courtesan, Vasantasena, for the good merchant Charudatta, who is now fallen to poverty; the love of his little son, Rohasena, who is peevish because his father is so poor now that he can buy him only a toy cart of clay; Vasantasena gives the boy her jewels to buy a toy cart of gold. Santhanaka, the king's brother-in-law, whose insulting offers Vasantasena has spurned, meets her in the park, and being again repulsed, strangles her and leaves her for dead. A Buddhist monk revives her and leads her off to a monastery. Santhanaka accuses Charudatta of robbing Vasantasena of her jewels and murdering her. On the way to his execution Vasantasena returns, and is thus able to save Charudatta's life. Arayaka, the herdsman, having escaped from prison, kills the king and takes the throne. Charudatta is to be rewarded, and Vasantasena, by royal edict, is to be freed from the bonds of having to live as a courtesan.

"The characters in *The Little Clay Cart* are varied and

unforgettable. The quality of the play cannot be conveyed in any brief account. Everywhere the sentiment and the action is gracious, noble and delicate at the same time. The flavor is one of grace and lyricism and wit. It has the quality of poetry, common sense, proverbs and ballads. And all these qualities, together with the action and words, whether romantic, satirical or droll, seem to move in one crystal medium, unbrokenly. *The Little Clay Cart* is an example of art that expresses a popular life imbued with the poetic. In India everywhere it still survives in that spirit. At the Neighborhood Playhouse it makes one of the most admirable entertainments in town.

"Thinking over the attraction and delight of this performance in Grand Street, we may look about for reasons. And the long ago age of *The Little Clay Cart* appears as one of the sources of its glamour. This play has on it ten centuries and something more of life. During all that time it has been given in India and after every fashion. Sometimes it has been conventional, sometimes popularized in the dialects, sometimes in modern clothes and Victorian settings. But all the while it has belonged to the people; it has been theirs in their own terms. In a performance of the old piece we see what ideas emerge as having that in them which can hold the human race so long a time. Life old and new, ancient and modern, has been capable of living itself in the region of the play. For us *The Little Clay Cart* is Indian, it is ancient—far off, indeed, in two senses; but it discovers an ideal region in which space and time are a dream. In this pure realm the play moves. What happens, the loves, the robberies, the villainies of parasites, the gambling, the just and unjust deeds, all move in an untouched and pristine world of idea, feeling, racial tradition; and all are seen in a mutual radiance and charm. . . .

"The production of *The Little Clay Cart* is an interesting case of *bona fide* treatment when we come to foreign or classic plays. Obviously, any drama, Greek, Indian, French or Elizabethan, is alive for us only in so far as it still expresses life. It was at the beginning a body discovered for some informing idea or soul. The necessity in every case of revival or production is to find a new form which does not violate the play but restates it under the conditions that are to be met. To give *The Little Clay Cart* exactly as it was given in its first performance, even if that were possible, could not any longer convey the truth of the play to us. The interest in such a performance would tend too much to the anti-quarian or academic. On the other hand, to give *The Little Clay Cart* in a manner always conscious that this is an old, quaint, foreign piece, to rub in its naïve oddities, would be to make something out of it which it is not.

"The producers at the Neighborhood Playhouse hit a happy medium in this problem. They allow the play its strangeness, its age, its convention, but always in a wise proportion to the real substance in it. They do not ask us to be overtickled at such conventions as throwing leaves where there are no leaves to throw, or riding a horse that does not exist; they merely flavor the scene with these foreign stage conventions. They do not guy the piece. They play with it happily, but they give every chance to the poetry and ideas behind it."

CHAPTER TWENTY-NINE

A VISIT TO JOYCE

In an early essay on the Irish theatre, James Joyce defined the artist by saying "his true servitude is that he inherits a will broken by doubt and a soul that yields up all its hate to a caress; and the most seeming-independent are those who are the first to reassume their bonds." He might have been speaking of the character of Richard, the writer, in James Joyce's *Exiles*, which followed *The Little Clay Cart* as the second production of 1924–25.

Like *Time Is a Dream*, *Exiles* was interesting for its psychological slant. But *Exiles* had far more stature as a play; in fact, at the time, it seemed to hold so much significance that one could only hope Joyce would make further use of drama as a medium.

The theme, dealing with the relationships between two men and two women, required, naturally, a psychological treatment to make its point—a point which had significance for me if the two men, Richard and Robert, were seen as the two parts of one man, namely Joyce: his conscious and unconscious nature. In this case the four characters might be seen in the light of the total personality, including the feminine elements. As I was unable to be in New York at the time of the production, which was directed by Agnes Morgan, my only contribution to it was a visit to Joyce living in Paris at the time, to see how he stood toward such a possible interpretation of the characters.

He received me cordially and with unfeigned surprise that his one and only play was to be produced in New York. Immediately, I confided my reactions to the play and asked him if he had intended to indicate the two men as different aspects of one man. He admitted that the idea had never occurred to him, but it was quite possible and an interesting angle. "But," he continued, "the artist is not concerned with the interpretation of his work." He, for one, left that to his readers.

That problem settled, we spoke of other things. His entourage and the little Paris flat, quite dingy and colorless, was apparently a makeshift. I asked him about his sojourn in Paris, if he wasn't homesick for Ireland. He said he was, very, but his problem was how to get back! There was an impenetrable wall, the English Channel.

"Are you afraid of seasickness? It can be wretched," I knew. "But surely not as bad as homesickness?"

"It isn't that," he said, in the most despairing tone. "You see I can't cross water. I'm stuck here. I want to leave and I can't."

Then I understood the impression I had of his being imprisoned in partial darkness. Later on, I asked myself if that was a provision of nature to hold him to those depths out of which his imagery grew? In relation to this problem I wondered later if *Ulysses* were not a form of whale from which, through the grace of his creative spirit, he might ultimately be disgorged.

I never met him in Zürich where he lived later on, but a Swiss-acquaintance who visited him quite often gave me an additional insight into his relation to his inner world. Apparently the night was his time for creative work. Each thought was scribbled on a small piece of paper and tossed on the floor—the precious seeds were gathered up in the morning by his wife. But I was not quite sure how the harvest was actually produced.

Though the visit did not throw light on the production of *Exiles,* I was grateful for the human touch and appealing aspect of his personality I should otherwise have been denied.

CHAPTER THIRTY

THE DYBBUK IN EMBRYO

During my absence from New York, I was staying in a tiny medieval village in the Bas Alps, full of ghosts of the long past, of ruined walls and rushing torrents. I had the script of *The Dybbuk* with me and as I read it the characters seemed to emerge from the pages, with irresistible appeals to become enformed. Henry Alsberg had made a revised translation of the play from the original Yiddish text by Ansky, a Russian student and ethnologist, who had gathered the material of the Chassidic sect, the background of the play, on his many journeys in remote sections of southern Russia.

The quality of *The Dybbuk* came through in translation, but could its atmosphere, so foreign, so strangely remote, be recaptured for the stage?

At the time, I merely knew of the existence of Chassidism as a mystical sect of Judaism which developed in the eighteenth century. In perspective it might be thought of as a protest against dogmatic ritualism, in which rabbinical law dominated. The Chassid expresses, in contrast, his relation to God through mystical enthusiasm or ecstasy. Deity, for him, as in other mystical cults, is imminent in nature, religion expressed as his personal, daily experience, rather than as creed. The outpouring of his emotional nature is accepted and furthered through the dance, through song, and in that intensified relation to the holy man, or Zaddik (a religious mediator and ruler in the community), who calls forth, on a human level, the worshipful attitude of man, through love and fear of the divine spirit. And spirit manifests for him through the warmth of relatedness.

These images and many more are interwoven in the background of *The Dybbuk*. Coupled with its folk expression is the more profound symbolism of the Kabala, a mystically toned theosophical doctrine stemming from the sixth century A.D.—for example, the marriage between Channon and Leah, the leitmotif of the play, is based upon the mystical or divine marriage in Kabalistic lore, between spirit and nature, corresponding in a sense to that in alchemy. But here in *The Dybbuk* it is poignantly expressed in its human guise, that is the attempt to break through the destined unio mystica in the effort to incarnate the sacred marriage. This conflict between the two worlds is suggested throughout the play, reaching a climax in the trial of the Dybbuk, that is, the soul of one who has died and returned to inhabit—in this case—the body of the beloved. In the Catholic Church the trial would be analogous to the rite of exorcism.

As *The Dybbuk* was written by an ethnologist, the dramatic structure was by no means its main feature. The value lay rather in revealing types, traditions, and fragmentary episodes associated with this little-known Chassidic sect in South Russia. The author succeeded in creating an atmosphere through which grotesque and mystic elements interweave as light and shade.

The thread of the drama is not easy to follow without an understanding of its background. The central theme, as indicated, revolves around the marriage of Channon, a young rabbinical student absorbed in the occult or secret teaching of the Kabala, and Leah, the daughter of a prosperous widower who, according to custom, is the patron of the religious student. It is merely inferred that Channon, though he had formerly lived in her father's house, is a dreamlike beloved presence to Leah. Their chance meeting in the synagogue, in the first act, foreshadows the mystery underlying the play and its link with the "sacred marriage" which, in the folk culture of the Chassid, is treated as a personalized experience.

Channon and Leah are destined to marry because of a vow made by their parents before the children were born, stipulating that if one couple should be granted a boy and the other a girl, these offspring should marry. To be affianced before birth reflects the mythological image of the hierosgamos (sacred marriage) as a dedication to God. Originally the sacred marriage was conceived as the prerogative of the god and goddess, or as service to the god enacted by the priest and temple hierodule to symbolize the relation between heaven and earth, that which is eternally renewing and that which transcends the life of the earth.

In the play this underlying destiny is crossed by human limitations. Light and dark forces interplay in the all-too-human threads of the drama. Channon is dominated by his hunger for God, infused with the hunger for Leah; while Sender, Leah's father, a robust man of the earth, breaks his vow in order to secure a suitable wealthy husband for his daughter. The motherless Leah is like a soul caught in a mystical sphere, not yet borne to earth.

In our first introduction to the lovers in the synagogue, they give the impression of birds on the wing carried to an eternal fate. This scene is followed by Channon's sudden, mysterious, yet self-determined death, which occurs in a moment of illumination, as he penetrates the secret name of God. But we are also led to assume that, involved in this enlightenment, is the foreknowledge of the broken vow and separation from Leah. Though not present thereafter, Channon plays a continuous role in the play, which is experienced on two levels of reality, the poignantly human and the ghost world strangely interwoven. For the Dybbuk is a ghost, in this case the soul of Channon, which at his death enters the body of Leah. This suggests a clue for Channon's unmotivated death: to obstruct Leah's marriage to the husband of her father's choice. Toward this end the Dybbuk makes use of the Beggars in the second act. They appear first in the wedding scene as a sinister yet ambiguous chorus. According to custom they are the guests of the father and have the privilege of dancing with the bride. In the course of the dance we become aware of their demoniacal nature when, in the frenzy of retribution, they carry off the bride. The climax of the scene is reached when Leah returns, apparently as bride, yet possessed by the Dybbuk which now speaks through her.

In the next act the trial of the Dybbuk takes place as a religious ceremony. It is conducted by the Zaddik, who upholds the righteousness of the Law, or God of Justice. Opposing him and equally potent is the Dybbuk, the demonic power controlling the soul of Channon, which unappeased by his death has entered Leah, his soul's mate. We can even assume that this incorporation of the dark spirit is a further step to insure Leah's union with Channon, promised before birth. For Channon has asserted in an earlier scene that the satanic spirit "is an aspect of God and therefore must contain also a germ of holiness." We can infer, then, that the trial involves more than the problem of overcoming the Dybbuk and its evil magic. According to the Kabala, the potentiality of spirit is evoked from darkness; so Channon, in allying himself with the dark nature of God, has in a mystical sense entered the darkness in order to be reborn or redeemed.

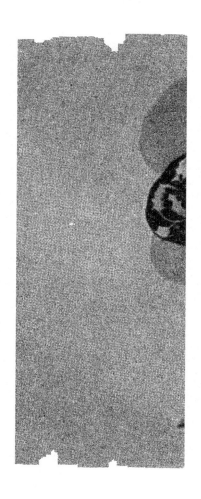

The Dybbuk by Ansky, 1925–26.

18. Wedding scene. Frade, Dorothy Sands, dances with beggar.

19. Leah's father, Marc Loebell, reveals to the Bathlonim
and others her betrothal.

A growing tension between the light and dark aspects of God dominates the scene, climaxing in the Dybbuk's defiance of all the powers of heaven and earth. Finally, through the instrumentation of a profoundly solemn ritual, the Dybbuk is exorcised and releases Leah from its possession.

But the mysterious, inevitable fate is still to be fulfilled on a plane transcending the power of the Zaddik. After the ceremony Leah awakens from the trance, hears the voice of Channon from afar, calling as a bird to its mate. As if in a dream she listens to the voice of her beloved chanting from the Song of Songs and rises to follow his call by crossing the magic circle holding her to earth.

These and many more subtle and grotesque incidents are the woof and warp of a legend which, though Chassidic in character, stems from a symbol universally significant: the attempt of man the world over to realize an image of wholeness, dark and light, divine and human. This basic need anticipates a state beyond the conflict of opposing forces, through the perception of a reality in which two shall be one or at one.

The image of harmony as dual unity has been expressed in mystery cults from time immemorial. But can we not also find in *Romeo and Juliet* a parallel to the tradition underlying this folk play? In both, the searching need of a perfected love transcends destructive forces, always threatening the living spirit. In both, the lovers eternally young are dedicated to the spiritual nature of love "as boundless as the sea." Here in *The Dybbuk* fate also places its seal upon the symbolic nature of the union by brushing aside the inadequacies and barriers of time and space. The magic circle which the Zaddik draws around Leah after the exorcism—uniting two worlds of reality—is such a symbol. But it is used by the Zaddik as a magical device to guard Leah against the world of

dark spirits and their disrupting influence. In stepping out of
the circle when she hears Channon's voice, she leaves the
boundary of its magical protection and dies. But in the
language of the play the predestined marriage has been
fulfilled on a plane transcending the dark magic of Channon,
or the white magic of the Zaddik, as indicated in the ritual
and circle, or any tricks or plans of man.

It is not easy to follow the process of Channon's transformation, for his hunger for God and hunger for Leah, at first
indistinguishable, require separation before the erotic and
the spiritual nature of love, symbolically expressed as earth
and heaven, can be united. A clue to his need of redemption
from desirousness is indicated in Act I in a dialogue with
Chennoch, another rabbinical student. In a discussion of
the problem of the greatest sin that is, love for a woman,
Channon passionately declares: "And when you have
cleansed this sin in a powerful flame then this greatest un-
cleanliness becomes the greatest holiness. It becomes the
Song of Songs."

The testing he undergoes during the trial is comparable to
this flame. The Dybbuk, at first defiant, finally succumbs
and releases its power over Leah. In abandoning his daemonic
will, Channon is cleansed in the "powerful flame" and thus
redeemed. This is merely suggested through the Song of
Songs [1] which he sings at the beginning and at the close of the
play. In the first act the song is a passionate outburst in the
synagogue, interrupted by Leah's unexpected entrance. As

---

[1] The Song of Songs has far more significance for the Kabalist than is
apparent to the uninitiated. Its value is expressed by Rabbi Akiba, a great
teacher and mystic who lived during the second century of our era, and
who is mentioned by Channon in the second act of the play as the great
Father of Kabalistic lore: "All the world is not worth as much as the day
upon which the Song of Songs was given to Israel. All the scriptures are
holy but the Song of Songs is the Holy of Holies" (quoted by Prof. G. Scholem
of the University of Jerusalem).

the final note of the play we again hear Channon's voice in the distance as a ringing echo of the Song of Songs. Leah, awakening from the trance, rises to follow its call and glides out of the magic circle binding her to earth.

In the play, as in many mystery cults, the image of this destined union beckons from "the other shore," the divine value is intuited as a future state.

Thus far we have followed Channon's transformation and redemption in relation to the mystical marriage, symbolized for him in the Song of Songs. And we have seen how he resorts to the use of black magic, personified in the Dybbuk, in order to possess Leah who reflects for him the divine attributes of the Song of Songs.

Leah's part in the mystical experience is more subtle. Does she play a purely reflective role as the soul image of Channon? In that case she would typify the feminine aspect of Channon's nature rather than characterize the woman in herself as partner in the marriage. Such a possibility is suggested in her apparent passivity in accepting the earthly bridegroom her father has chosen, also in the feeling she conveys of not being rooted to earth. These motives in the play are, however, reminiscent of a mythological background. I am thinking of Persephone as a figure neither quite linked to earth nor to the underworld, but epitomizing the maiden reflected in every woman whose potentialities have not quite bloomed.

A closer analogy can be seen in the "Hadesian" power of the Dybbuk by whom Leah is forcibly carried to the dark world just as she is to be married to the earthly bridegroom, inferring that she is undergoing a process of transformation. Her release in death is made possible, as we have seen, not through the spiritual power of the Zaddik, but through Channon's regeneration in withdrawing his black magic or compulsive power. In the myth, Persephone is restored through the intercession of Demeter, the mother of life; while Channon's transformation reflects the spiritual demands of a patriarchal culture.

Mythologically perceived, this moment is suggestive of the "light penetrating darkness," anticipated here in Leah's restoration to the light world after the dark journey in the underworld. But we must bear in mind that this situation is also a central motive in ancient Mysteries as in many forms of ritual drama. Perhaps we can read in it an eternal truth, that enlightenment or widened consciousness is rarely attained without a collision with the inferior elements in our nature. Leah's active participation in the drama begins at this point and is indicated in her crossing the magic circle intended to hold her to earth and the traditional life of a Chassidic woman. The hurried preparations for the wedding to follow immediately after the exorcism show that the tension and conflict are not yet resolved. The culmination of the play, its ultimate resolution, lies in Leah's silent acknowledgment of the sacred marriage, for which she yields her life as Channon his power. Religiously perceived, this implies the sacrifice of the personal value for the spiritual claim. To the Kabalist, as we have learnt through Channon, God has not only a light but also a dark aspect, which could imply psychologically that the divine drama is being enacted within the soul of the participants undergoing a process of transformation. The predestined union can then be seen as a suprapersonal reality.

May we not read in the overwhelming response the play has received in many lands an indication of the universal appeal inherent in this symbol? Its age-old significance is reaffirmed by the lovers in their need of an experience uniting the transient or erotic nature of love with its eternally creative reality. In the utter simplicity of its unfolding we experienced the core of drama, that is, the mysterious process of transformation taking place in the soul, whether heeded or unheeded by the individual, a process whose goal, directed toward such unity, involved the lovers in a conflict with supranatural forces.

To try to extract its motives out of the fantastic network of folklore and mystical teaching leaves the play threadbare. Its humanness yet "otherworldness" could only be suggested in the playing as if an indefinable "presence" were hovering between two worlds. To review the play it has alas been necessary to fill in the gaps which on the stage could be sensed through the emotional intensity of the experience.

The text of *The Dybbuk* is more like an outline for improvisation than a completed structure. This is indicated in the many versions of the play that exist, differing not only in language but in interpretation. For example, the highly stylized and symbolic treatment of the Habima production, or again the wholly folk expression of a German version. The French, as I recall it, had a classic touch; while in ours the mystical values were stressed.

In transforming the imagery of an ancient teaching into folk experience the Chassidic sect, as the author of the play, preserved it by way of the heart.

CHAPTER THIRTY-ONE

THE DYBBUK IN PRODUCTION

While I was pondering over the strangely gripping character of *The Dybbuk,* so real yet so
remote, a cable arrived from my colleagues in New York
suggesting that I go to Moscow to confer with the director of
the Habima, the original producers of *The Dybbuk.* The
idea, however, did not appeal, for I felt that the play would
have to grow out of our own experience and that the Russian
method, however brilliant, might somehow inhibit our spontaneous approach. So I lingered on in the medieval village,
where spooks and remoteness carried me even further into
the Dybbuk world. Soon another message came from my
colleagues, saying that David Vardi, a member of the original
Habima production, had presented himself at the Playhouse,
eager and apparently equipped to help with *The Dybbuk* if
we decided upon its production. Suddenly all obstacles
vanished and I hurried back into the ring.

The day I arrived in New York I met Mr. Vardi, a tiny
man expertly groomed, suggesting in no way the ravages
of the recent revolution through which he had lived. At
the first interview, although he knew practically no English,
his mobile face and expressive gestures revealed far more than
any kind of discussion or lecture. We sensed without words
the point of view of the Habima organization and its definite
departure from the Moscow Art Theatre methods. Mr.

Vardi's sympathy and imaginative gesticulation showed an Hebraic background vital to the production of *The Dybbuk*. Without delay we engaged him to serve as our interpreter and guide to the Chassidic sect, its character, customs, and religious principles.

Born and brought up in a village similar to Brainitz in *The Dybbuk*, Mr. Vardi was familiar with all its folkways and melodies. From his own experience he could describe to us a trial between the living and the dead, the episode which played so important a part in the drama; he could reveal contrasting attitudes between the Kabala and Talmud, not in an intellectual way, but so that our lay minds could grasp the conflict between the formal creed of the latter and the symbolic imagery of the former. Vardi was still so related to his experience that *The Dybbuk* had become his religion, and the ecstasy of its characters was reflected in him. Ansky, the playwright, had with consummate sensibility been able to penetrate the crust of that curious world, releasing a spark buried in what appeared to the naked eye as common clay.

Through Vardi, we were able to probe into the inner strata of the Bathlonim, the professional prayermen of the synagogue, shunned and outcast, but still hanging like gargoyles to the structure for spiritual and physical support. To the world outside, they were merely dregs, but in themselves they were strange shadows of the past. They had no contact with life as it was, nor did they even make any effort to struggle. They just sat by the fire, basked in its warmth when it was lighted, and froze when the fire died out. But they never ceased to glow inside with memories of their heroes, the Rabbis, the lore of the Talmud, and legends of the faith. And as they sat there and talked of these things in hushed voices, they were taking a chance as terrific as inhabitants of the "underworld" of today, for they believed that at any moment an evil spirit would emerge to destroy them. So their whispered tales fairly clung to the walls of the synagogue.

In *The Dybbuk* it is all this world of ghosts and spirits, forms and shadows of the past, that Leah instinctively feels when she comes into the synagogue. Frade, her foster-mother, accepts the synagogue with all its traditions; for her it has a homely meaning; it represents all the known world of comfort and security and she revels in it as a background. But to Leah, sensitively tuned to inner experience, it repels even while it calls from her a longing she cannot understand. Channon, her betrothed, becomes a symbol to her of that longing, the spirit within herself trying to release itself, or perhaps the symbol of all the ancient world of spirits, trying to release themselves from the wall.

Is it love? Is it fear? Is it the wonder and mystery of the unknown calling again from the soul of Channon? Gittel, her friend, sees nothing of all this. For her, each object is an ordinary fact, provoking childlike interest. How simply the author threads his theme as it winds itself about the synagogue, making us sense with the characters the throbbing pulse of its ancient heart!

Channon and Leah as old souls are caught in a moment of their pilgrimage. They still have a long road to travel, for earth, according to the Kabala, is one of the stations of life eternal. To Leah, Channon contains all the mystery that speaks to her in the synagogue, and the synagogue is simply another form of the personality of Channon. To Channon, Leah is a dream figure. Yet their unquenchable longing, their youthful ardor, cannot be precipitated upon the stage, but has to be suggested merely by the actors who have absorbed something of the intangible forces out of which *The Dybbuk* originally took form.

About three weeks after our first meeting with Mr. Vardi, we introduced him to the Playhouse company. He rose and stood silently before the group for what seemed a minute or more; then, haltingly at first, but gradually with more and more fluency, he addressed them in English. He was never at a loss for an explanation. If the words did not offer themselves, he immediately presented a picture of each character in its relationship to the play and to its background through colorful pantomime and expression.

Then followed the exciting and tedious work of selecting a company, which meant try-outs for parts. All of our permanent company in turn were given the opportunity of reading the part each felt qualified to play. Without any hesitation, most of the girls selected Leah, and an equal number of the men were candidates for the part of Channon. Hardened as I had been by the years of training and try-outs, the disappointment of each candidate at each refusal tumbled upon me like an avalanche. The desire to play a particular role is like an acute disease which spends itself in frenzied fevers. To have an entire company more or less afflicted at the same moment gave the Playhouse for a while the atmosphere of a plague center.

Meanwhile we were encouraging Broadway applicants to read for us. Day after day, processions of actors descended upon the Playhouse, those who had been called, others who had read of the forthcoming production, and still others who had some vague notions of its distinguished Moscow production. There were many more who just wandered in, or who had been recommended by agents or other managers.

Those first weeks of the prospective casting seemed the most difficult part of the production. The actors who considered themselves qualified, Jewish actors of Broadway, proved themselves least suited, because their whole approach and emphasis was upon obvious values, and they had no relation to mystical feeling. To us the Dybbuk world had become a reality, and each newcomer, as he presented himself, seemed a being outside the pale. Often the candidate would look wholly mystified and walk away, sensing that he had trodden taboo soil.

After days and weeks of the Broadway recessional, it became apparent that we could not hope to assimilate in the role of Channon an actor born into and bred with the standards of Broadway. We decided to abandon all further search outside our own group, and awarded the part to Albert Carroll. But there was still a Leah to be found!

The part remained unfilled till the eleventh hour, although it was not for want of applicants. Rehearsals could naturally not proceed without Leah, so for many weeks I rehearsed the part with the company, and was just as gripped by the fascination and possibilities of the role as all the applicants; in fact it was one of the greatest conflicts of a lifetime to release Leah to another. At last the die was cast, and Mary Ellis won the much-sought treasure, while my task was to lavish the intensity of undivided responsibility upon the production, which would not otherwise have been possible.

The preliminary rehearsals of *The Dybbuk* were in many instances improvisations without text. These, as well as the ground plan of the types, were directed by Mr. Vardi. The Playhouse group, for the most part the Festival Dancers under Irene's direction, labored unceasingly upon the improvised themes. Frequently a scene in which the text was tersely abbreviated developed into a mounting experience through improvisation. So, for example, the situation between Sender, Leah's father and Frade, her foster-mother, was built up to a scene scaled in intensity upon the words:

"Where is Leah?" This was so meaningfully experienced in the roles by Dorothy Sands and Marc Loebell that it still stands out as one of the creative moments of the play.

From realistic studies of their types through improvisation of the background and homelife of the characters, the actors had to undergo a process of gradual transformation until they could realize their supernatural prototypes. Day after day in rehearsal the Beggars fought among themselves, grumbled, growled, suffered, grabbed, and gobbled food, at first politely and decorously, then with growing abandon, until at last their beggarhood seemed to take to itself supernatural attributes and ultimately the grotesque stature of fiends let loose by the disembodied Channon to capture his promised bride.

Though rehearsals were now shaping themselves through concentrated experiment, we realized that the usual four or five weeks would be wholly inadequate, and boldly decided upon ten. Even that seemed a terrifyingly short time in which to rehearse, organize the production, develop and build it, and also complete the translation. With Mr. Vardi's assistance, Henry Alsberg and Winifred Katzin incorporated parts of the version by Bealik which was used by the Habima. To integrate this with Ansky's text it was essential to change scenes as well as phrases after each rehearsal. For weeks the actors had to adjust to the vagaries of an improvised text, and it never ceased to be a miracle that the manuscript, molded from Hebrew and Yiddish and then pruned down into English, still held its natural flow and character. This was of course greatly helped by the musical themes that wound themselves in and out of the scenes, not as accompaniment but as an integral part of the text. Some of these scenes, as for example, the crooning chants of the Bathlonim, were unrecorded melodies rooted in Chassidic culture, yet pointing to a far older origin. They were given to us by Mr. Vardi, who sang them into the phonograph from which they were transcribed. The musical episodes directed by Howard Barlow, the Playhouse musical director, contributed a colorful folk flavor and especially enhanced the supernatural mood underlying the wedding scene in the second act.

The score written by Julius Engel for the Habima production was used for the scenes in the second act, the dynamic current of which was carried by the beggars' dance, climaxing in Leah's possession by the Dybbuk. The choreography of this episode, as well as the movement of the whole scene, was developed by Irene, who also played one of the beggars.

Settings and costumes for *The Dybbuk* presented serious problems. Chassidic types and the architecture of synagogues of the eighteenth century were obtainable through photographs and cuts, but neither a photographic nor a conventionalized interpretation was suitable. For the quality of *The Dybbuk* could not be sensed either through an external or an abstract treatment. Aline Bernstein rose courageously to the challenge, especially in her intensive and patient mothering of the costumes which, after they had been developed for type, form, and color, were molded into character. With the Bathlonim and Beggars, the line between the actor and his costume was, like the equator, purely imaginary, for the materials were literally treated as if of clay molded to register the distinct personality of the being it contained.

For the Habima Players, *The Dybbuk* had significance as a tradition from which they, as its inheritor, were in revolt; therefore they viewed it neither tenderly nor in a romantic twilight. Dissociating themselves root and branch from the old "superstitions," they naturally swung into another dimension and were impelled to treat abstractly symbols that to them were outworn. With us, who saw the drama from a more distant and less personal perspective, the grotesqueness of its character became mellowed, and that which was sharpened by the Habima through actual contact was, with us, veiled through poetic imagery.

It was that remote, half legendary quality which we found so illusively alluring, so tantalizing to suggest, yet ardently pursued by designers and workshop directors. Despite the lavish emphasis of ten weeks on rehearsals, the physical side of the production was scrupulously held within the limits of a modest budget. In the way of economy, even the most venerable costumes and flats, that might have been pensioned for honorable service, were surgically treated and mustered again into action.

These strenuous weeks of absorbing Chassidic culture had cast their spell. The afternoon of the opening I found myself at the Playhouse because elsewhere I felt queerly aloof and disassociated. When I walked into the auditorium, there was Mrs. Duffy cleaning far earlier and with more vigor than usual, as though she too had been haunted by the Dybbuk. In the dressing-rooms a number of the cast had already gathered, strangely silent. They admitted the need to return to the Dybbuk world, confessing in turn that it was impossible to stay at home.

The Dybbuk was now to be let loose and soar, or drop with a dull thud. For ten weeks we had worked, strained, struggled, endured together, with faith in the experience we shared, even if at times we secretly doubted the result. Could the quality we felt surrounding each scene be a form of self-hypnotism? Yet could the intensity, the discipline of the weeks, fail to create the spell, to sound the note that held for us some strange attachment we could not explain?

The night of the opening I stood at the back as usual,

reliving each inflection. Every flaw seemed magnified, each note of beauty more intense. For instance, a loss of tempo threatened to frustrate an entire scene, or again the Frade of Dorothy Sands suddenly assumed a stature and dignity beyond every promise at rehearsal.

At last the final curtain, silencing the faraway call of spirit to spirit. Channon and Leah had dared all, suffered the fire and brimstone of earthly damnation, and could soar now each to each in an eternal embrace. Silence! Darkness! All too soon the house lights would proclaim the unreality of a world "un*Dybbuked*."

The next morning the unanimous praise of the critics created a situation for which we were once again unprepared. From early morning till late at night, the box-office telephone never ceased ringing. Members of the playing company were besieged by private calls with pleading requests for seats. Under this avalanche of public interest the Playhouse staggered a bit at first, and then proceeded quietly on its way.

What had called forth so much enthusiasm? Why had the production made so universal an appeal? Was it merely a reflex of critics or was it that for a moment an audience was drawn, sucked away from the confusion of tangible reality into the spell of a profound inner experience?

In the light of subsequent events it is easier to analyze some of the contributing causes than it was at the time. There had been just as much of an element of chance about this manuscript as there is in any. We had entered into it because it spoke directly to the heart and allowed us to feel our way into a drama in which two worlds of reality interplay as light and shadow. To the cast, the play was so convincing that the faith, fervor, and mood jealously guarded during the long intensive preparation could be released. Although as drama *The Dybbuk* was loosely constructed and offered little opportunity for brilliant acting, its value lay in the interweaving of the threads binding the characters under an aura of the transpersonal experience.

The transition from our all-too-natural doubt of "landing the ship" to a tumult of recognition had occurred overnight. Night after night increasing numbers of people were turned away. How meet this widened response? Tempting offers came from Broadway managers to move to an uptown theatre for an indefinite run, with the indication that similar opportunities awaited future productions. The possibility of a degree of security for later productions could not be wholly ignored. In addition, the author's estate, the translator, and Mr. Vardi all added their weight to the rational end of the scale. Such were the first easily defined values but others were more complex.

For instance, how plan for an indefinite run of *The Dybbuk* when we were already committed to our subscribers for three more productions that season, and to our actors for a variety of parts? How transplant the production, scaled to our small theatre, without seriously marring its quality?

Any production demands the initial fervor of a new venture. Could this force be directed into two channels simultaneously? Could we hope to re-create the production while developing a new one? What of the danger of crippling our energies by deflecting them into what, for want of a better name, was the salesmanship of theatre? When we actually faced the organization of a second company and all it entailed of repetition and revitalization, we knew conclusively that we could not, upon sudden demand, repeat the experience, or rebuild the fire that had taken so much time to kindle. At best the effort would have been stillborn. So the glittering vision of relief from financial pressure, of experiment in wider fields, soon faded.

The cast, at first divided in its reactions, gradually realized the inevitability of the decision, but in that decision we dimly foresaw a crisis in the life of the Playhouse. The moment for expansion and a widened career had come and gone, leaving in its wake a shadow of that which we had to face more clearly a year later: the realization that another epoch had ended and a reshaping of plan was again imperative.

CHAPTER THIRTY-TWO

DECISION TO TEST REPERTORY

As our organization grew in size and complexity, the need for further technical development was daily more acute. Each department cried out for more intensive and creative experience. Yet such development was not possible under conditions of financial pressure and the multiple demands of organization. Even with the overwhelming response *The Dybbuk* attracted, it was unable to earn more than the cost of running the production. With the increasing overhead, as well as maintenance of productions, the problem was becoming insurmountable; one failure in a season could cripple the entire organization. And yet without the freedom to fail, to court adventure with all its recklessness, without the privilege of discard and discovery, how could the Playhouse be fed? How exist if fear and doubt lurked behind every gesture, and each production needed the shelter of success?

There seemed to be no constructive answer to this inevitable dilemma. But one possible way to salvage the immediate situation was to test repertory and in this way to reduce the number of new productions. I doubt if the ironical twist struck us at the time, for here we were extending the run of *The Dybbuk* and planning for a series of revivals, although a few months before, when response to *The Dybbuk* was at its zenith, the opportunity to transfer it to Broadway, necessitating a new production equivalent to a revival, had been turned down. This indicates at least how attitudes and values have their time and place.

As a matter of fact, we were confronting a wholly new situation in the theatre world. The comparative freedom and independence to operate as and how we wished was being threatened by the rigidity of the stagehands union, which now not only dictated the number of stagehands but forced us to accept whomever they sent. Furthermore, the union watched the clock, so that rehearsals had become a luxury. It ordained ludicrous restrictions; for example, the director no longer had access to his stage, that is, the right to touch an object on it. We had coped with the music union for years, but this new foreign body, with its negative re-sponse to creative values, was a menace anticipating the doom of an individual enterprise. Experimentation in ways and means to exist had now to be underscored.

By the end of March 1926, we were committed to playing *The Dybbuk* during the mid-week, while rehearsing for a wholly new lyric bill scheduled for weekends. The scope and bizarre character of the lyric bill—involving no less than three plays of widely varying quality—engulfed the work-shop, actors, and directors in prodigious experiment. The light, frolicsome nature of the triple bill, undertaken to con-trast with the exacting demands of *The Dybbuk,* needed, in the end, considerable resourcefulness to compensate for its tenuous content.

Not only did these contrasting episodes require special technique in operating, but each called for a wholly in-dividual treatment. *Kuan Yin* and *The Apothecary* were linked only through the periods which bound the Eastern and Western hemispheres in modes of eighteenth-century Baroque. The Burmese Pwé, however, with its age-old roots, was still a living form at the time of the production, as it doubtless is today.

The Apothecary, a slight one-act operetta by Haydn, with the most fragmentary text, was translated by Anna Mac-Donald and directed by me. Its eighteenth-century artificiality and mannered froth, touched with burlesque, hinted that it belonged to the many "divertissements" produced by Haydn as command drawing-room entertainment for the Freiherr von Furnberg, his original patron.

The point of these extravagantly spoofed, lovelorn scenes has entirely escaped me, but the romantic Primadonna, for example, and the Dottore, were undoubtedly relics of the types familiar to the audiences of the Commedia dell' Arte a century before. Having lost their original vitality, they lingered on as a diversion for the salon and served as themes for the composer's skill, sandwiched between his more serious works.

The only tension offered by this musically charming divertissement was in synchronizing speech and movement to the theme played on a harpsichord on stage. The incidental arias, treated to simulate sustained tone, and the dances, were supported by a chamber ensemble in the pit, all of which added a peculiar detachment which enhanced the artifice of its stylized form. Aline Bernstein's costumes and settings were a suitable frame for this vignette whose mood, approximately two centuries old, had not only to be resuscitated but given a reflected charm for us.

Kuan Yin, the next episode in the triple bill, an extravaganza in Chinese opera form, was composed by A. Avshalom-off, who was also responsible for the libretto. Never had the Playhouse been flooded with such barbaric splendor, for the baroque quality dominated rather than the more familiar classic background of Kuan Yin, the Goddess of Mercy, as she appears in Chinese art and myth. The text afforded scope for the conventional movement of the Chinese theatre touched up with Russian fantasy.

Kuan Yin was also a study in the synchronization of form, line, movement, and sound that carried Irene and her corps of dancer-actors into the most complicated fields of expression. The costumes had architectural proportions, so that each gesture of the humans inhabiting them had to be magnified to scale with the daemonic, yet florid, grandeur of the characters.

Another problem of synchronization was handled by the Chinese orchestra, impersonated by members of the Festival Dancers. The instruments they used were forms of percussion in wood, brass, and drums. This was one of the most convincing and pictorial elements of the production. For the orchestra, seated Chinese fashion on a raised rail gallery, stage rear, formed a most interesting and colorful portrait background in natural form, while the figures on the stage were scaled to superhuman proportions, inverting the usual order. Here we had the miniature proportions of human beings seen on a balcony above, in contrast to the giantesque forms of demigods striding the earth. Something of their dynamic spirit infected all backstage servitors, for I remember how one had to hoodwink these demigods for the favor of a rehearsal of the Haydn, as they devoured not only space but time with a gusto restricted wholly to giants.

Mere human energy underwent incredible transformation in the process. I think of the workshop directors battling with the fabulous dress of the heroes and of the heroic task of the actors weighted down under their costumes constructed for the most part of rubber. This achievement remains one of the unwritten epics of the Playhouse. Ernest de Weerth's designs, though brilliant, required the ingenuity and enthusiasm of super-helpful spirits to carry through.

The difference in style and treatment of the Eastern and Western opera forms of the same period provided an unimaginable scale of contrasts. Nor had the Playhouse ever before indulged in such an orgy of color. How pale, how confined, the coquettish artifice of Europe's eighteenth century in relation to the giantesque stride of Chinese demigods. And, in contrast to both, the naïve simplicity of the Burmese Pwé, last of the episodes, with its exotic sophistication, conjured a fairylike world. For it was as limpid and lilting in a pictorial sense as the colorful score composed for it by Henry Eichheim. Irene succeeded in conveying the quality of a pwé without in any way injecting a photographic slant.

That the beguiling mood of a Burmese ritual could be conveyed by young Americans had never really seemed probable. Intricate movement and posture, quiescent yet forceful, concentrated in the body encased in the tightest of garments, was conveyed with apparent ease by Blanche Talmud and Paula Trueman, who had "imbibed" this conventional form after months of strenuous application. Likewise, the Burmese rhythms were painstakingly studied by the intrepid Festival Dancers, who succeeded to a remarkable extent in bringing to life the bathala, that zitherlike instrument as decorative to the eye as enchanting to the ear. Though played independently of the orchestra as accompaniment of the dances, it added a touch of magic to these elfin beings with whom we, the audience, felt ourselves sailing to the land of fée.

The triple bill undoubtedly provided an enriching experience and wholly new fields of technique for all concerned

with the production. But during the process of preparing
the exotic feast, the actors, simultaneously playing in *The
Dybbuk*, were taxed to the limit; and when a performance
of *The Dybbuk* seemed to flatten to a mere shell, in spite
of the weekly tuning-up rehearsal, it seemed wasteful and
destructive of those values we had labored to develop. It
would have needed the renewing waters of the Castilian
Spring to emerge from the clanging world of the Chinese
operetta to restore the atmosphere of Chassidic folk in faraway untrammeled Brainitz in southern Russia.

How cope with the mounting pressure? As any natural
growth, life demanded more life. In the theatre, where the
heightening of experience is called for, tension develops to
the explosive point. The creative daemon in us cries for
more expansion, adventure into unexplored forms, and at
the same time for substance, content, the urge to sound
deeper levels of experience.

The problem stared at us. How sustain one production
in its original impetus and simultaneously build up another
with the same company? Though the spirit delighted in the
variety of experience, groans of fatigue and protests at the
hours of work echoed through the building, and it was evident that the theatre was living us.

While we were still immersed in the rehearsals of the
triple bill, its successor, *The Romantic Young Lady* by
Martinez Sierra, with Mary Ellis in the title role, was
announced. The cast of *The Dybbuk*, who were already
alternating in the triple bill, were now scheduled for this
effervescent comedy.

The values of *The Romantic Young Lady* were in its deftness, its whimsical nature, and the touch of fantasy. Much

of the Spanish theatre reflects a hovering between romance and the actuality of the everyday world. It is as if the Spaniard seeks to escape from the sombre force of his setting, characterized in the landscape, in order to create a world in tune with the spirit of play. This interplay between romance and immediate reality, reflected in the modern Spanish playwright, is also deeply rooted in Spain's traditional theatre, for example, in the plays of Lope de Vega. If we play with him, we too must sense the fairy tale in life. The element of fée was sensitively brought out by Helen and Harley Granville-Barker in their translation.

The production might have been criticized for leaning toward a treatment in characterization and setting too realistic for the atmosphere of the play. On the other hand, it had all the earmarks of a popular success, a surprise to the director, Agnes Morgan, and the cast.

CHAPTER THIRTY-THREE

THE PACE QUICKENS

Throughout the summer of 1926 we debated the pros and cons of repertory. True, the hasty output of the first season was hardly a test; with proper apportioning and careful manipulation, the new repertory plan had a fighting chance—thus spoke reason. The slightly worn spirit's answer was: "If that is the garment we must wear, the sign of our day, then, at least, let us cut it to our own measure." It seemed obvious that we could not advance in two directions simultaneously and, at the same time, grow from within; realize our direction, develop its trend more consciously.

As the outlook for new plays was not promising, we decided to resurrect and refurbish *The Little Clay Cart*. During rehearsals the directors were at a loss to know why the exquisite lyric quality of the original production could not be recaptured. Again and again, I heard inadvertent sighs—why was it so difficult to restore the grace and unexpected charm that lived on in memory? In the same way, the dynamic verve of the original production of *The Dybbuk* would soon be missing in its revival. So at the beginning as at the end, the problem of revival remained an open question, determined by the shifting winds of production plans, the particular play, and the particular situation.

Involved in the dilemma was an attitude. Few of us in the West have the desire to repeat the pattern of our lives; for here we demand invention, change at any price. The routine of mechanized life exacts an incessant variety of new sensations and experiences.

The capacity to sense Nature as a mold out of which man, individually and collectively, unfolds, belongs to the perspective of an old culture. The subtle values of its art forms show this. Until comparatively recently, the same legend and image of India and China continued through the centuries to stimulate a response from their people. In Europe, where people have lived and worked in a traditional way, they look reverently at their monuments and their art, they kneel in cathedrals where their ancestors have worshiped, structures filled with a culture belonging to them. But in America, with an assorted but limited background in time, we are stimulated by the future and the new. And because of this tremendous eagerness for the new, the experimental and inventive here and now, the past with its traditions, positive and negative, has naturally little appeal. We are less aware of the significance of what has been, in the sense of its meaning for us.

Of course this could be immediately challenged in regard to the appreciation of music, the growing interest in museums and in various cultural enterprises. But I am referring to an instinct for invention and change versus the old and traditional, an unconscious response rather than the cultivation of aesthetic values. I can think, for example, of the Comédie Française continuing as a tradition until the last petit pois disappears from the land. But is there any force in our United States that can make even a hero endurable for more than a fraction of a span? Doesn't the same hold true of the fairy tale in relation to childhood?

Even Bible stories are presented with a new comic look.

The force of the creative spirit emerges out of a dual and conflicting impulse—an insatiable longing for fulfillment or completion, the urge to realize what has been, along with the desire, perhaps the need, to invent new modes, to unleash new experiences. The tipping of the scales on either side results in exotic or eccentric expression. And that center, or balance, is perhaps like the perennial voice of spring, calling us again and again to the wellspring of Nature, neither to be absorbed by her, nor yet to exploit her.

Theatre can hold its lamp so that a light may radiate in all directions. The familiar need never pall if translated into terms of a new idiom, and the "unbeknown" need never be too remote if we have a feeling relation to the material—or if we respond like the primitive, whose imagination has to be violently stimulated before he can undertake the simplest of tasks.

Pinwheel, produced in 1927, required some such ritual, for it presented a world close, yet remote, not easy to reach via feeling. It could hardly be ranked as a play; rather it was a collection of scenes characterizing unidentified inhabitants of Manhattan, a kaleidoscopic impression of its dramatis personae swung in the dynamis of work and play.

The city was the protagonist. The masses, caught in its undertow, struggling against yet yielding to its pressures, were personalized in two human beings, indicated as The Guy and The Jane. The drama was like a code which compressed the whole into an incident, suggestive of a close-up. Thus without offered interpretation its author, Francis Faragoh, a newspaperman, suggested a wider aspect of a drama, the outline of which was more than covered in the newspaper columns, or on the beaten thoroughfares and pleasure grounds of the city.

Nothing but the eagerness to enter into the very rhythm of the mass, feel its pressure, sense its dynamo, could have compelled such sustained effort to indicate mass behavior in the rehearsals of the subway-crush scenes. In fact, this was done in defiance of broken limbs, for "traps" were in continual use behind the scenes. It was also a test of endurance to support the explosion of sound that provided the "music," or dissonances, in the accompaniment, not to mention the tension supplied in the "lingo" itself.

Donald Oenslager designed the settings and costumes for *Pinwheel*, and his quick perception and ingenuity were of immense help in solving the innumerable problems of staging this experiment, which was a challenge to us all. I still recall the enthusiasm with which he entered into the production. His première in design for the New York theatre had occurred at the Playhouse two years earlier, when he did the settings and costumes for *Sooner and Later*, a dance satire by Irene, with music by Emerson Whithorne. Soon he was moving to the frontiers of scenic art. Later on, Yale seized him, and from that moment on, he combined his gift as artist with that of teacher, his influence reaching out through our land. Since 1946 the Neighborhood Playhouse School has been fortunate to have him in close association as president.

The impetus of movement, the main feature of *Pinwheel*, impersonated by the mass as a dynamic force, was, in a sense, analogous to the chorus in a Greek drama. Here, the commentary, unlike that of the Greek chorus, was not voiced but indicated in the mechanized gestures enhanced, in turn, by stiffly angular costumes. The designs splashed boldly upon them gave the impression of ceaseless motion without form or direction. Looked at singly, each costume was a patchwork, but together they suggested a dizzy repetition of formless line which not only overshadowed but blotted out any vestige of personality in the wearer. Though we did not use masks, the make-up was stylized, erasing any individual feature of the character.

In the first act we are introduced to this macabre corps at Coney Island, where fantastic and explosive sound vie with each other in a confused turmoil. The masses reappear in the next scene in the aggressive confusion of a subway station, en route to work. The Guy and The Jane, emerging from the mass, now become focused as if in a close-up. Hereafter we follow the drama through them, as personalized replicas of the crowd. This two-dimensional, shifting pattern was indicated through the impressionistic treatment of the mass, set against the realistic treatment of The Guy and The Jane. They appear in one lurid episode after another until, at the end of the play, again re-emerging from the formlessness of the down-and-out lost in the mass, they confront each other in a deserted park after a long separation. Homeless and abandoned, The Guy and The Jane are forced bodily together against the bleakness of the night. In the distance, the lights of the city are gleaming.

All associated in the production of *Pinwheel* were so gripped by the play of forces so close to us that we needed this impressionistic treatment to avoid the banality of photographic realism until, in the end, from whatever angle one approached, the drama was seen as though through the wrong end of an opera glass. One moment, scenes would be sharpened to their essentials, intensity focused upon The Guy and The Jane; the next moment, The Guy and The Jane were lost in the flux of mass movement.

These were some of the production problems boldly suggested in the manuscript. It was difficult to resist the challenge of looking on as if perched on top of the Woolworth Tower, from there to see the passing show. Even if the play moved, at times, in the guise of caricature, still we tried to hold it to its beat, and not to lose sight of the submerged humanity in this chaos of movement. To find a balance between the substance, text, idea and their expression in movement, color, form, and sound, was the end we struggled to achieve.

Perhaps it was to our audiences' credit that *Pinwheel* did not commend itself warmly to them, in spite of the excellent characterizations of The Guy and The Jane played by Marc Loebell and Dorothy Sands, both of whom had won distinction in *The Dybbuk*. And the beggars, individualized in the chorus of *The Dybbuk,* were now called upon to evoke the daemonic power of Manhattan which was, in the Coney Island blare and subway crush, a tour de force.

Was the reception due to what was, at that time, a bizarre treatment? Or had *Pinwheel* as a pioneer attempt to dramatize the forces of Manhattan, not come through convincingly?

In retrospect, this failure to make the grade to a convincing production might well have been due to the fact that dynamis in and of itself leads to stagnation. The Guy and The Jane, who might have emerged even momentarily from chaos, remain in the confusion of the mass. The play indicated, not actually in the script but by way of production, the deterioration of instinct through uprootedness. And yet, however unsatisfactory *Pinwheel* was as drama, it served as a first attempt to deal with material which, a decade later, became a recognized and popular form. The individual is seen on a wider canvas—in coping with the trend of collectivism. In other words the human being struggles as of old with the giants, here the tremendum of collectivity.

In this connection, I cannot resist referring to *Our Town* which, when I saw it about a decade after *Pinwheel,* seemed to have achieved a completed form for the modern stage. With its utterly simple theme of transformation, childhood, youth, marriage, death, and rebirth form a cycle experienced with a conviction and directness which gives the play its quality of uniqueness. And yet this typically New England product links us with the theme of mystery cults the world over.

My reaction to *Our Town* at the time was a feeling of release. Someone had done it! Someone had perceived the here and now through the frame of a wider dimension. And yet, there was no break in time or mood; life flowed naturally in its own rhythm. And we, as audience, had the privilege of participating in the experience as a ritual.

In the language of the stage manager, as commentator in *Our Town,* "I don't care what they say with their mouths, everybody knows in their bones that something is eternal, and it ain't houses and it ain't names, and it ain't earth, and it ain't even stars—everybody knows in their bones that something is eternal, and that something has to do with human beings."

Life, death, rebirth are knit as a pattern into the lives of the folk at Grover's Corners, so simply and unobtrusively that we experience with them and, like the stage manager, look on objectively. These two perspectives give *Our Town* a distinction which carries beyond the frame of immediate reality, and yet it never loses the pulse of being "just so." Death is experienced as rebirth, and rebirth as a fuller awareness, by Emily who returns from death to celebrate her twelfth birthday once again. Coupled with the joy of the child is the throb of a fuller consciousness in *knowing* that she is experiencing.

The memory of *Our Town* as concept, as form, as production is still profoundly meaningful and remains for me an experience that has widened the horizon of modern theatre. In this sense, it has epochal value.

CHAPTER THIRTY-FOUR

THE DOORS CLOSE

The landslide of interest for the earlier Playhouse productions had dwindled to the barest attendance at *Pinwheel*, and in spite of its continued appeal to those who felt the sting of its satire, we were forced once again to reconsider the problem of our direction. For it was not merely *Pinwheel* that evoked a lukewarm response; other plays which had been enthusiastically received a short time before were also showing signs of declining attention.

Repertory was unquestionably failing, not only, we felt, at the box office but at the core, because of our lack of conviction in repertory as a form. We had from the beginning been committed heart and soul to unexplored fields, as well as to synthesizing the media of expression. Repertory had been undertaken as a concession to circumstances rather than an urge, and commitment to its form was in contradiction to our essential values. This reservation might in turn have found a echo in the audiences.

The final program for the season 1926–27, characteristically lyric, included the *The White Peacock,* a composition by Charles Griffes, the *Ritornell* by Béla Bartok, and a reconstructed fragment of the Commedia dell' Arte, all of which were staged and directed by Irene. *The White Pea-*

22. UPPER: *Fleur et Blanchefleur,* Neighborhood Play

Anna Sokolow, third from le

23. LOWER: *Ein Heldenleben,* orchestral dance drama t

performed at the Manhattan Opera House in 1929 wi

Martha Graham and Charles Weidman

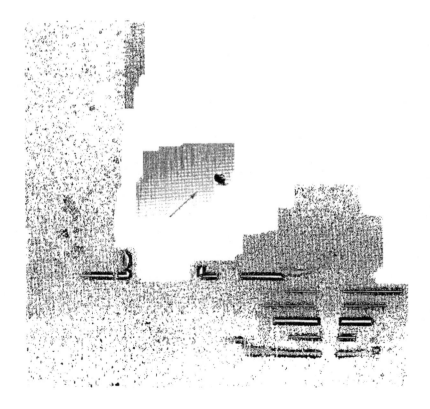

cock had an exotic quality and distinctive form, musically as well as through the choreography Irene developed. The *Ritornell,* with its swishing rhythm, fire, color, freshness, revivified appraisals of the productions as "the spirit of The Playhouse." For the abandon, the refreshing spontaneity of the movement, the electric verve in the ensemble had a quality of uniqueness.

The Commedia, however, demanded of the actor a form and robustness beyond the possibilities of the cast. This was also due to the fact that the text arranged and adapted by Anna MacDonald from the original fragments translated by Amelia Defries supplied little dialogue, so that the characterizations demanded a keen sense of improvisation. The problem that we could not solve was to draw individuality out of a form stamped by a conventionalized tradition.

Nothing is more difficult for the actor of today than to enter into rapport with another period. In spite of all the techniques of reproduction we are reminded that the bridge between our consciousness and that of cultures lying behind our epoch has been destroyed. The restlessness of our time has had its reverberations in theatre. A competitive spirit is now ruling out individual expression; this is evident in personal as in collective experience. Theatre, which serves as a mirror of contemporary life as of the past, demands of its craftsmen the quality of reflection. Such insight, rather than technical equipment, needs fostering. Stress upon artifice soon leads to a form of masquerade. To find within oneself echoes of another age, or to realize its values, requires not only imagination but the power to absorb and reflect.

The Neighborhood Playhouse had developed an individual attitude not only as a group but in stimulating each member to recognize his own values and expressiveness. Could it do more at this point? Could we individually and collectively retain our direction within the maelstrom of a threatening system? Actors, workers, members, friends, cleaving as they did to the Playhouse, were bound in loyalty and affection. Still, how many were prepared to travel a stonier way? How many equipped to meet new tests? They were young, and each had his life and career to mold.

Had we originally come together with more maturity and accord in the sounding of values, even then the fine balance between group and individual would have required extraordinary poise to survive the increasing pressure and tempo of the day. For art was no longer a receptacle through which to assimilate and release images; rather the standards of an industrial age were setting their seal upon artist and craftsman. Perhaps it was inevitable that each should leave the nest, meet the challenge in his own way, and so arrive at a fuller stature.

But how could we contemplate dissolution? The thought was intolerable, physically and humanly, for the Neighborhood Playhouse had entered as a force and fraternity into the very fiber of experience, giving a poignancy and lift to each day. Despite all its unfulfilled dreams, there it was, alive, ardent, vital. In retrospect the Playhouse assumed the form of a beloved being who had, under all conditions, pleaded for its life. Was life now to be denied? An inevitable destiny was hanging grimly in the balance. The time had come at last when a final decision had to be faced, and once made, nothing could stay it.

It is no longer possible to reconjure all the probing and weighing of values, the sorting out of negative and positive reactions to the problem of closing the doors of the Playhouse. Nor could I venture to describe the task of breaking the ultimate decision to the company and staff. But there still hovers a sense of the muted silence that followed, as if the death warrant of a beloved comrade had been passed.

The final night, May 31, 1927, Béla Bartok's *Ritornell* carried such verve that it seemed as though all that had ever been dreamed or hoped for over the years had suddenly been released. Far, far more than swishing rhythm, scintillating color, graceful characterization, or poignant melody came across the footlights. The drama stirring within each player transcended performance, seeming to lift the audience with it. The magical mingling of light and shadow still clings to the memory of that night, making the years of our working and playing but the transient tick of a deep, unsounded experience.

The Neighborhood Playhouse was drawing to a close. Ominously, silently, the dreaded moment came for the decision to be made to the public. The statement was brief, decisive. Factual circumstances could only be indicated— financial pressure, the increasing handicap of location, the realization that we had outgrown the physical dimensions of the building, the growing intensity of the work. Reflection and study of the situation as a whole were necessary before future plans could be shaped. Once said, how coldly obvious it seemed beside the depth of emotion stirred. Silence was the only acknowledgment—a deep, throbbing, rending silence. The Neighborhood Playhouse as it had existed was dissolved.

The weeks that followed brought the real testing. How much easier to continue under some plan, however inadequate, than to tear up the roots and have to bear the "slings and arrows" of doubt and self-questioning! It was strangely difficult to live through those unending days, severing bit by bit contacts steeped in meaning, and discarding objects, some of which seemed suddenly transformed into holy relics. Even the wardrobe filled with the magic of characterization now seemed wantonly bare and sinisterly leering. Then the inevitable adjustments—weighing and considering, trying to hold taut the line between desire to continue and the realization of its impossibility under existing conditions. And the nights of reliving more than the problems of each day!

For weeks after the announcement of the closing, in the tearful atmosphere of the Playhouse, one seemed to feel that death had passed, leaving a household of mourners drawn together by the new, strangely tender impact of suffering. In the world without, the brief statement, coldly unrevealing as it was, touched wide areas of response. From far and near, newspapers and magazine comments, editorials, letters from members of the audiences unknown to us, offered sympathy and expressed a sense of loss. Bewildering as the external situation was, nothing could have foretold what the wrenching of roots, so deeply imbedded, would cost.

That was over thirty years ago. Today, as I think of the Neighborhood Playhouse almost half a century after its beginning, it seems as though it lay there at peace, a page untouched, unread, invitingly alluring, filled with expectation. In every corner of my memory there lurk effervescent sparkles, recalling a discovery here, a keen edge of recognition there, workshops crowded with the pageantry of doing and undoing, stageways teeming with a constant flow of movement. I feel again the moments of release, then suddenly the crowding on of pressure, the reckless plunging into work and the breathlessness of pushing against time. There are memories of opening nights with their brimful counterplay of fear and radiance.

Through the years, barriers, walls, obstructions disappear. A thousand shadows ride swiftly by, too numerous to see at once, too indistinct of pattern as they hurry past, but an outline here, a profile there, of that beloved host of makers and creators, sharers of the years—all eager to serve, to pool gifts, knowledge, youth, desire, the great ones and the small, each with each to suffer, to create. Not one has disappeared, not one has dissolved in shadow. Each played a part, each lives on in the timelessness of the deep experience we called the Neighborhood Playhouse.

Actually, there was no thought of abandoning the experience of the years at the time the Neighborhood Playhouse closed. Though we had to face dissolution, there was the hope of some further development, but at the time the new pattern did not present itself. It was not long, however, before the vitality of the original image opened the way to further enterprises.

A series of orchestral dance dramas created and developed by Irene soon brought a renewal of life to the lyric programs. Daringly conceived, these productions were intended to treat movement, not as an accompaniment of music, but rather as a visualized expression of the orchestration, as if the musical structure were being interpreted through a composite orchestra of dancers and musicians. In their form and movement, they were scaled to the proportions of a spacious stage and to the breadth and fullness of a symphony orchestra.

The first of these orchestral dramas was Ernest Bloch's "Israel," performed in 1928 at the Manhattan Opera House in collaboration with the Cleveland Symphony Orchestra under the direction of Nikolai Sokoloff, who was an enthusiastic participant in this new adventure. The sculptor Jo Davidson provided the design for the setting, the powerful score suggesting a background of chiseled rock—the Wailing Wall. The monumental character of the setting and the beauty in the composition of the figures were deeply stirring. Static or in movement, the dancers gave the impression of shades hovering about an ageless sculptured edifice which in turn was linked with the weeping heart of Israel. As symbol it had a moving appeal inspired by the creative fervor of Bloch's composition, which did not call for solo characterization. Martha Graham, Doris Humphrey, and Charles Weidman, though part of the mass, were distinctive figures lending a sense of leadership and direction to hapless beings who had lost the visible presence of their ancient heritage. On the same program Debussy's "Images" was danced by Martha Graham and Michio Ito, and a group led by Gluck-Sandor completed the program with Russian dances drawn from Borodin.

The following year the Cleveland Orchestra again collaborated at the Manhattan Opera House in the production of Richard Strauss's tone poem, "Ein Heldenleben." In this most ambitious of all the productions, Irene read into the musical theme a drama of heroic dimensions, developing the libretto and choreography in strictest relation to the orchestration. Martha Graham and Charles Weidman gave eloquent support to this venture with the central characterizations. Charles Griffes' "White Peacock," with Blanche Talmud as leading dancer, and Enesco's "Roumanian Rhapsody," with Gluck-Sandor, rounded out the program.

In 1930 the scene shifted to Mecca Temple, where Martin Loeffler's "A Pagan Poem," "La Procession Nocturne" by Henri Rabaud, and "New Year's Eve in New York" by Werner Janssen were performed. That same year, the company was invited to Cleveland as part of the dedication program for Severance Hall.

In 1931, in response to a commission by the Elizabeth Sprague Coolidge Foundation, a program was presented at the Library of Congress in Washington and repeated later in New York at the YMHA. This production included Ernest Bloch's String Quartet, performed by the Jacques Gordon

String Quartet and danced by Doris Humphrey, Charles Weidman, and Blanche Talmud; The Toccata and Fugue in D Minor by Bach, played on the organ by E. Powers Biggs and danced by Benjamin Zemach and a group. The final number, "Music of the Troubadours," was arranged by Carlos Salzedo for a quartet, led by Mr. Salzedo at the harp. The dancers were Eugenia Liczbinska, Blanche Talmud, and Charles Weidman.

Apart from its quality and intention, this pioneering attempt had significance as a stimulus to the later development of the dance in America during the period that followed the first World War. Louis Horst, who has made a unique contribution to modern dancers through the musical quality he has brought to their language, has said that "these orchestral dramas gave dancers the necessary push to express dramatic and emotional values which up to that time had been conceived more or less abstractly." Significantly, Martha Graham's "Primitive Mysteries," her first extended dramatic work, was introduced in 1931, the final year of the orchestral drama series. Another value not to be overlooked in these productions was their extension of the lyric form developed at the Neighborhood Playhouse. They also offered specially qualified students of the Neighborhood Playhouse School of the Theatre (inaugurated in 1928) opportunity to participate. It was in these programs that Anna Sokolow and other members of the original Neighborhood Playhouse classes had an outlet for their training.

The place of folk expression in the modern theatre, always supported at the Playhouse, was to receive a further impulse through the collaboration of Kurt Schindler, distinguished musical scholar and director of the Schola Cantorum. He undertook a special research in Spain for sources of folk music and material that might lend itself to theatre production. This plan had a wider scope for continued research in Mediterranean countries. Unfortunately the work had to be abandoned because of his long illness and subsequent death. But material from his valuable Basque collection was adapted for a folk ballet and produced by Irene at the Booth Theatre in 1929.

The Costume Institute was another enterprise to emerge as a creative adventure out of the original germ of the Neighborhood Playhouse. The place of costume as a cultural value for the theatre was a vital consideration at the Playhouse. But naturally during those intensive years it was not possible for all these aspects of production to become differentiated. A limited number of folk costumes gathered during our travels was always at the service of the productions and designers. From time to time exhibitions were informally held, and a small costume library, including charts of historical dress as well as designs for production, was occasionally shown. But it remained for the Costume Institute to realize the full potentialities of this aspect of theatre.

The Institute, conceived and founded by Irene, drew to it the cooperation of leading personalities of the theatre and allied arts, among them Aline Bernstein, Lee Simonson, and Clarence Stein, who, with Irene, became the incorporators in 1937. With Irene as first president, a position she held until her death in 1944, the Institute soon grew to an active many-faceted organization, a further expression of her gift of careful nurturing through the growing pains of trial and effort. Its function from the beginning was to devise ingenious and effective exhibitions of costumes both traditional and period, and simultaneously to work out a method for exhibiting, recording, and storing its materials; also to make its records and the details of costume available to students of design. The exhibitions were for the most part gathered as loans or gifts from private sources. In its new approach to presentation it was startling to see the living quality that mere static figures assumed when manipulated with loving care, a dramatic sense of values, and a knowledgeable touch in assembling and selecting suitable details so meticulously that not a figure but a personality stood before you.

Later the fashion industry was won to the opportunity the Institute offered in providing a cultural background for designers of fashion and also for those associated with various branches of textiles and allied fields. The industry's realization of this value is both symbolized and expressed today in the indefatigable services of the current president, Dorothy Shaver.

Polaire Weissman, who had been closely linked with the Playhouse workshops, was installed as Irene's first aide, and remains at the Institute today as the uniquely endowed executive director. Her association was not limited to developing techniques for conserving, recording, and presenting the growing collection; she soon discovered a pedagogical capacity as well in directing the large classes of students who flocked to the Institute.

In retrospect one can see how the emphasis upon technical training was a spontaneous outgrowth of the original Playhouse image in which traditional crafts and a symbolic use of costume were inextricably bound with ritual and, in the course of historical development, were preserved through folk festivals. This extension was not determined by a rational plan, but evolved out of a need rooted in the original perception of theatre as a composite structure through which varying media could be synchronized.

After Irene's death, her cherished dream of affiliating this new venture with the Metropolitan Museum was realized under the auspices of the Institute's next president, Aline Bernstein. Undoubtedly the Museum's responsiveness to this idea was due to its vision of a museum as a living force and cultural expression in the collective life of the community. The plaque on the entrance wall of the Costume Institute, dedicated by the Museum as a memorial to Irene, expresses the recognition of her creative contribution. It reads in part:

HER INSPIRATION IN THE FURTHERANCE OF THE IDEALS FOR WHICH THE COSTUME INSTITUTE STANDS WILL BE A CONSTANT TESTIMONIAL TO HER DISTINCTION AS A CITIZEN AND HER DEVOTION TO THE ARTS.

The first child of the Playhouse to develop a continuity and a life of its own is the last to be mentioned here, the Neighborhood Playhouse School of the Theatre. The historical background of the School has already far exceeded that of the parent organization. Starting with a modest roll call of nine students in 1928, it has had an unbroken continuity in plan, direction, and guiding values for over thirty years. But its unhistorical background dates from a still older* period. For the School grew out of the desire to realize what had not been possible at the Playhouse, where the pressure of production, exigencies of an audience, and demands of a continuous program hindered adequate concentration on the technical or the cultural values of production.

At the School, technical training was planned not as a system but as a way toward integrating varied media for theatre. Its plan, scope, and fundamental values were the result of a unique partnership. For Irene confided the direction of the School to Rita Morgenthau, our associate in the early days of the Henry Street Settlement, who had remained a loyal comrade and wise counselor in relation to many problems of the Playhouse as a member of its advisory board. In this new enterprise Irene served as adviser, cooperating in details of organization and curriculum based on the experience of the Playhouse, and she worked enthusiastically with the students. The heightened awareness due to the direction of two such creative personalities provided that extra source of energy upon which the School thrived.

No inheritance could be luckier for the School than that of Rita Morgenthau, who as director today still brings to it not only years of experience to generations of young people, long and tested understanding of educational and social values, but also a genius for relationship. As the School has been a source of inspiration to her, so it in turn receives the quality and sensibility of a rare personality. Every detail is considered in the service of the whole, which means a meticulous sense of adjusting to each problem with warmth and responsiveness, highly seasoned with humor, then with the next breath a scrupulous demand for perfection. With Donald Oenslager, president since 1946, Rita Morgenthau works in harmonious 'partnership, their relation to the School unencumbered by barbed-wire judgment of what "should be" or what is expected. Together with the Board of Directors, executive and teaching staff, students, and household staff they form a spirited family circle. This attitude is reflected even in the polish of the doorknobs, and in the keen eye for aesthetic values in the proportions and simple dignity of the rooms designed as a frame for work, yet to which some personal touch has been added. For example, no library could offer a more inviting pilgrimage to study than that which has been dedicated to Irene.

An intimate relation exists at the School between technical work in the classroom and research into details of production. Neither preparation nor demonstration appears subordinate to the other value. Then where, one might ask, is the point of emphasis? Apparently not in an academic or technical approach—how to produce tears or laughter, fall or faint, enter a room or retire, stylize speech or gesture. Isn't it rather in the attempt to approach reality in the experience? The gift of acting a role is supported largely by the ability to undergo the transforming experience anticipated or realized by the dramatis personae. Naturally, an attitude of this kind can only be appreciated by the exceptional individual who not only has a flair for acting but also the desire to understand what he acts.

The sum total lies in the attempt to form an organic language out of a collection of different techniques: acting, movement, mime, speech. Nevertheless this intensive training does not suggest an outwardly applied accomplishment as equipment of an actor or dancer, but rather a varied experience offered to and absorbed by the student as his natural or individual pattern. Perhaps one could say that the spark which influenced the establishment of the school was the capacity to feel into the heart of youth, remain in step with its dreams and groping conflicts which reflect in a measure the transforming process at the core of drama, or more correctly, the realization of drama as the projected experience of a process taking place in the individual.

The fascinating stimulus and influence of theatre explains to a certain extent the degree of warmth poured into the

School by its co-workers. In one sense the students are carriers, in another they are the vessel into which the rare stuff of experience, imagination, and cultural values has been poured. The increasing demand for admission to the School in spite of the exacting standard proves the soundness in an attitude and approach to theatre which has been nursed and guarded for more than thirty years. Probably it is this same feeling for essential values that stimulates an increasing response to the performances, and spontaneous demonstrations from friends and colleagues, seasoned members of the professional theatre, and scouts hunting talent. It is not surprising that former students, whose names are now legion, have won distinction in the professional world of theatre and training for theatre not only throughout the country but in lands across the sea.

From the first, collaboration of rare creative personalities has been the treasured inheritance of the students. We need only think of the good fortune of Martha Graham's association over the thirty years, offering not only her inspirational qualities as an artist, and the unusual gift of her specialized technique, but also her responsiveness to the needs of each student, her understanding as friend, her evaluation of and devotion to the School. The same holds true of Louis Horst, who thirty years ago, in cooperation with Irene, developed his unique course in the relation between music and dance forms as a stepping stone toward characterization and choreography. He remains at the School today, honored for his consistent guidance toward the vision he holds.

Laura Elliot, one of the original associates at the old Playhouse, was another contributing spirit to the School. Here she found an avenue for further experimental work in choral speech, which had been a feature of Playhouse productions, and also for her individual method in cultivating the voice and diction for the stage. Her death in 1940 was an incomparable loss.

Another leading figure whose personality has been stamped upon the School is Sanford Meisner, who from 1935 to 1958 wielded the baton for the acting department and the plays. His association with the School, while he was also achieving success as actor and director in the professional theatre, gives a clue to his devotion to an enterprise wholeheartedly indentured to the creative spirit. During the summer of 1958, David Pressman became the director of the summer session and continues today as director of the dramatic department of the School, from which he graduated in 1936. His record as actor and director on the professional stage as well as his long association with the acting department of the School have equipped him admirably to carry on the work so firmly established by Sanford Meisner.

Craftsmanship for the structural side of stage production is an important feature of the program. Building, carpentry, painting, lighting, technique for stage management are necessary elements of the process, offered simply as work to be done for the plays. Here again the students have the rare chance of applying themselves under the leadership of Paul Morrison who combines these varied functions of the craftsman with the sensitivity of an artist. His association with the School since 1945 marks another record of uninterrupted partnerhip, remarkably harmonized with his active career as stage designer in the professional theatre.

We cannot disregard the significance of the words "drama" and "theatre" in a discussion of the School. Drama expressed to the Greeks an activity—to do, or enact, or to be involved in an activity. Theatre on the other hand was used in a more static sense, as the place from which to behold or envision the contents of drama. Yet the roots of drama were associated with rituals and these in turn with regenerative forces in nature, which in the belief of primitive man were furthered by means of his magic devices—song, dance, incantation, votive offerings, and so forth. When we think of the dance, music, poetry, painting, can we help but realize that this wholly personal experience was originally a magical means to restore order? That is, to harmonize the demonic powers in nature and the guardian spirit, powerful, terrifying, grotesque, benignant, not comparable of course with spirit in the Christian sense.

Perhaps we can draw a slight analogy between these activities of original man and our relation to drama which, after all, is based upon a similar conflict incorporated, however, in the dramatis personae. For example, the villain or witchlike woman appears in opposition to the hero or to those personalities who express a spiritual or conscious attitude. And all the devices of theatre—props, stage equipment, light, and color— are used as a means to further the experience of the transforming process taking place in the characters. The drama of antiquity presented this conflict between light and dark forces through mythological figures who fulfilled their roles as representatives of nature, its continuous round reminding the audience no doubt of man's fate: birth, growth through conflict, death, yet with the promise of rebirth. With us, the dramatis personae is to a large extent self-determining; nature, one might say, is seen through man. He becomes the stage upon which the drama of transformation with its motive of growth, death, rebirth is played.

Such images are not arbitrary, but have grown out of the source of all creativity and culture, the unplumbable areas in the human soul. Whether in viewing or in acting we are involved in a process which has universal validity yet which, like the perennial voice of spring, is eternally new, belonging to this moment here and now. Perhaps we could say that the fascination of theatre does not depend upon the particular situation or upon this or that personality but rather upon its ageless background which, in releasing a magical spark, lends drama its stimulus and significance.

PRODUCTIONS OF THE
NEIGHBORHOOD PLAYHOUSE

Prepared by Alice Owen

Exclusive of Revivals and of Performances by Visiting Companies

* First time in New York; ° Created by the Neighborhood
Playhouse

Productions Prior to the Opening of the Playhouse

1912–1914

THE SHEPHERD	by Olive Tilford Dargan. Directed by Sarah Cowell Le Moyne with Agnes Morgan.
THE SILVER BOX	by John Galsworthy. ?
* WOMENKIND	by Wilfred Wilson Gibson.
* THE PRICE OF COAL	by Harold Brighouse.
* RYLAND	by Thomas Wood Stevens and Kenneth S. Goodman.

At the Neighborhood Playhouse

February–June, 1915

*° JEPHTHAH'S DAUGHTER, a dance drama based on an incident in the Book of Judges	Music by Lilia Mackay-Cantell. Arrangement, choreography, direction and design by Alice and Irene Lewisohn.
TETHERED SHEEP, an American folk play	by Robert Gilbert Welsh. Directed by Agnes Morgan.
THE GLITTERING GATE	by Lord Dunsany. Directed by Agnes Morgan.

THE MAKER OF DREAMS	by Oliphant Down. Directed by Agnes Morgan and Alice Lewisohn.
CAPTAIN BRASS-BOUND'S CONVER-SION	by George Bernard Shaw. Directed by Agnes Morgan. Scene designs by Clifford Pember and Warren Dahler.
* THE WALDIES	by J. G. Hamlen. Directed by Agnes Morgan and Alice Lewisohn.

1915–1916

*° THANKSGIVING, festival on elemental forces	Arranged, choreographed and designed by Alice and Irene Lewisohn.
WILD BIRDS, an English folk play	by Violet Pearn.
* THE SUBJECTION OF KEZIA	by Mrs. Havelock Ellis. Directed by Agnes Morgan.
PETROUCHKA, a ballet	Adaptation by Irene and Alice Lewisohn. Music by Igor Stravinsky. Choreographed by Louis Chalif. Designed by Frank J. Zimmerer.
* A MARRIAGE PRO-POSAL	by Anton Chekhov.
* WITH THE CURRENT	by Scholem Asch. Directed by Alice Lewisohn.
* A NIGHT AT AN INN	by Lord Dunsany. Directed by Agnes Morgan.

1916–1917

| * GREAT CATHERINE | by George Bernard Shaw. Directed by Agnes Morgan. Design by Warren Dahler. |
| * THE INCA OF PERU-SALEM | by George Bernard Shaw. Directed by Agnes Morgan. Design by Warren Dahler. |

*	THE QUEEN'S ENEMIES	by Lord Dunsany. Directed by Agnes Morgan and Alice Lewisohn. Designed by Howard Kretz-Coluzzi and Warren Dahler. Costumes by Aline Bernstein.
*	THE MARRIED WOMAN	by Chester B. Fernald.
	HOLIDAY	by Wilfred Wilson Gibson.
*°	THE KAIRN OF KORIDWEN, a dance drama from an ancient Celtic legend	Music by Charles T. Griffes. Adapted and directed by Alice and Irene Lewisohn. Designed by Herbert Crowley.
	BLACK 'ELL	by Miles Malleson. Directed by Agnes Morgan and Alice Lewisohn.
*	A SUNNY MORNING	by The Quinteros; translated by Anna S. MacDonald. Directed by Agnes Morgan and Alice Lewisohn.
	THE PEOPLE	by Susan Glaspell. Directed by Agnes Morgan.
	LA BOITE A JOUJOUX, a ballet, children's production	Music by Claude Debussy. Story by André Hellé. Directed by Irene Lewisohn and Blanche Talmud, choreography by Irene Lewisohn. Designs by Esther Peck.

1917–1918

*°	A RUSSIAN FOLK-SCENE	
	PIPPA PASSES	by Robert Browning. Directed by Agnes Morgan and Alice Lewisohn. Designs by Warren Dahler.
*	TAMURA, a Japanese Noh play	by Zeami. Translated by Ernest Fenollosa and Ezra Pound. Arranged and directed by Alice and Irene Lewisohn.

FORTUNATO	by The Quinteros. Translated by Anna S. MacDonald. Directed by Agnes Morgan and Alice Lewisohn.
FREE	by Mme. Rachilde. Translated by Anna S. MacDonald. Directed by Agnes Morgan.
° FESTIVAL OF PENTE-COST, based on Old Testament themes	Arranged and directed by Alice and Irene Lewisohn.

1918–1919

* ° THE FEAST OF TABER-NACLES, based on Old Testament themes	Arranged and directed by Alice and Irene Lewisohn.
* GUIBOUR, a 14th Century French Miracle play, as arranged by Yvette Guilbert	English version by Anna S. Mac-Donald. Directed by Agnes Morgan and Alice Lewisohn. Designs by Robert Edmond Jones.
THE ETERNAL MEGALOSAURUS	by Justina Lewis. Directed by Agnes Morgan. Designs by Warren Dahler and Howard Kretz-Coluzzi.
* THE NOOSE	by Tracy Mygatt. Directed by Agnes Morgan. Designs by Frank Stout.
EVERYBODY'S HUS-BAND	by Gilbert Cannan. Directed by Agnes Morgan and Alice Lewisohn. Designs by Esther Peck.
MA MERE L'OYE, a ballet, children's production	Music by Maurice Ravel. Choreography and direction by Irene Lewisohn and Blanche Talmud.

1919–1920

MARY BROOME	by Allan Monkhouse.

LA BOUTIQUE FAN-
TASQUE, a pantomime
ballet

Music adapted by Frederick
Jacobi from Rossini-Respighi.
Scenario, choreography and direction by Irene Lewisohn. Designed by Esther Peck.

THE FAIR, a folk play   by Violet Pearn.

1920–1921

* THE MOB

by John Galsworthy. Designed
by Warren Dahler.

* THE WHISPERING
WELL

by F. H. Rose. Designed by
Frank Stout.

THE GREAT ADVEN-
TURE

by Arnold Bennett. Designed
by Frederick Bentley.

* INNOCENT AND
ANNABEL

by Harold Chapin. Directed by
Agnes Morgan.

THE HARLEQUINADE

by Harley Granville-Barker
and Dion C. Calthrop. Music
arrangement by Lily May Hyland. Dances staged by Albert
Carroll. Designed by Esther
Peck.

THE ROYAL FAN-
DANGO, a Spanish bal-
let

Book and music by Gustavo
Morales. Costumes and setting
by Ernest de Weerth.

1921–1922

THE MADRAS HOUSE

by Harley Granville-Barker. Directed by Agnes Morgan and
Alice Lewisohn.

* DANCE PATTERNS, a
mid-week interlude

CLAVILUX, a mid-week
interlude

Thomas Wilfred's color organ.

THE CAFE OF THE
BROKEN HEART, a
mid-week interlude

by Anna S. MacDonald; based
on the story by Leonard Mer-
rick.

THE SUICIDES OF THE RUE SOMBRE, a mid-week interlude	by Agnes Morgan; based on the story by Leonard Merrick.
A MORALITY PLAY FOR THE LEISURE CLASS, a mid-week interlude	by John Lloyd Balderston.
* A NORSE FAIRY TALE, pantomime	Arranged by Roshanara. Music by Frederic Chopin.
THE FIRST MAN	by Eugene O'Neill. Directed by Augustin Duncan.
THE GREEN RING	by Zinaida Hippius. Stage designs by Warren Dahler. Costumes by Aline Bernstein.
*° SALUT AU MONDE, a lyric drama	Adapted from Walt Whitman's poem. Scenario and choral design by Irene and Alice Lewisohn. Designed by Esther Peck. Music by Charles T. Griffes.
* MAKERS OF LIGHT	by Frederick Lansing Day. Designed by Warren Dahler.
*° THE GRAND STREET FOLLIES of 1922	by Helen Arthur & Agnes Morgan. Dances by Albert Carroll.

1922–1923

THE LITTLE LEGEND OF THE DANCE, a medieval interlude	Story by Agnes Morgan. Music by Lily May Hyland. Children's production.

1923–1924

THE SHEWING UP OF BLANCO POSNET	by George Bernard Shaw. Directed by Richard Boleslavsky.
* THE PLAYER QUEEN	by William Butler Yeats. Directed by Richard Boleslavsky.
* THIS FINE-PRETTY WORLD, an American folk drama	by Percy MacKaye. Directed by Agnes Morgan and Alice Lewisohn.

*° AN ARAB FANTASIA, an impression of Arab life

Scenario and choreography by Irene and Alice Lewisohn. Music by Anis Fuleihan.

BUFFOON! (Chout) a farcical pantomime ballet

Scenario adapted by Irene Lewisohn. Music by Sergei Prokofieff.

TIME IS A DREAM

by H. R. Lenormand. Translated by Winifred Katzin.

*° THE GRAND STREET FOLLIES, Second Edition (1924)

Book and lyrics by Agnes Morgan. Music by Lily Hyland. Staged by Helen Arthur & Agnes Morgan. Costumes and settings by Aline Bernstein. Masks by Jo Davidson.

1924–1925

THE LITTLE CLAY CART, a Hindu drama

attributed to King Shudraka. Translated by Arthur William Ryder. Adapted by Agnes Morgan. Directed by Agnes Morgan and Irene Lewisohn. Designed by Aline Bernstein.

* EXILES

by James Joyce. Directed by Agnes Morgan. Designed by Russel Wright.

*° SOONER AND LATER, a dance satire

Scenario, design and direction by Irene Lewisohn. Music by Emerson Whithorne. Designed by Donald Oenslager.

THE CRITIC

by Richard Brinsley Sheridan. Directed by Agnes Morgan and Ian Maclaren. Settings by Aline Bernstein. Music arranged by Lily May Hyland.

*° THE GRAND STREET FOLLIES, Third Edition (1925)

Book and lyrics by Agnes Morgan. Music by Lily May Hyland. Designed by Russel Wright and Aline Bernstein. Dances by Albert Carroll.

1925–1926

* THE DYBBUK — by S. Ansky. Translated by Henry Alsberg and Winifred Katzin. Directed by David Vardi in association with Alice Lewisohn. Settings and costumes by Aline Bernstein.

*° A BURMESE PWE, an impression of Burma — Scenario, choreography and direction by Irene Lewisohn, assisted by Blanche Talmud. Music by Henry Eichheim.

THE APOTHECARY, an opera bouffe an adaptation of "Der Apotheker" — by Joseph Haydn. English version adapted by Anna MacDonald. Score adapted by Howard Barlow. Directed by Alice Lewisohn. Costumes and setting by Aline Bernstein.

*° KUAN YIN, The Goddess of Mercy, a Chinese fantasy — Music by A. Avshalamoff. Story by K. L. Shi, adapted by Carroll Lunt. Directed by Irene Lewisohn. Costumes and setting by Ernest de Weerth.

* THE ROMANTIC YOUNG LADY, a gentle comedy — by G. Martinez Sierra. Translated by Helen and Harley Granville-Barker. Directed by Agnes Morgan. Settings and costumes by Aline Bernstein.

*° THE GRAND STREET FOLLIES, Fourth Edition (1926) — Book and lyrics by Agnes Morgan. Music by Lily May Hyland, Arthur Schwartz and Randall Thompson. Staged by Agnes Morgan. Settings and costumes by Aline Bernstein.

1926–1927

THE LION TAMER, a satirical fable — by Alfred Savoir. Translated by Winifred Katzin. Directed by

Agnes Morgan. Settings and costumes by Aline Bernstein.

*° A GATEWAY IN PROVENCE, children's production

* PINWHEEL   by Francis Edwards Faragoh. Music by Howard Barlow. Directed by Alice and Irene Lewisohn. Design by Donald Oenslager.

*° TONE PICTURES and THE WHITE PEACOCK, lyric dramas   by Charles T. Griffes. Scenario and choreography by Irene Lewisohn. Settings and costumes by Aline Bernstein.

*° COMMEDIA DELL' ARTE   Text translated by Amelia Defries. Acting version by Anna MacDonald. Music arranged by Howard Barlow. Directed by Irene Lewisohn. Setting and costumes by Aline Bernstein.

*° RITORNELLE, a dance romance, Hungarian folk scenes   by Irene Lewisohn and Francis Edwards Faragoh. Arranged to Béla Bartok's Dance Suite by Howard Barlow. Choreography and direction by Irene Lewisohn, assisted by Blanche Talmud. Designed by Esther Peck.

*° THE GRAND STREET FOLLIES, Fifth Edition (1927)   Sketches and lyrics by Agnes Morgan and others. Music by Max Ewing and others. Costumes and settings by Aline Bernstein.

The text and music of many of the productions in this list can be inspected in the Theatre Collection of the New York Public Library.

INDEX

NP refers to Neighborhood Playhouse
pl. refers to plate or illustration

CPSIA information can be obtained
at www.ICGtesting.com
Printed in the USA
LVOW04s0828270216
476959LV00027B/823/P